Sue Dengate is a psychology graduate and former high-school teacher who became interested in the effects of foods as a result of her own children's experiences. Over the last 15 years, Sue has published five bestselling books and a DVD on the topic and spoken to many thousands of parents all over the world. Sue's husband, Dr Howard Dengate, is a food scientist. Together they founded and run the Food Intolerance Network through the website www.fedup.com.au.

FULLY UPDATED AND EXPANDED

The Failsafe Cookbook

Reducing food chemicals for calm, happy families

Sue Dengate

RANDOM HOUSE AUSTRALIA

Random House Australia Pty Ltd
Level 3, 100 Pacific Highway, North Sydney, NSW 2060
www.randomhouse.com.au

Sydney New York Toronto
London Auckland Johannesburg

First published by Random House Australia 2007

National Library of Australia
Cataloguing-in-Publication Entry

Dengate, Sue.
The failsafe cookbook.

Rev. ed.
Bibliography.
Includes index.

ISBN 978 1 74166 876 6 (pbk.).

1. Cookery. 2. Food allergy – Diet therapy – Recipes.
I. Title.

641.56318

Original cover design by Greendot design
Cover photograph by Austral International Photo Library
Typeset by J&M Typesetters, Victoria
Printed and bound by Griffin Press, South Australia

Acknowledgements

The surge of interest in food intolerance took me by such surprise that there has been a long delay in getting updated information to the many thousands of readers who have telephoned, emailed and written, but here it is, thanks to your encouragement. I couldn't have done it without you, nor without the loving support of my family, especially my food scientist husband Howard, for helping to create recipes, and for test-cooking and editing, and my children, who showed it really can be done. A special thanks to Doctors Anne Swain, Velencia Soutter and Robert Loblay at the Royal Prince Alfred Hospital Allergy Unit in Sydney, Australia, whose elimination diet based on their research changed our lives, and to dietitians Jan Branch, Marion Leggo, Liz Beavis and Melanie Reid.

Thanks also to the hard-working local contacts and group leaders, particularly Kathleen Daalmeyer and Jenny Ravlic in Melbourne, Brenda Hunting in Brisbane, Bronwyn Pollnitz in Adelaide, Jennifer Berthold in Sydney, Bernard and Marie Trudgett in Wollongong, Jan Cafearo in the UK, and Robin Fisher and Linda Beck in New Zealand.

Thirteen years ago, when we embarked on the RPAH elimination diet, we thought that we were the only family with these problems. Now we belong to a strong, supportive network of more than 4000 members who know that reducing food chemicals really can create calm, happy families.

For contributing recipes, hints or quotes, many thanks to readers all over the world for sharing your experiences and successes over the years.

There are almost too many people to list, but I must thank: Helen Ampt (Italy), Nick Avery, Maree Baggaley, Ruth Beaver, Libby Benson, Trudy and Hugh Bland, Ingrid Boyle, Cherie Braham, Geoff Brewer (UK), Susan Bridgman, Vicki Cana, Tania Cannons, Alison Cliff, Margie Cole, Nelida Contreras, Darani Cooper, Annette Cowie, Mary Cowley, Tami Cox, Liz Cullen, Kylie Dallow, Jenni De Carli, Leal De Carli, Sharon Delpol, Jane Figg, Sharon Fishlock, Lynda Gaebel, Caroline Garner, Kate Geyle, Julie Gilfoyle, Chris Griffiths, Trish Hale, Deborah Halliwell, Vena Halliwell, Deborah Harding, Beth Hennessey, Julieanne Hensley (USA), Dani Hewton, Rosy Hill, Jenny Hodgkinson, Dianne Hunt, Anne

Hurman, Celia James, Lesley Joiner, Jill Joy, Nicole Judge, Michelle Jurgens, Elaine Keeley, Dagmar Krautloher, Deanne Langford, Sally Lauder, Juliette Lee, Pat and Kevin Little (USA), Max Luck, Grace Lyons, Kerry MacDowell, Joanne Mahmood, Bernadette Martin, Faye McCarthy, Bunitj Miles, Susie Moen, Helen Monger, Jane Moore, Janet Morgan, Jill and Richard Newton, Debbie Newton, Rosemary Norwood, Jeanette O'Brien, Johann Packer, Julie Patterson, Julie Pegrum, Tracy Percival, Vanessa Peterson, Deb and Ross Porter, Cindy Ridden, Bennitta Robertson, Caroline Robertson, Emma Roffey, Katrina Rooke, Jim Rothwell (USA), Carlene Royan, Jenny Saal, Gwen Sculley, Kate Serisier, Birgit Setiawan, Moni Shuttlesworth (USA), Sheryl Sibley, Debbi Smith, Lynda Smith, Tracey Smith, Andra Somerville, Janelle Spicer, Eleanor Staude, Melita Stevens, Vivienne Stewart, Tracy Stoves, Diane Sylvester, Faye Taylor (Sweden), Sam Tinsley, Maria Townsend, Margie Turner, Carlia van den Hoek, Joanne van Os, Teresa Ventris, Erica Waite, Heather Waldron, Kerry Walker, Llewellyn Wall, Dr Alison Walsh, Judith Webster, Diane Wilson, and members of all the failsafe email groups.

If I have failed to record your name, my apologies, and please let me know.

Finally, my sincere thanks to Roberta Ivers at Random House Australia for never losing faith that this book would one day be back in your hands.

Contents

Are You Affected by Food Chemicals?   **1**

What Every Parent Should Know About Food Intolerance   **5**
Avoid these additives   15
How we did our elimination diet   17
A rating scale   23
The 13 Commandments   25
The Fridge List   26
Failsafe substitutes   27

Weights and Measures   **28**

Breakfasts   **31**

Lunches and Snacks   **39**
Lunches   40
School lunches   49
Snacks   52
Finger food for babies and toddlers   59
Drinks   60
Icypoles and icecups   66

Main Meals   **69**
Soups and stews   69
Meat   73
Chicken   90
Seafood   99
Vegetables and vegetarian meals   102
Salads   118
Eggs   121
Pizza and pasta   124

Something Sweet   **132**
    Desserts   132
    Muesli bars, muffins, cakes, biscuits and slices   158
    Sweet treats   173

Others   **183**
    Fats and oils   183
    Spreads   185
    Dips   188
    Sauces   190
    Odds and ends   194

Food for Special Occasions   **199**
    Birthday parties   199
    Christmas cakes and puddings   202
    Easter   204
    Salicylate and amine recipes   204
    Eating out   209
    Failsafe weight loss   211
    Travelling, camping and hiking   214
    Failsafe gardening   218
    Medications and remedies   221
    What about nutrition?   224

Gluten-free Cooking   **228**

Shopping List   **247**

Checklist of Common Mistakes   **255**

Frequently Asked Questions   **262**

Symptoms of Food Intolerance   **269**

Support and Further Information   **297**

Notes and References   **299**

Index   **305**

Nasty Additives Wallet List   **315**

Are You Affected by Food Chemicals?

What we eat has changed dramatically over the last 30 years, and so have our children. Behaviour and learning problems, asthma, depression, youth suicide and teenage violent crime are all increasing. Many parents find that raising children is not the joyful experience they were expecting, and I was one of them.

When my first baby was born, my life revolved around trying to get an unsettled baby to sleep. Then she grew into the terrible twos and never grew out. On good days she was charming, adorable and clever, but on her frequent bad days she was demanding, dissatisfied, grouchy, easily annoyed, argumentative, defiant, took hours to get to sleep and woke frequently. We had expected her to do well at school but she struggled with schoolwork.

For 11 years I did the rounds of doctors, baby-health nurses, psychologists, teachers, school counsellors, alternative practitioners, tutors, physiotherapists, dietitians and many more. I was told I was a bad mother; to use better behaviour management; to pour myself a stiff gin; to learn to live with it; that I needed medication; that she needed medication. After years of sleep deprivation, my marriage was at breaking point, and so was my sanity.

Of all the remedies we were offered, most helped a little. We tried various diets, for six years avoiding additives, sugar and dairy foods, but it wasn't until she did a 24-hour water-only fast in hospital at the age of 11 that I finally saw the daughter I'd always wanted. Under our eyes she became settled, calm, polite, interesting, intelligent and fun to be with. 'That's the child I want!' I said. Our paediatrician finally believed that her problems were food-related, and we started a three-week trial of a low salicylate diet.

A magic answer

Like most parents, I was reluctant to limit salicylates – which are found in fruit and vegetables – but within days the agreeable, compliant child we'd met in hospital returned, this time to stay. The magic answer for our daughter turned out to be additive-free, dairy-free, low-salicylate foods.

We were surprised to find that everyone in our family was affected, although in different ways and to a different range of food chemicals. It was like emerging from a nightmare. 'No one should have to go through that,' I thought, and started writing.

This book is intended to support families who are doing the diet that was such a miracle for us. It is based on the Elimination Diet developed by Doctors Swain, Soutter and Loblay at the Royal Prince Alfred Hospital Allergy Unit in Sydney, Australia. The recipes and hints can also be used by families who want to know how to reduce their intake of food additives and other chemicals.

> General information about food intolerances, along with comprehensive charts showing the content of natural salicylates, amines and glutamate in the most common foods, is available in *Friendly Food* by Anne Swain, Velencia Soutter and Robert Loblay (Murdoch Books, Australia, 2004). *Friendly Food* and additional information about the RPAH Elimination Diet and challenge protocols can be obtained online via the Royal Prince Alfred Hospital (RPAH) Allergy Unit website: (www.cs.nsw.gov.au/rpa/allergy).

Thirteen years on, every day I hear from grateful parents whose lives have been transformed like ours. 'Salicylates are our nemesis,' wrote a Sydney mother of two. 'I get cranky, stressed and short-tempered, my daughter gets teary at the drop of a hat.'

It is frustrating that the people in charge of our children's health are so reluctant to accept the implications of our changing food supply. It takes 30 years to notice the results of a national diet change, and effects are easier to understand if you can see them – as with the obesity epidemic – rather than when they manifest in the complicated issue of children's behaviour and learning.

One mother who was just starting the elimination diet with her son and already seeing improvements was devastated when her school counsellor dismissed the diet, saying 'there's no scientific evidence to prove this theory'. Experts who say that are ignoring the evidence. Negative diet-behaviour studies in the 1970s were mostly food-industry-funded, and we now know that the outcome of scientific research is likely to be favourable to the source of funding.

Independent scientists who conducted an extensive review concluded that the evidence strongly suggests that some children's behaviour is affected by some foods (see p. 299). They recommended that • food regulators should consider banning artificial colours • parents should try diet before medication for children's behaviour problems, and • schools should minimise the use of additives that may contribute to behaviour problems.

Schools following this advice see that it works. When TV chef Jamie Oliver introduced fresh, natural, additive-free school meals for 16,000 schoolchildren in the UK, after four weeks the teachers at Wingfield Primary School in London reported improvements in behaviour, reading, writing and concentration. They noticed that the children were calmer, and none of those who normally used asthma medication at school had needed their medication since the program began.

Similar findings were reported from Appleton Central School in Wisconsin, USA, where behaviour problems had been so extensive that the school required its own policeman. The numbers of school dropouts, expulsions, drug use, suicides and weapons violations dropped to zero after a similar eating program was implemented.

In Australia, most school principals are unwilling to initiate changes on this scale. In 2005, I took part in a simple two-week trial at Palmers Island Primary School where 120 students were shown how to read labels, asked to avoid 50 additives and provided with additive-free breakfasts. Staff, parents and students all saw changes – students were quieter, calmer, 'stopped yelling out in class', had better self-control, concentrated better, and classes were more harmonious. When the children again ate artificially coloured treats at the end of the study, they exhibited noisy, argumentative, 'in your face' behaviour, as shown on our

DVD (*Fed Up With Children's Behaviour*, available from www.fedup.com.au).

Meanwhile, parents are learning that diet is effective by trying it for themselves. 'Your DVD is currently doing the rounds of our kinder and all the mothers are commenting on the difference in their children!' wrote a mother from rural Victoria.

Some children improve just by avoiding a few additives, while others do best on the elimination diet, with fine-tuning supervised by a dietitian.

One father I'll call Robert emailed:

> 'I am an inch away from losing my temper again with my six-year-old son, who is driving us all to exasperation. When he is good he is a wonderful angel, but when he becomes oppositional, which can happen in a second, he is appalling. I love my boy, and I can't bear this. Do you have a straightforward page that I could attach to the fridge that says: Buy these things – feed him these things – and see what happens over three weeks???'

So Robert started with the Fridge List on p. 26. It's what we've kept in our pantry and eaten in our home since diet provided a magic answer for our daughter's behaviour 13 years ago.

Robert soon found that his son was very food sensitive. As well as avoiding additives, salicylates and amines, he had to avoid dairy foods and gluten. The family also needed some fine-tuning hints from the Checklist of Common Mistakes (p. 255) during the first six weeks.

After five months, Robert wrote that the improvement had been extraordinary: 'At the beginning of the year he was diagnosed with ADHD and ODD, and you wouldn't believe it now,' he said.

I wish you the same success.

What Every Parent Should Know About Food Intolerance

1. Food intolerance is not the same as a food allergy

When my daughter was born, I knew she was at risk of allergies because her father had hayfever and a food allergy. If Howard ate even the smallest amount of broccoli, within minutes the inside of his mouth started itching, his throat started swelling and he needed antihistamines. True allergic reactions like this – a reaction to the proteins in foods – are generally easy to identify. They can be confirmed by skin-prick tests and can be life-threatening.

> Hamidur Rahman had never had a severe reaction to peanuts but he avoided them because they made him feel itchy. Although his mother informed the teacher in charge of a school excursion about his peanut allergy, Hamidur died in 2002 at the age of 13 after taking part in a peanut butter challenge during the excursion trivia night.
>
> Peanut allergy is increasing. Helpful information about food allergies for parents and schools is available from www.allergyfacts.org.au.

So I followed the allergy recommendations of that time. I breastfed fully for five months and delayed introduction of known food allergens, avoiding peanuts during pregnancy and breastfeeding because I rarely ate peanuts anyway. As it turned out, my daughter didn't develop allergies.

What I didn't know at that time was that food *intolerance* – reactions to chemicals such as additives and salicylates in foods – is much more common than allergy. The behavioural reactions to foods that would come to dominate our lives were due to intolerance, not allergy, although it is possible to have both. In theory, everyone can be affected if the dose is high enough, but some families, like ours, are more sensitive than others.

2. You won't know if you are affected

Research shows that consumers will make the connection between what they eat and how they feel only if the reaction occurs within 30 minutes. As true food allergies – such as a reaction to peanuts – generally result in a quick response, they are relatively easy to identify. On the other hand, most intolerance reactions can be delayed for hours, even days, or build up slowly. If a child has a bad day on Monday, few parents think, 'That's because we had takeaways on the weekend.' Yet that's the way it happens, so most people who are affected by food additives don't realise they are affected.

3. Food intolerance can disturb every area of child-rearing

Parents assume that they will know if their children are affected by foods – or that someone will tell them – but that's not what happens. As the levels of potentially harmful food chemicals have slowly increased in our foods, their effects have crept up and have gradually come to be regarded as 'normal', or as new illnesses that require medication.

If one person in a family is affected you can be sure there will be others in the family who are food sensitive too, although they will probably be affected in different ways. It is common for mothers to comment: 'I thought I was doing this diet for my son's overactivity, but now I realise we all need to know about it.' Symptoms of food intolerance can include the following (and there are more details on p. 269):

The quiet ones
• inattentive, dreamy or lethargic • anxious, depressed, has panic attacks or self-harms • speech delay, learning delay • grizzly, miserable (in babies and young children).

The restless ones
• irritable, restless, easily distracted, restless legs • wakes at night or goes to bed like a jack-in-the-box • loud voice, talks too much, makes silly noises.

The defiant ones
• loses temper, argues with adults • refuses requests, defies rules • deliberately annoys others, blames others • touchy or easily annoyed • angry and resentful.

The others
• hives, eczema, nappy rash, cradle cap, thrush, other rashes • sensitive stomach, e.g. colic or reflux, recurrent mouth ulcers, constipation and/or diarrhoea, stomach aches, bloating, bedwetting, sneaky poos, incomplete evacuation • asthma, stuffy or runny nose, frequent colds, flu or ear infections • headaches, migraines.

It is possible to have symptoms from more than one category, and adults can be affected just as much as children.

Who is most likely to be affected?
• people from food intolerant families • people with exposure to environmental chemicals such as pesticides • people who eat the highest amounts of suspect food chemicals • people from low-income areas, because they eat more junk food • people who are ill, stressed or sleep-deprived • people who are taking medication • babies and young children, because they eat, drink and breathe proportionally more than adults – and reactions are related to dose • females – premenstrually, postnatally and on the contraceptive pill • seniors, due to decreasing ability of kidneys and liver to detoxify the blood.

Food intolerance in babies

Symptoms of food intolerance in babies can include • frequent crying • difficulty settling to sleep • frequent night waking • reflux • colic • 'cappuccino poos' • nappy rash • thrush • eczema • cradle cap • other itchy skin rashes • bronchiolitis or asthma • frequent colds, flu and ear infections. For breastfed babies, food intolerance can also cause feeding problems such as breast refusal 'as if the milk doesn't taste right' and sore nipples from breastmilk with an irritant effect. Although breastfed babies are not supposed to be constipated, babies who go for 10–14 days without a bowel movement generally turn out to be food intolerant later on.

Food chemicals eaten by the mother can pass through breastmilk to affect babies. Problems can be made worse by • frequent takeaways brought home by helpful dads • keeping up fluids with additive-laden commercial soft drinks or strong tea • rewards such as artificially coloured chocolate biscuits • a 'healthy' diet very high in salicylates or amines • bingeing on dairy products because it is supposed to be good for the baby. Some breastfeeding mothers see a huge improvement in their babies just by avoiding additives such as artificial colours in their own diet. For extra sensitive babies, breastfeeding mothers can do an elimination diet supervised by an experienced dietitian (see p. 17).

Formula-fed babies with food intolerance may need special formulas, see p. 266.

Other problems for food intolerant babies include • teething gel with salicylates • artificial colours, flavours and/or preservatives in infant medications, painkillers and skin lotions (see p. 221) • perfumed airfresheners and aerosols (see p. 299) • preservatives in fruit juice drinks • salicylates and/or amines in weaning foods such as avocados, broccoli and bananas. Mothers who can trace the onset of their child's problems back to the introduction of solids often didn't recognise food intolerance at the time because they were looking for a quick allergic reaction rather than the slow build-up of fluctuating 'good days and bad days' that characterise food intolerance.

Testing for food intolerance

Contrary to what many alternative practitioners say, there are no scientifically proven laboratory tests for food intolerance. There are literally thousands of elimination diets, but the diet that I recommend as the most scientific and effective in the world is the low salicylate elimination diet introduced in the United States by Dr Ben Feingold in the 1970s, and refined over many years by Australian researchers.

This is how the elimination diet works. For three to six weeks children have to avoid • certain food additives • some natural food chemicals called salicylates (in most fruit and some vegetables), amines (in protein foods) and natural flavour enhancers called glutamates • in some cases, dairy products and wheat or gluten • perfumes and perfumed products such as aerosols and air-fresheners.

> The key with any elimination diet is to stick strictly to the shopping list. If a food isn't listed, don't eat it. If this seems restricted, just think about the Few Foods diet – it typically starts with rice, turkey, pears and lettuce.

The next step is to reintroduce one group of food chemicals at a time as *challenges* to find out exactly what's causing the problem. Some people are affected by only one food chemical and some react to all of them.

> **Q**. What does *failsafe* mean?
> **A**. It's a kind of dyslexic acronym meaning free of additives, and low in salicylates, amines and flavour enhancers.

Additive creep

Most parents are unaware of how much our food supply has changed since the early 1900s, when it was rare for families to eat out, there were daily deliveries of fresh meat, bread and milk, and most Australian families grew vegetables and fruit in their backyards. In the 1970s, when processed food became widely available, consumers started to eat daily food additives, and the levels have been slowly increasing since then.

A few children go ballistic soon after eating food colours, but what most people experience is a slow build-up of food chemicals leading to fluctuating symptoms that seem unrelated to foods. If you have ever, even once, seen your child react to any of the foods listed below, it means your child is food sensitive and is probably affected by many more food chemicals than you realise.

Common problem-causing foods

When a mother called Sophie started reading labels because of her five-year-old's behaviour, she was amazed at what she found.

- *Additives in junk*: soft drinks, cordials, sweets, flavoured snacks, chips and biscuits, ice-creams, ice tubes, takeaways and family-restaurant meals.

- *Additives in 'healthy foods'*: like bread (preservative 282), yoghurt (colour 160b, preservative 202), muesli bars (preservative 220), butter or margarine (preservative 200, antioxidant 320), cheese slices (preservative 200, colour 160b), juice (preservatives 211, 223), sausages (preservative 223, flavour enhancer 635).

After Sophie cut down on additives, she saw a 'fantastic' change in her son in three weeks. 'He seems a whole lot calmer,' she wrote. 'I was blaming my son's behaviour on immaturity, but I look back on the food I've been providing for my kids and I feel like such a fool.'

For some families, avoiding food colours and preserved bread is enough to see an improvement. Others need to take natural food chemicals seriously too:

- *Salicylates and amines* in some fruits, juice, dried fruit, vegetables and flavours, especially tomato paste and sauce, oranges, grapes, sultanas, broccoli and mint.

- Additives, salicylates and amines can pass through *breast milk* to affect babies.

Natural food chemicals

All foods are made up of hundreds of naturally occurring compounds that can have varying effects on us, depending on how much we eat and how sensitive we are.

'It may taste nice, but lunch is a bundle of chemicals whose impact we should seek to understand' – Tom Jaine, food writer, publisher and former editor of *The Good Food Guide*.

What are salicylates?

The effects of salicylates have been studied extensively over the last hundred years, largely through the effects of aspirin or acetylsalicylic acid, one of the salicylate family. When aspirin was first introduced it was regarded as a wonder drug with no side effects. Now the known side effects of aspirin are so extensive that one group of researchers described them as the 'protean manifestations' of salicylate toxicity, Proteus being an ancient Greek god who could assume any shape.

Doctors noticed in the 1960s that children's behaviour could be affected by salicylate medication, and one reported a patient who attacked him with a knife while 'under the influence of salicylates'. In the 1970s, American paediatrician Dr Ben Feingold noticed that children's behaviour could also be affected by natural salicylates in foods, but his diet achieved mixed results because it used an outdated food list that was not really low in salicylates.

In the mid-1980s Australian researchers published a new analysis of salicylate contents in foods, showing that there were salicylates in many more foods than previously thought. For people who had already been following low salicylate diets, the new salicylate information was a revelation. 'When I found the Australian salicylate lists I was so excited,' wrote a salicylate-sensitive asthmatic from New Mexico. 'I could finally understand what was happening – I had inadvertently been eating salicylates every day.' (See story 228 on www.fedup. com.au.)

Salicylates occur in varying amounts in • all fruit except pears • most vegetables (some of the lowest are potatoes, beans, cabbage and leeks: see Shopping List, p. 247) • in other plant foods such as herbs and spices. They are concentrated in processed foods such as dried fruit, sauces and strong fruit flavours.

Most parents are reluctant to consider a low salicylate diet. 'How can children live without fruit?' they ask, but it is only very recently that children have had constant access to a huge range of out-of-season fruits from distant countries.

Nearly two thousand years ago, the ancient Greek physician Galen, considered to be the co-founder of modern medicine, wrote that his father had lived to be a hundred by avoiding fruit. A low fruit diet can be healthy if vegetables are eaten. There are many more vegetables at the low end of the salicylate scale than fruit, and the latest research shows that some failsafe vegetables have much more powerful antioxidant effects than any fruits (see p. 105).

For people from food-intolerant families, salicylates are more likely to cause problems than any other food chemical, although, unlike artificial additives, one dose in food is unlikely to cause a reaction. Nearly every mouthful we eat contains salicylates, so what usually happens is that effects build up slowly, and fluctuate due to varying daily exposure to salicylates eaten in foods, absorbed through the skin and inhaled from perfumed products. Most people never realise they are salicylate sensitive until they do an elimination diet with challenges. For more details see the 'Salicylate' factsheet on the website www.fedup.com.au.

What are amines?

Biogenic amines such as tyramine in cheese and histamine in wine are common chemicals formed by the breakdown of proteins in foods. Probably best known as migraine triggers, amines can be associated with the usual wide range of food intolerance effects, including hyperactivity, aggression, depression, eczema, asthma and irritable bowel problems.

In my experience, more children are affected by salicylates than amines, but for those who are affected, avoiding amines can make a huge difference.

Foods that are known to contain varying amounts of amines include: fish, cheese, wine, some meats, some fruit such as bananas and avocados, some vegetables such as mushrooms, and fermented foods such as chocolate, sauerkraut and soy sauce, but basically any protein food can contain amines depending on the way it is handled. The amine content of foods varies greatly due to differences in processing, age, ripeness, handling, storage, the variety of the fruit or vegetable, cooking method and many other factors.

As with salicylates, amines are eaten many times a day every day, so most people who are sensitive to amines have no idea they are affected until they do an elimination diet. For more information about amines, see the 'Amine' factsheet on the website www.fedup.com.au.

How many people are affected by food intolerance?

Less than 1 per cent of the population are affected by food additives, according to scientific studies that have failed to understand the difference between allergy and intolerance. The food industry is happy to support this figure, arguing that so few people are affected they are not worth worrying about. More recently, the conservative World Health Organization upwardly revised its estimate of the number of asthmatic children affected by sulphite preservatives from less than 4 per cent to 20–30 per cent, meaning that in the general population about 10 per cent of Australia children are affected by this one food additive alone, not counting those who react with eczema, behaviour problems or irritable bowel symptoms.

When schools remove food additives they always report an improvement in their students, whether making extensive changes like Jamie Oliver's or asking children to avoid additives as in the Palmers Island trial and the Dingle School in the UK, where nearly 60 per cent of parents of an entire class of six-year-olds reported an improvement after two weeks additive-free. For many more examples, see the 'Schools go low additive' factsheet on www.fedup.com.au.

In theory everyone will react if the doses are high enough, so, as doses of food additives and salicylates and amines continue to increase in our food supply, we would expect to see more children affected every year, and that appears to be what is happening.

> 'I think your next book should be *How to tactfully suggest that someone else's child is a food responder*. I am just staggered at how much of our son's behaviour we see in other children whose parents insist that they do not react to food.'
> Reader, Melbourne

Considering all this, you'd think it would be sensible to reduce the number of additives in our food supply. We all have to live with the effects of difficult children in our schools or the costs of chronically ill people in our health-care system. Many families assume the government will protect

them, but that is not what I have found. Food manufacturers do not want to be told what to do by regulators, although they will listen to the demands of consumers.

In the last five years in the UK, many major supermarket chains including Sainsbury's, the Co-op, Marks & Spencer and Iceland have removed additives such as artificial colours and preservatives from own brands, and Nestlé Rowntree have switched to natural rather than artificial colours in their icon Smarties brand. In Australia, major bakeries have removed bread preservative (282). If enough consumers want additive-free foods, manufacturers will provide them.

How to avoid additives
Find a list on the product label headed 'Ingredients: ...' and check whether the additives listed following appear on the label. Numbers not included in the list are unlikely to cause reactions. There are hundreds of additives that have to be listed by name or number, as well as thousands of flavours that don't have numbers and don't have to be specified by name. So far, about sixty additives have been associated with symptoms of food intolerance, as well as some flavours. This leaves hundreds of additives that are unlikely to cause reactions, such as vitamin C (300), Vitamin E tocopherols (306), vegetable gums such as guar gum (412), and emulsifiers such as lecithin (322). If the food is unlabelled, ask the supplier what it contains. If the supplier doesn't know or won't tell you, don't eat it.

AVOID THESE ADDITIVES

COLOURS	
Natural colour annatto (bixin, norbixin) 160b **Artificial colours 102, 104, 107, 110, 122, 123, 124, 127, 128, 129, 132, 133, 142, 143, 151, 155** Allura red 129 (red 40 in USA) Amaranth 123 (red 2 in USA) Azorubine red, carmoisine 122 Brilliant Black 151 Brilliant Blue 133 (blue 1 in USA) Brown 155 Erythrosine 127 (red 3 in USA) Fast Green 143 Green S 142 (green 3 in USA) Indigotine 132 (blue 2 in USA) Ponceau 4R 124 (red 4 in USA) Quinoline yellow 104 Sunset yellow 110 (yellow 6 in USA) Tartrazine 102 (yellow 5 in USA) Yellow 2G 107	**USED IN** a wide range of sweet and savoury foods, drinks, confectionery, medicines, US breakfast cereals. Rarely used in Europe. **SAFE ALTERNATIVES** Riboflavins 101, Cochineal and carmines 120 (WARNING: some allergic reactions), Chlorophyls 140, Chlorophyls, copper complexes 141, Caramel (plain) 150, 150a, Vegetable carbon 153, Carotenes, beta Carotene 160a, Titanium dioxide 171, Iron oxides 172, Saffron, crocetin, crocin 164. *Plant-based natural colours, may contain salicylates:* Curcumins 100, Alkanet 103, Paprika oleoresins 160c, Lycopene 160d, Carotenal 160e, Carotenoic esters 160f, Flavoxanthin 161a, Lutein 161b, Kryptoxanthin 161c, Rubixanthin 161d, Violoxanthin 161e, Rhodoxanthin 161f, Beet Red 162, Anthocyanins 163.

PRESERVATIVES	
Sorbates 200–203 Calcium sorbate 203 Potassium sorbate 202 Sodium sorbate 201 Sorbic acid 200	**USED IN** processed fruit and vegetable products, drinks, cheese, ice-cream, breads and pasta, processed meats, dips, sauces, wine. **SAFE ALTERNATIVES** to many preservatives include refrigeration, freezing, ascorbates 300–304, improved hygiene, aseptic packaging. Fresh is best.
Benzoates 210–219, especially 211 in soft drinks Benzoic acid 210 Calcium benzoate 213 Potassium benzoate 212 Sodium benzoate 211 Ethyl 4-hydroxybenzoate 214, Sodium ethyl 4-hydroxybenzoate 215, Propylparaben 216, Sodium propylparaben 217, Methyl paraben 218, Sodium methylparaben 219*	**USED IN** most soft drinks, diet drinks, cordials, juice drinks. Also in semi-preserved fish products, desserts, dips and snacks. **SAFE ALTERNATIVES** How is it that some Schweppes drinks don't need this preservative?
Sulphites 220–228 Calcium hydrogen sulphite 227 Calcium sulphite 226 Potassium bisulphite 228 Potassium metabisulphite 224 Potassium sulphite 225 Sodium bisulphite 222 Sodium metabisulphite 223 Sodium sulphite 221 Sulphur dioxide 220	**USED IN** wine, beer, bread, processed meat like sausages, seafood like prawns, prepared salads, fruit salads, fruit and vegetable products like drinks. Very high in most dried fruits. **SAFE ALTERNATIVES** to many preservatives include refrigeration, freezing, ascorbates 300–304, improved hygiene, aseptic packaging. Fresh is best.

Names and numbers from Australia New Zealand Food Standards Code (to Amendment 87, 2006)

* permitted in food colours, ointments and medicines in Australia and New Zealand

Nitrates and nitrites 249–252
  Potassium nitrate 252
  Potassium nitrite 249
  Sodium nitrate 251
  Sodium nitrite 250
	USED IN processed meats like ham, salami, devon, and in cheese.

	SAFE ALTERNATIVES to many preservatives include refrigeration, freezing, ascorbates 300–304, improved hygiene, aseptic packaging, and, for meats, salt and sugar.

Propionates 280–283, especially 282 in bread
  Calcium propionate 282
  Potassium propionate 283
  Propionic acid 280
  Sodium propionate 281
	USED IN many breads in Australia and the US, and in cheese, jam, fruit and vegetable products. Very rare in Europe. Also added as fermented whey powder.

	SAFE ALTERNATIVES See above. In bread, a safe alternative is better bakery hygiene, such as wiping surfaces and machinery with vinegar.

SYNTHETIC ANTIOXIDANTS

| **Antioxidants 310–321**
  BHA 320
  BHT 321
  Dodecyl gallate 312
  Octyl gallate 311
  Propyl gallate 310
  TBHQ 319 | **USED IN** oils and margarines to prevent rancidity, chips, fried snack foods, fast foods. Not necessarily listed on labels where vegetable oil is a component. |
| | **SAFE ALTERNATIVES** Ascorbates 300–304, Tocopherols 306–309. Keep oil in refrigerator, protected from air and out of direct light to slow rancidity. |

FLAVOUR ENHANCERS

| **Glutamates 620–637, 640, 641 (MSG is 621)**
  Calcium dihydrogen diglutamate 623
  Disodium guanylate 627
  Disodium inosinate 631
  Ethyl maltol 637
  Glycine 640
  L-Glutamic acid 620
  L-leucine 641
  Magnesium diglutamate 625
  Maltol 636
  Monoammonium glutamate 624
  Monopotassium glutamate 622
  Monosodium glutamate 621
  Ribonucleotides 635 | **USED IN** tasty foods like flavoured noodles, snack foods, chips, crackers, sauces and fast foods. Glutamates are in hydrolysed vegetable (HVP) and plant protein, yeast extract, caseinate, broth, stock, soy sauce and 'natural flavourings'. |
| | **SAFE ALTERNATIVES** Salt. Glutamates were introduced into Western food after WWII and ribonucleotides in the last 10 years. Do we really need hyper-tasty food? |

ARTIFICIAL FLAVOURS

| No numbers since they are trade secrets | **USED IN** many foods, particularly where flavour has been damaged by processing. |
| | **SAFE ALTERNATIVES** Some natural flavours, including vanilla in small amounts. |

The letter E preceding a number (e.g. E102) stands for European regulations but the numbers are the same.

How we did our elimination diet

Before we started our elimination diet we had already gone additive-free. Some families can see big improvements by • switching to preservative-free bread (see shopping list, p. 247) • drinking water – it can be filtered, bottled, spring, mineral, soda water or tap water if it tastes good – but avoid soft drinks, cordial or juice, except for magic cordial (p. 63) as an occasional treat • avoiding nasty additives, especially artificial colours, preservatives and flavour enhancers (p. 15) • cutting down on some of the worst of the natural chemicals by avoiding tomato sauce, broccoli, citrus, grapes and dried fruit • switching to A2 milk (p. 267) • using the recipes in this book and *Friendly Food* (p. 298).

For us, cutting down didn't help enough. We achieved our greatest success by doing the elimination diet supervised by a supportive dietitian. The whole point about elimination diets is to get them right by sticking strictly to the foods in the shopping list, and the key is to be organised.

1. The diet that was a magic answer for us is called the RPAH Elimination Diet from the Royal Prince Alfred Hospital Allergy Unit in Sydney, Australia (www.cs.nsw.gov.au/rpa/allergy). It is best to be supervised by an experienced dietitian. **Our list of supportive dietitians** is available from confoodnet@ozemail.com.au. Dietitians are also available through www.daa.asn.au (Find an Accredited Practising Dietitian, Area of Practice: allergy and food sensitivity), the dietitians' department at your local hospital or community dietitians. Local failsafe contacts and failsafe email support groups (listed on www.fedup.com.au) can also recommend local dietitians. The benefits of a supportive dietitian include • increasing the chance of success • a dietitian's written report helps with schools – and, sadly, with courts during custody battles • dietitians can check nutrition • dietitians will provide a very useful diet booklet. There are numerous salicylate lists on the internet but they can be misleading. For example, if cauliflower appears on the low end of the scale, the list is out of date.

2. We had already consulted many doctors and knew that our daughter's problems were not due to a medical condition, but there are a few stories of people embarking on diets for **conditions that need medical treatment** so it's worth checking first. Medication for ADHD makes it much more difficult to achieve success on the diet, so families of medicated children often ask their doctor if they can start the diet during school – and thus drug – holidays.

3. The dietitian weighed our daughter and we continued that once a week at home. Caloric supplements such as Polycose can enhance appetite **if weight loss is a problem**, but we only used it a few times years later during an illness.

4. We had to decide whether to avoid **dairy foods and gluten** as well. We already thought dairy was a problem so after discussing it with our dietitian we chose to go dairy-free but not gluten-free (see p. 266). That turned out to be a good compromise, although years later I twice developed gluten intolerance after severe gastrointestinal infections.

5. When I first saw the dietitian's booklet, like most mothers I was overwhelmed. 'This is too hard!' I said. The trick was to **stop focusing on what we couldn't eat**, and to look at what we could eat. Compared to the Few Foods diet – turkey, rice, pears and lettuce – it's easy.

6. Ingredients change frequently and some of the products on the shopping list were already out of date. That's why we established the **Product Updates** on www.fedup.com.au so that readers could easily check on the latest changes.

7. We established **a failsafe house** by eating or giving away all the unsuitable food in our kitchen. It is best for the whole family to do the diet for support. It is common for fathers to refuse to do this, but at least they can appear to support the diet while at home. Children who are expected to stick to this diet while others at home eat tempting foods beside them will very reasonably sneak food or money.

8. I negotiated **incentives** with our children – 'What's this worth to you?' Daily credit points and weekly rewards with a bonus after three weeks worked better than one big bribe. In our case our children settled for cash, but I bargained them down. Some mothers have to negotiate for the support of their partner or others in the household.

9. We marked **D-day** – diet day – on our calendar, waiting until special occasions like birthday parties and school camp were out of the way.

10. I wrote down what we normally ate then drew up a **week's menu plan** (p. 26) using the **Shopping List**. The important thing was to find foods our children would eat. Some families have a lot of home-made chicken and chips in the first three weeks, when the most important thing is to get over food cravings and withdrawals.

11. The first **shopping** trip was hard. I took a list of the ingredients I needed for the week's menu plus the shopping list for other ideas and the list of additives to avoid (see card). It took a long time because I had to read labels. These days, shopping is quicker and cheaper because I know exactly what I want and there's so much I don't buy.

12. I tried out some **recipes** before D-day. I cooked and froze some meals and treats, such as failsafe mince, pear muffins and biscuits, and had magic cordial, pear jam and icypoles ready.

13. I scored my child's behaviour on a **rating scale** like the one on p. 23 so that there was a starting point against which to measure progress.

14. On D-day, **we started the diet**. I found the first few days were difficult, and a few times we had a bowl of Rice Bubbles because I couldn't think of anything else, but after that we settled into it.

15. I would have found it helpful to talk to others in the same situation. That's why we started failsafe **email groups** and local supports, so parents can discuss the diet and suitable products in their area (see www.fedup.com. au). There are also regular newsletters with updates about product changes, recipes and inspiration – send an email with 'subscribe' in the subject line to failsafe_newsletter-subscribe@yahoogroups.com.

16. I kept a **diary** of food and symptoms. It should also include toothpaste, medication and anything that goes on the skin. I noted changes in behaviour, learning and health. Mothers find it is easier to see results when reading the diary than when surrounded by the hurly-burly of family life. Positive behaviours such as 'fell asleep within minutes', 'fed dog without being asked', 'went to bed without arguing' can be the first sign of improvement. In our case we saw virtually immediate improvements in sleeping, but

we had already been additive-free for years. People who are starting from scratch may take a week or more to see improvements. In retrospect I should have been looking more at physical symptoms in the rest of us.

17. **Withdrawal symptoms** often occur within the first two weeks, in our case on days four and five. These can be • feeling tearful and overwhelmed • strong food cravings • irritability • any symptoms that existed before the diet • flu and other illnesses (see p. 274) • mouth ulcers • any other physical symptoms. Howard and I were both surprised by my uncharacteristically aggressive outburst when he ate a mango in front of me (he didn't do that again!). Because I've been through it, I feel strongly that children shouldn't be punished for outbursts during withdrawals, but should be kept home from school if possible and away from stress. It's not their fault. We probably made our withdrawal symptoms worse by bingeing on fruit and take-aways the weekend before starting.

18. It is extremely easy to make a mistake that stops the diet from working. That's why I wrote the **Checklist of Common Mistakes**, see p. 255 (the website also has a constantly updated version). There are lots of foods allowed on the dietitians' lists that affect our family and other readers, so many newbies find their diet needs fine-tuning. Some children improve within days; others improve slowly, going through the second week blahs and only coming good in the middle of the third week. Success is the greatest motivator. Families who see huge improvements are highly motivated to continue, so it is worth getting the diet right. If there is no improvement after a week or two, dietitians, failsafe contacts and email groups can offer suggestions.

19. **Children cannot be punished into sticking to this diet.** My children told me years later that what helped them most was the example I set by sticking to the diet too. I also gave them lots of extra love and hugs, spent extra time on outings and board games, and praised them lavishly for sticking to it. We treated it as a family adventure that we were all in together. When we started the diet I had been at the end of my tether so I had to work on rebuilding love, positivity and fun. Laughter therapy really works, so we had family nights with comedy videos.

20. As soon as the diet kicked in, my daughter became more amenable to discipline, so we introduced a **behaviour management** program that doubled the effect of the diet. Since then I have discovered *1-2-3 Magic*

(www.parentmagic.com or www.parentshop.com.au), which seems to be the easiest and most effective program on the market. Over the years I have seen many readers achieve magic results with it – but all agree it doesn't work until the child is failsafe.

21. There were such massive improvements in my daughter by the end of two weeks that we started our **first challenge**, but another week would have been better. Challenges consist of the reintroduction of one group of food chemicals at a time and recording their effects, as described in the dietitian's booklet. In retrospect, we didn't do challenges for long enough, focused too much on behaviour, and missed many physical symptoms. There's a good example of a challenge diary on p. 204. Discussing challenges with others in the failsafe email support groups can be very helpful. We skipped additive challenges because we already knew they affected us. Over the years, occasional mistakes have confirmed their effects. We were all affected by salicylates with many different symptoms. In addition, two of us were affected by amines, and three of us by dairy products. You can do anything as a challenge, so we did a sugar cube challenge, twice – I was amazed to see that my daughter passed – and a Mars Bar challenge (failed). Fish-oil supplements, vitamins, untested foods, anything can be done as a challenge, but it has to be done according to the rules in dietitians' booklets. It is never enough to eat one serve and conclude that an item is safe. At the end of challenges, those who passed their amine challenge were able to reintroduce amine-containing foods, so in our family two people can have unlimited bananas, yellow pawpaws, tinned or frozen fish, additive-free ham and bacon – from organic suppliers – unflavoured chocolate and cocoa. As well, the one who is okay with both dairy and amines can have unlimited milk, cheese and yoghurt. Two of us have subsequently passed an A2 milk challenge (www.a2australia.com.au) and now drink that, and one is yet to do that challenge, but we are less hopeful.

22. After failing the challenges, we had to work out our **tolerance** for that chemical. Some people who fail the amine challenge find that chocolate is a disaster and they can manage a little banana, and some are the reverse. Unfortunately, I am one of the latter – I simply can't eat commercial bananas, although I can eat large quantities of the small old-fashioned variety with seeds in Bali and Nepal. With salicylates, we were instructed to introduce

half a cup of salicylate foods (such as carrots, sweet potatoes, Chinese greens, snow pea sprouts, mangoes or Delicious apple) every second day for two weeks, then daily for two weeks, then one cup every second day for two weeks, and so on, until we reacted. Then we went back one step. We all have differing sensitivities – from the most sensitive on half a cup every second day to the least sensitive managing one cup every day plus occasional treats (peaches, rockmelon, watermelon). Our daily sensitivity depends a lot on varieties, ripeness, and our own stress levels. When we are on holidays we can manage much more. We generally tighten up on the diet during illness or medication, stress such as exams or deadlines, premenstrually, and when short of sleep. Regular enjoyable exercise and relaxation increases our tolerance. Our daughter is the most sensitive and doesn't proceed beyond the first level during term; the males of the family have higher tolerances than the females.

23. After we had finished challenges and settled into a new way of eating, we went back to our dietitian and had our **nutrition** checked, particularly because we had to avoid salicylates and dairy products. I was pleased to find we were doing fine in all respects, except that my dairy-free son who doesn't like soymilk had to work at getting enough calcium – not an issue for him now that he can manage A2 milk.

24. During our elimination diet we changed our washing powder, deodorant and toothpaste, but didn't take **environmental chemicals** seriously until years later when we stayed in a friend's strictly smell-free home and realised how good it felt. We now avoid a wide range, including • aerosols • perfumed household cleaners • sunblock • personal care products (see p. 247 for alternatives) • solvents, glues and paints • new furniture unless made from non-smelly products • pesticides • house renovations, unless low chemical. I have seen children affected for months by house renovations. Avoidance of environmental chemicals can be important for anyone, but even more for people with chronic fatigue syndrome (CFS), autism, lethargy and eczema.

25. Most children like to eat fatty and sugary foods while being weaned off processed food, and mine were no exception. As our tastes settled down, we reduced our intake of fats and sugars, and ate more **permitted vegetables.** There are many hints in this book about how to get vegetables into children, and I figure I must have succeeded because my children have continued to eat permitted vegetables, including Brussels sprouts, in soups and stews since they left home and started catering for themselves.

A rating scale

Assessment

Some people use rating scales to assess behaviour so they can see changes before and after diet or behaviour management, but the one I have found the most useful is a list I made myself. I wrote down the ten things that bothered me most about my child, and rated each item for how much it bothered me, on a scale of 0–3, where 3 is worst. I repeated this after the diet, as well as before and after a behaviour management program.

Possible problems are • sleeping (falling asleep, waking, night terrors) • eating (fussy eater, won't try new foods, won't eat breakfast, craves certain foods) • gut problems (reflux, bedwetting, sneaky poos, other) • asthma • oppositional behaviour (defiant, argumentative, always says no, always breaks rules) • forgetful and disorganised • anxious, depressed, panic attacks • restless, can't sit still • irritable, easily annoyed • inattentive • loud, makes silly noises, talks too much, stutter, speech delay • learning problems (maths, reading, writing), coordination problems, social problems • won't do chores when asked, won't do homework • won't go to bed • fights constantly with siblings. See other possible symptoms on p. 269.

SYMPTOM	SCORE BEFORE DIET/AFTER DIET	
e.g. often takes hours to get to sleep	3	1
1.		
2.		
3.		
4.		
5.		
6.		
7.		
8.		
9.		
10.		

- During the diet, I kept a daily food and symptom diary so I could look back and see changes. I added comments like 'fed the dog without being asked – for the first time ever!'
- We experienced withdrawal symptoms on days four and five (can be anger, anxiety, weeping, bad behaviour, physical symptoms, etc.) but they can occur any time in the first two weeks.
- For families where the diet doesn't seem to be making any difference within ten days, I've included the Checklist of Common Mistakes (p. 255) made up of readers' mistakes. There are many helpful email groups: see email support on www.fedup.com.au.

The 13 Commandments

1. **Failsafe your house** by getting rid of all unsuitable food – eat it or give it away.

2. **It's easiest for the whole family** to do the diet, at least for the first three weeks (usually except Dad – they can just appear to do the diet while they are at home).

3. **Arrange a bribe** with your child. Ask 'What's it worth to you?', then negotiate. Daily payments are better than one huge bribe at the end. Negotiate also with ex-partners and any others who care for the children.

4. **If your children make mistakes**, thank them for telling you. Discuss with them how to avoid that situation in future; for example, offer a reward for refusing off-diet foods at school, and have a slice of failsafe birthday cake in the freezer at preschool.

5. **Don't worry too much about fussy eaters** in the first few weeks, just find something they will eat from the main meals section (such as chicken and chips) until they get over their withdrawal symptoms and food cravings. After that they will probably eat better than ever before.

6. **Be prepared to avoid all suspect foods** – when a mother writes 'my son loves yoghurt so much he would be devastated if I took it away from him', I am suspicious, because whatever you find hardest to give up is most likely to affect you.

7. **Encourage a happy home**. Most families come to the diet as a last resort when they are utterly desperate. Reduce conflict by avoiding confrontations. Treat each other with the respect and kindness you would show to strangers, and laugh often.

8. **Do one thing at a time**. This diet works far better when followed 100 per cent, not in combination with other supplements or medication. Allow at least six months to give it a really good go before leaping into other therapies. It is possible to use both diet and medication for ADHD but get the diet sorted out *first*.

9. **Stop blaming giftedness for bad behaviour** or depression. Gifted children often have food intolerance that is more likely to cause these problems than boredom.

10. **Read the Checklist of Common Mistakes**, many times. Everyone thinks 'this doesn't apply to me', but it does.

11. **Include regular exercise** in your routine. It's a great way to burn off the effects of nasty food chemicals, overcome stress and depression, control appetite and avoid weight problems.

12. **Turn off the TV** to avoid food advertisements. Studies show that food advertisements really work. We hired videos instead. Some people tape their favourite shows so they can fast-forward through the ads.

13. **Home-cooking is best**. Supermarket foods often have hidden ingredients and flavours. I know cooking seems like a lot of work but in the long run it's worth doing it yourself to get it right.

The Fridge List

Breakfast

Rolled oats, porridge (p. 31)

Rice Bubbles, Weet-Bix (limit to 2 every second day at first)

Milk, A2 milk, soymilk, ricemilk

Eggs (boiled, scrambled, poached, toad in the hole, French toast) (p. 121)

Toast with butter only; or with pear jam, golden syrup, cashew spread

Pancakes with pure maple syrup (p. 35)

Pear smoothie (p. 61)

Lunch

Sandwiches, rolls or wraps, e.g. chicken, egg and lettuce (p. 40)

HFC chicken nuggets (p. 90)

Fried rice (p. 57)

Hard-boiled egg, omelette, leftover frittata

Failsafe salad with beans and pasta (p. 43)

Baked potato with cream cheese and chives

Chicken pasta (p. 48)

Home-made pie or sausage roll (p. 44)

Chicken and/or vegetable soup/stew (p. 71)

Main meal

Home-made chicken nuggets and chips (p. 90)

Failsafe burger/pizza/frittata (p. 74)

Spaghetti with garlic mince topping (p. 125)

Ten-minute stir-fry (chicken, beef, lamb, egg, vegetables) (p. 80)

Home-made fish fingers or pan-fried fresh fish (p. 99)

Grilled lamb/steak/chicken/failsafe sausages with vegetables (p. 75)

Roast chicken/beef/lamb with vegetables (p. 94)

Chicken and chickpeas (p. 99) or Irish stew (p. 85)

Drinks

Water – filtered, bottled, spring, mineral, soda, tap (if no nasty taste) · decaf coffee · unflavoured milk, A2 milk, soymilk, ricemilk, So Good Soyaccino soymilk · magic cordial (p. 63).

Snacks

Fresh ripe peeled pear or equivalent (limit 2 per day) · Diced Pear Fruit Cups in syrup, can be frozen (see Shopping List) · plain or buttered wheat crackers such as Saladas · home-made muffins · Brumby's white iced finger buns · plain rice cakes with failsafe hummus (p. 189) or butter/margarine and home-made pear jam (p. 186) · trail mix made from unsulphited dried pears, Chickadamias and raw cashews (see Shopping List) · home-made icypoles (p. 66) · home-made chicken noodle soup (p. 43) · home-made scones or pikelets (p. 52) · home-made potato wedges (p. 54) · sandwiches · beans on toast (p. 106) · anything from the lunch or main-meals menu, e.g. pasta · plain or vanilla yoghurt (see Shopping List) · plate of crunchy failsafe salad vegetables, e.g. celery sticks filled with home-made cashew paste (p. 187) or failsafe hummus (p. 189) · home-made rolled oat bars (p. 160) or other biscuits · toast and home-made pear jam or other spreads · Kettle plain chips

Treats and lollies

See Something Sweet (p. 132).

Vitamins

See Vitamin icypole recipe (p. 68).

Toothpaste

See Shopping List.

Failsafe substitutes

These are what my family uses as failsafe substitutes for common foods.

alcohol	gin, vodka, whisky
baked beans	kidney beans or canned butter beans with pear ketchup
biscuits	shortbreads/home-made (p. 170)/ commercial biscuits on shopping list
bread	preservative-free (see Shopping List), rice cakes, Saladas
breadcrumbs	rice crumbs (p. 194)
brown sugar	light brown sugar – not dark and coloured with molasses
burgers	home-made (p. 74)
butter	pure butter, Mainland Butter Soft, Nuttelex
cakes	home-made (p. 158)
cheese	preservative-free ricotta or cream cheese
chips	Kettle plain chips (infrequently), also see hot chips below
chocolate	carob instead of chocolate, cocoa, Milo
cooking oil	see failsafe oils (p. 183)
cordial	see magic cordial recipe (p. 63)
crumb mix	see breadcrumbs (p. 194)
dried fruit	unsulphited dried pears (see Shopping List)
fish fingers	home-made (pp. 59, 93)
'flavours'	no need for added flavours, we enjoy fresh, natural, quality ingredients
fries	home-made, see hot chips below
ginger	in gingerbread, use brown sugar instead
gluten-free	see gluten-free section (p. 228)
hot chips	see chips recipe (p. 104) or use Logan Farm frozen oven fries
icypoles	home-made (p. 66)
jam	pear jam (p. 186); pawpaw jam if amines are okay (see Product Updates) on www.fedup.com.au
juice	water, home-made icypoles, magic cordial (p. 63)
honey	maple syrup, rice malt, golden syrup
KFC	HFC (p. 90)
lemon juice	'citric' lemon juice (p. 194)
'lite'	means more additives; eat smaller portions of full fat foods less often
margarine	Nuttelex, and see Shopping List (read labels carefully)
milk	A2 milk (www.a2australia.com.au), soymilk, ricemilk
noodles	uncoloured noodles, no flavour sachet (see Shopping List)
nuggets	home-made (p. 175)
Nutella	Deborah's cashew paste variation (p. 187)
pasta topping	see pasta section (p. 128)
peanut butter	failsafe hummus (p. 189); Deborah's cashew paste (p. 187); soy butter (p. 188)
pizza	home-made (p. 124)
salt	use for flavour – failsafe eating is naturally low in salt
soft drinks	see magic cordial recipe with soda water (p. 63)
soy sauce	golden syrup
tomato sauce	Howard's bean paste, pear ketchup, pear puree, mayo (see sauces)
toothpaste	plain, unflavoured toothpaste or wet brush (p. 256)
sweets	toffees, caramels, butterscotch (for others, see shopping list)
takeaways	plain BBQ chicken if available – no stuffing, no seasoning, no seasoned salt; own Brumby's or Bakers Delight rolls, salad; grilled fresh fish, maybe a tiny amount of hot chips; own fresh rolls, salad; potato-cart baked potato, own Nuttelex or cream cheese and chives; steak sandwich, no sauce, no onions, use own bread
Vegemite	buttered toast with salt
vitamins	permitted supplements (see Vitamin icypoles)

Weights and Measures

Liquid measures

Cups and tablespoons used throughout are Australian metric. A standard teaspoon is the same (5 ml) in Australia, America and Britain. An Australian metric tablespoon equals 4 teaspoons (20 ml), different from America and Britain, where 1 tablespoon equals 3 teaspoons (15 ml). One metric cup equals 250 ml in Australia and is the same size in America (8 fl oz).

Weights

GRAMS AND OUNCES APPROXIMATE CONVERSION TABLE

ozs	1	2	3	4	5	6	7	8
g	25	50	75	125	150	175	200	225
ozs	9	10	11	12	13	14	15	16 = 1 lb
g	250	275	325	350	375	400	425	450

1000 g (grams) = 1 kg (kilogram) = 2 lbs 4 oz

Oven temperature

CENTIGRADE		FAHRENHEIT
110°C	very cool	225°F
130°C	cool	260°F
180°C	moderate	350°F
220°C	hot	425°F
240°C	very hot	475°F

Some Australian–American terms, with thanks to the Failsafe USA group

- Biscuits: crackers or cookies
- Caster sugar: powdered sugar, very fine white sugar, e.g. processed plain white sugar in your food processor
- Cordial: a drink base similar to Kool-Aid but sold as a liquid
- Cornflour: corn starch
- Cold pressed: expeller pressed
- Eggs (raw) shouldn't be eaten in the USA (see warning, p. 61).
- Esky: cooler
- Fairy floss: cotton candy
- Fruit and vegetables:
  choko: chayote, vegetable pear
  marrow: squash
  pawpaw (yellow, amines): papaya (if red, amines and salicylates) or pawpaw
  rockmelon (salicylates): cantaloupe (green version is honeydew)
  shallots: green onions
  sultanas: golden raisins
  swedes: rutabaga, yellow turnip
- Glucose syrup: White Karo syrup (corn based)
- Golden syrup: make a substitute by combining 1 cup white sugar, 1 cup brown sugar (not raw) and 1 cup water. Boil on low heat in an open saucepan for about 20 minutes, until the temperature is 110°C (230°F). Cool and store in a glass jar at room temperature. Lyle's Golden Syrup is available in USA but contains some salicylates.
- Grilled: broiled (the Australian barbeque is the USA grilled over open flame)
- Icypoles: popsicles
- Icing: frosting
- Icing sugar: confectioner's sugar (sometimes containing added cornstarch in both countries)
- Jam: jelly
- Jelly: jello
- Lamingtons: cubes of sponge cake, normally dipped in chocolate and coconut

- Lamington tin (swiss roll tin): similar in size to the American standard 13" × 9" pan
- Mince (as in beef): ground beef
- Muesli: muesli if uncooked 'raw' oat grain breakfast cereal, not sugared and often with dried fruit; but granola if baked oat grain cereal, always sweetened, often with dried fruit and nuts plus flavourings
- Nuttelex is a dairy-free margarine: Shedd's Willow Run dairy-free soybean margarine (if you can tolerate soy), phone toll free 1800 735 3554.
- Paracetamol (e.g. Panadol): acetominophen (e.g. Tylenol), often with cornstarch as the filler
- Rice Bubbles: Rice Krispies (contains malt, not gluten-free – Erewhon Gluten Free Crispy Rice Cereal is a USA brand that is gluten-free and very tasty)
- Rissoles: beef or lamb patties
- Sports drinks: thirst quenchers, e.g. Gatorade and Pedialyte
- Soft drinks: soda, soda pop, pop
- Soda water: club soda
- Scones: biscuits
- Sugar: pure refined white cane sugar. Beet sugar may contain sulphite residues that can affect extra-sensitive individuals. Corn and cane syrup may contain some salicylates
- Sweets, lollies, confectionery: candies

Brand-named foods recommended by US readers

See 'Product Updates' on www.fedup.com.au. For more information from the failsafe USA email discussion group send 'subscribe' in the subject line to failsafeUSA-subscribe@yahoogroups.com.

Breakfasts

Five-minute oats (may contain gluten, see box below)

Oats are the new health food in Britain, where sales have increased 80 per cent in the last five years due to their excellent nutritive value – oats are low in saturated fat, low in salt, high in fibre and have a naturally low GI (glycaemic index).

½ cup plain rolled oats per person
1 cup water per person

Place oats in a large microwave-safe bowl and microwave on high for 1 minute, stir, then microwave again for a further 4 minutes.

VARIATIONS • For a creamier texture, make cooktop porridge by placing rolled oats in a small saucepan with cold water and bring to the boil. Reduce heat and simmer for five minutes, stirring constantly while the porridge thickens • For an even creamier texture, particularly with very chewy rolled oats, the traditional Scottish method of soaking oats overnight then cooking to a creamy consistency works well using 2 parts water to 1 part oats • With quick-cook oats, simply pour over boiling water and stir.

Gluten in oats is due to contamination from other crops. In Sweden, oats that have been specially grown, milled and packaged so as not to become contaminated with wheat, rye or barley are available from food manufacturer Semper AB. In Australia it is now possible to buy certified contamination-free oats from Freedom Foods (www.freedomfoods.com.au).

Processed cereals

Rice Bubbles and puffed rice (many brands) are the safest packaged cereals. Plain, additive-free, wheat-based processed cereals are permitted, but many children with behaviour problems cannot tolerate the wholegrain of wheat in products like All Bran, Weeties, Vita Brits, Weet-Bix and Special K (see box below).

Cereal toppings

Serve rolled oats and cereals with any of the following from the shopping list according to your tolerance: pears, whichever form of milk you are using (regular, A2 milk, soymilk, ricemilk), yoghurt or soy yoghurt, light brown sugar (not coloured with molasses), maple syrup, golden syrup, rice malt or rice syrup. The two in our family who have passed their amine challenge have sliced bananas. Those of us who can manage a few more salicylates can sometimes have stewed rhubarb from our salicylate allowance – rhubarb is another traditional food making a big comeback in Britain.

VARIATIONS • *Gluten-free*: malt-free rice cereals, puffed millet, puffed amaranth, puffed buckwheat • buckwheat pancakes • porridge made from rice flakes • millet porridge (p. 236) • sago, tapioca or rice pudding (p. 152) • malt-free yoghurt • *Dairy-free*: use rice or soymilk, colour-free soy yoghurt • see Shopping List for product suggestions.

Avoid corn-based cereals like Cornflakes and Nutri-Grain, and any cereal containing artificial colours, natural colour annatto (160b), fruit, honey or raw sugar. Note that 'all natural' cereals can contain colour (160b) listed as annatto extracts. Some people, including children with behaviour problems, are affected by a natural chemical in wholegrain products such as wholemeal bread and wholewheat cereals – these people tolerate refined cereals, white flour and white bread better than wholegrains. For more details see Checklist of Common Mistakes.

Rice porridge

½ cup medium-grain plain white rice

1 cup water or milk, A2, soymilk or
  ricemilk

Place rice and water in a small saucepan and bring to the boil, stirring occasionally. Reduce heat, cover and simmer for 12–15 minutes. Sweeten to taste with maple syrup, golden syrup, plain white sugar, or rice syrup.

VARIATION • For babies, puree in blender. Baby formula can be used instead of milk.

Toasted muesli

This recipe can compete with commercial cereals because of the high sugar content. Reduce quantities of sugar as children learn to live without processed foods.

1½ cups rolled oats

2 tbsp brown sugar

2 tsp white sugar

1 tbsp failsafe oil (p. 184)

Combine all ingredients in a large bowl and mix well. Stir mixture in a hot frying pan for a few minutes until golden brown and smelling delicious. Remove from heat immediately to prevent burning. Serve muesli with yoghurt for a healthy breakfast.

VARIATION • Add 2 crushed Weet-Bix, ½ cup puffed amaranth, ½ cup puffed millet, ½ cup Rice Bubbles and ½ cup All-Bran to cooled mix above. Store in airtight container.

Gluten-free muesli

Try different brands of puffed rice – they can vary from large and chewy to small and crunchy.

1 cup puffed rice

1 cup puffed millet

1 cup puffed amaranth

1 cup rice bran

1 cup chopped cashew nuts

Mix together and store in an airtight container. Serve with milk, soymilk or ricemilk, yoghurt or soy yoghurt, pear and sweetener.

> Amaranth is an ancient Aztec grain, which is enjoying a revival thanks to its extraordinary nutritive values: 11 per cent fibre, 17 per cent protein (which is the highest of any cereal), and an amino acid composition close to optimal for human nutrition. Eat it in combination with other cereals, in muesli bars (p. 159), or alone. Don't confuse amaranth the grain with amaranth the nasty artificial colour 123 (Red 2 in USA).

Toast

Use toasted failsafe bread or croissants (p. 40) topped with failsafe spreads (p. 40).

VARIATION • *Gluten-free*: use gluten-free bread (p. 234), toasted or heated in the microwave for 10–20 seconds until hot and steaming.

Home-made yoghurt
This is a cheap, simple way to make fresh yoghurt.

yoghurt-maker with a very clean container
milk or soymilk (not successful with
   ricemilk)
2 tbsp mild natural or vanilla yoghurt per
   half litre of milk as starter. For dairy-
   free use soy yoghurt or Easiyo soy
   starter.

Fill the container of your yoghurt-maker to the fill line with milk or milk substitute. Add starter and stir well. Leave for at least six hours, or as recommended by the manufacturer. Refrigerate when ready. For flavoured yoghurt, mix with pear jam or maple syrup.

VARIATIONS • For A2 milk, add 3 tbsp as starter • Use an Esky (Chilly Bin, cooler) with a hot-water bottle wrapped in a towel instead of a yoghurt-maker.

Potential problems with commercial yoghurt include natural annatto colour 160b, artificial colours, preservatives, malt (if gluten-free), inulin (possible allergy), fruit flavours or fruit juice sweetener (salicylates) or too much vanilla (vanilla is permitted but limited to 2 drops per day from all sources). Plain yoghurt that tastes strong and sharp can affect amine responders, so fresh, mild yoghurt is safest. As an amine responder, I find most plain commercial yoghurts including Easiyo are too strong for me in big quantities or unless very fresh. I prefer Vaalia plain yoghurt as the mildest, or to make my own. People who are affected by cows' milk need to avoid cows' milk yoghurt too.

Pancakes (wheat with gluten-free variation)
There are two types of pancakes: thick pancakes that rise because they are made with baking powder, and thin pancakes, or crêpes, made without rising agents. Thick pancakes are easier.

1 cup self-raising flour or gluten-free flour
   (p. 233)
1 large egg
1 cup milk, A2 milk, soymilk or ricemilk
failsafe oil (p. 184) or pure butter for
   frying

Blend together flour, egg and water until smooth: a wand blender in a jug is ideal. Cook in a hot, lightly oiled frying pan. When first side is golden brown, and top is dry, turn carefully with a spatula, and brown remaining side. Serve with pure butter or failsafe margarine (p. 183) and pure maple syrup, or stewed pears and yoghurt, or savoury fillings.

VARIATIONS • For amine non-responders, stir 1 ripe banana, thinly sliced, through batter just before cooking • *Gluten-free*: I use the Orgran buckwheat pancake premix, which is additive-free and has no added flavours.

There are permitted wheat-based and gluten-free commercial pancake pre-mixes, see Shopping List. Maple syrup must be pure with no preservative or added flavour.

Pancake for one

Family members using different kinds of flours can make their own mix. Cook the gluten-free mix first to avoid contamination.

1 large egg or 1 tbsp failsafe oil (p. 184)
3 tbsp flour (any type, from self-raising to
   gluten-free premix)
3 tbsp milk, A2 milk, soymilk or ricemilk.

Break egg into a mug. Beat lightly with a fork. Add flour and mix with fork until smooth. Add milk and beat until smooth. Mixture should be wet enough to pour smoothly. Add extra milk if necessary. Cook as for previous recipe.

Boiled or poached eggs (p. 121)

Scrambled eggs on toast

A quick nutritious meal that can be eaten at any time of the day.

1–2 eggs
1 tbsp milk or milk substitute per egg
salt to taste
knob of pure butter or failsafe margarine
    (p. 183)
fresh chives, chopped
2 slices sandwich or cob loaf bread,
    toasted

Beat eggs with milk and add salt. Gently melt the butter in a pan and stir in the eggs, stirring constantly until the eggs are soft, fluffy and nearly set. Eggs will become hard if overcooked. To serve, spoon the scrambled eggs onto toast and top with chopped chives. Serves 1–2.

French toast

4 slices failsafe bread (p. 40) or gluten-
    free bread (p. 234)
2 eggs, beaten
1 tbsp butter or failsafe oil (p. 183)

Soak bread in beaten egg. Melt butter in pan and cook bread on both sides, pushing down flat with egg slice, until golden. Serve with real maple syrup.

Aussie toad in the hole

As seen in the Palmer's Island school breakfasts on the DVD (p. 298).

1 egg
1 slice of failsafe bread (p. 40)
Failsafe oil for frying (p. 184)

Place a cookie-cutter or a small glass over the middle of your bread and press hard to make a round hole. Place the bread flat on the surface of a well-oiled preheated frying pan and crack the egg into the centre hole. Cook for about two minutes while the bread browns and the egg hardens, then flip and repeat on the other side.

VARIATION • Spread both sides of the bread with butter or failsafe margarine (p. 183), cut hole in the middle of bread and place the bread flat on a preheated but unoiled frying pan.

Plain omelette

1 or 2 eggs

1 tbsp water (optional)

salt to taste

failsafe oil (p. 184) or pure butter

Beat eggs. Prepare a medium hot frying pan with a little oil or butter spread evenly over the pan with a paper towel. Pour mixture into pan and cook until brown on the bottom. Loosen with an egg slice, turn over carefully and cook briefly, then fold over and serve at once, garnished with parsley and sprinkled with salt.

Pear smoothie (p. 61)

Gluten-free recipes (p. 228)

I'm the only one in the family who is gluten-free and this is what I usually eat • millet porridge made from millet meal such as Lotus Organic French Millet, although I prefer to get it really fresh by buying whole millet (Demeter organic) and grinding it in a hand grinder as required • puffed rice (often just crumbled rice cakes, I like them really fresh) as a cereal with A2 milk, yoghurt and canned pears or rhubarb (salicylates) • porridge cooked from plain rice flakes (definitely nothing with grape juice sweetening) • the Orgran buckwheat pancake mix is easy, and free of added flavours, so I use it for breakfast or lunch • gluten-free bread (p. 234) with butter or Nuttelex and pear jam or failsafe hummus (p. 189).

Lunches and Snacks

'Breakfast is easy, dinner is easy, it's the lunches and snacks I find hard on this diet.' Parent, Darwin

This is what three-year-old Ethan ate during his elimination diet in a menu that met or exceeded nutritional requirements for essential minerals and vitamins including folates:

- **Breakfast:** Soy smoothie with soymilk, carob powder, pear and egg or gluten-free toasted bread or riceflake porridge with pear puree and soymilk.
- **Lunch at school:** 4 rice cakes, home-made hummus or cashew spread with carob and chickpeas or gluten-free sandwich with rissoles.
- **Morning/afternoon tea:** soy yoghurt or pear muffin (Margie's lunchbox muffins) or baked muesli slice or pureed pear icypole or packet plain crisps (only on treat days).
- **Dinner:** Darani's amazing chicken noodle stew or spaghetti with failsafe topping or baked dinner or rice crumbed chicken nuggets and chips or mince and potato casserole with hidden green veggies.

It is best to minimise your child's intake of sugary treats. One mother was pleased to hear that you can feed children dinner recipes such as pasta, mince and veggies for lunch and snacks – 'I never thought of that,' she said.

A weekly menu plan can provide leftovers and frozen meals for lunchboxes and snacks, from frittata (p. 115) to chicken nuggets (p. 90) to roasts (p. 88).

Read through this chapter for suggestions about how to fill hungry stomachs between breakfast and dinnertime.

Lunches

Sandwiches

Use preservative-free bread, rolls, toast, croissants, toasted sandwiches, jaffles, gluten-free bread or rice cakes.

FAILSAFE BREAD

Avoid bread with • any preservative in the range 280–283, usually calcium propionate (282) • vinegar • sodium metabisulphite (223) used as a flour treatment agent • antioxidants 310–312, 319–321 (may be unlisted) • fermented whey powder or solids, a tricky method of adding natural calcium propionate although usually in smaller doses. As far as we know, whey cultured with unlisted propionates is used only in bakery products.

SPREADS • butter or failsafe margarine (p. 183) • preservative-free cream cheese with chopped chives • preservative-free cottage cheese (like Quark or Jalna) • egg, hard-boiled and mixed with a little warm milk and salt • failsafe hummus (p. 189) • cashew paste (p. 187) • cashew paste with or without golden syrup, pear jam or pure maple syrup • carob cashew spread (p. 187) • lentil spread (p. 189) • Howard's bean paste (p. 106) • bean dip (p. 189) • pear jam (p. 186) • magic spread (tastes like lemon butter, p. 85) • maple syrup jam (p. 185) • rice malt • golden syrup.

WHEN PERMITTED • mashed butternut pumpkin (salicylates) • mashed banana (amines) • canned fish like salmon, tuna (amines) • additive-free mild cheeses (amine and dairy).

FILLINGS • fresh or home-frozen chicken, lamb and beef with salt, lettuce, chopped shallots, mung bean sprouts, parsley or celery • rissoles • sausages • meatloaf with pear puree (p. 247) • steak sandwich (p. 44) • sliced hard-boiled egg or warm hard-boiled egg mashed with a little milk • fried egg • butter beans • fried tofu (p. 114) • Sunday roast – mashed leftover roast potato or butternut pumpkin (salicylates) with roast chicken or meat, salt, parsley garnish and lettuce.

OTHER LUNCH SUGGESTIONS • jaffles or toasted-sandwiches in an automatic toasted sandwich maker, using the same fillings as above, or left-over sausages with pear puree, or an egg, or butter beans with parsley • butter beans on toast or rice • slimmers' salad (p. 213) • egg and vegetable stir-fry (p. 122) • pies (p. 44), Cornish pasties (p. 47), pancakes (p. 35) • rice hoppers (p. 237) • three-minute spaghetti (p. 128) • garlic pasta (p. 129), Arran's fried rice (p. 57) • pizza, leftover pizza (p. 124).

Emma's bread (in the breadmaker)

This is a basic recipe for bread in an automatic breadmaker.

2½ cups of plain flour

190 ml water

¼ cup milk or soymilk

1 tbsp failsafe oil (p. 184)

1 pinch ascorbic acid (vitamin C) powder (optional)

1 pinch salt

1½ tsp of dried yeast

Put all ingredients in breadmaker, unless there is a separate container for yeast. Set the timer and wait for the wonderful aroma. The ascorbic acid helps to deliver well-risen bread every time. When finished, remove and cool before slicing. A good bread knife is essential.

VARIATION • If you don't have a breadmaker, this recipe works fine without: form dough in a bowl with all ingredients, turn out and knead thoroughly on a floured surface, replace in the bowl covered with a tea towel and stand in a warm place until doubled in bulk (60–90 minutes). Turn out and knead again, place in a greased bread tin, cover with tea towel and allow to stand again until fully risen (about 60–90 minutes). Bake at 200°C for 35–40 minutes. Turn out and cool, in the tea towel to soften top crust if desired.

Some commercial bread still contains preservative 282.

> 'If you can't persuade them to give up anything else, try to get them to give up bread containing calcium propionate (282) or any of the other related propionate preservatives (280–283). Also included in this is bread with whey powder added. Propionates seem to cause problems for more people than any other single food chemical.' Email discussion group member, Queensland

Super salad rolls or wraps

The secret ingredient for getting salads into kids is Mighty Mayo (p. 190).

1 failsafe roll or wrap
1 sliced hard-boiled egg
1 cup celery, lettuce, cabbage, shallots, finely sliced, plus grated fresh beetroot and/or carrot and/or sliced snow peas (salicylates) when permitted from your allowance.

Mix salad ingredients with 1 tbsp Mighty Mayo (p. 190) or Howard's bean paste (p. 106). Assemble all fillings.

Hot chicken roll

Split preservative-free bread roll in half but not quite all the way through. Spread thickly with failsafe mayonnaise (p. 190), Birgit's pear ketchup (p. 192), or pear puree and fill with sliced, cooked chicken. Cover and microwave on High for 20 seconds.

Slimmers' salad (p. 213)

Bean and pasta salad

1 cup cooked chickpeas or cooked
  chopped green beans
1 cup cooked butter beans
1 cup chopped celery
1½ cups spaghetti springs, macaroni or
  gluten-free pasta, cooked
Mighty Mayo (p. 190) or mayonnaise
  (p. 190)
salt to taste
1 tbsp chopped chives

Mix beans, celery and pasta together in salad bowl. Pour salad dressing over and toss. Add salt to taste and garnish with chives. Handy to carry in a lunch container.

Andra's Chicken Noodle Soup

This noodle soup makes a great one-pot dinner when served with garlic rolls.

3 tbsp canola oil
2 cups chopped cabbage
4 stalks chopped celery
1 chopped leek
1 small carrot (optional)
2 litres water
2 cubed chicken breasts (uncooked)
2 cups chopped green beans
250 g packet of 'Fantastic' rice noodles
  or equivalent
salt to taste

Gently stir-fry cabbage, celery, leek and carrot in oil. Add water and simmer 30–40 minutes. Add chicken and beans and simmer 5 minutes, then add rice noodles and simmer 10 minutes.

Chicken noodle snack

1 packet permitted noodles
  (see Shopping List)
home-made chicken stock
chopped cooked chicken

Bring stock to the boil, add noodles and chopped chicken and simmer until noodles are cooked. This is a good substitute for 2-minute noodles.

VARIATIONS • cook noodles and stir in ½ tsp sugar, 1 tbsp preservative-free cream cheese and drizzle golden syrup while hot • top with failsafe mince and bean mix (p. 76).

Two-minute noodles may contain artificial colours (102, 110) and synthetic antioxidant 320 in any oil, not necessarily on the label, which can be problems for sensitive children. Choose uncoloured noodles without vegetable oil. Throw away any 'flavour' sachets. These contain MSG and other flavour enhancers. Maggi two-minute noodles, chicken and corn flavour, contain flavour enhancers 621 (MSG), 635 (disodium 5-ribonucleotide), 637 (disodium guanylate), and 631 (disodium inosinate). You can make your own additive-free toppings like failsafe mince (p. 76), chicken and leek topping (p. 97) or pasta toppings (p. 125).

Steak sandwich with the lot

1 shallot, chopped
50–100 g thin beef or lamb steak
salt
2 slices failsafe bread
lettuce
mayonnaise (p. 190)
beetroot (optional, salicylates)

Stir-fry shallots in oil until transparent and put aside. Put steak into preheated medium frying pan. Sprinkle with salt and cook on first side until done. Turn steak, cook until done, at the same time making toast. Butter toast and assemble sandwich.

VARIATION • Use cooked chicken pieces instead of steak.

Pies

At the beginning of the elimination diet, many families find home-made pies are an easy way to wean children off processed food, but pastry is high in fat. A lower-fat option is to use mashed potato topping instead of pastry. Later, you can encourage foods lower in fat, like jaffles, or pie fillings over pasta or toast. Use commercial puff pastry, shortcrust pastry (p. 48) or gluten-free pastry (p. 48). For fillings, try failsafe mince (p. 76), left-over chicken and mashed potato, lentil mash (p. 107), or these delicious recipes.

'The best thing we ever bought was the pie-maker.' Reader, Alice Springs.

Beef and leek pie filling

500 g mince
whole leek, chopped
equal amount of cabbage to leek
cloves of garlic to taste, crushed
1–2 tsp cornflour
enough water to make sauce, about
    2 cups
1 tbsp golden syrup
2 shallots, chopped
salt to taste

Combine mince, leek, cabbage, garlic, water and cornflour, bring to the boil and simmer until reduced, then add golden syrup, shallots and salt. Cook together until soft. For pies, reduce longer for a firmer mix than for pasta topping.

Chicken and shallot pie filling

white sauce with garlic and shallots
    (p. 192)
2 cups cooked chicken
1 cup finely chopped celery
1 tsp finely chopped parsley
1 cup green peas if tolerated
    (glutamates)

Cook together until celery is soft.

Other pie filling suggestions from readers

'My recipe for the mince pie involves throwing everything into the pot – cabbage, Brussels sprouts, bean mix, swede, potato, etc. My kids won't eat vegetables cooked so I mash or blend the vegetables once they are cooked and add to the mince. Then I just put it all in the pastry and cook in the electric pie maker.' Reader, email.

'I use the garlic mince recipe [p. 76] and I make savoury egg ones too, cooking the eggs first like scrambled egg. I use eggs, chicken, shallots, anything really that I have in the fridge that looks like it could go in. I set out trying to make enough to freeze but they get eaten as fast as I make them.' Reader, Queensland.

Pies are the biggest seller in most school tuckshops. Almost all pies contain artificial colours (110) or annatto (160b) in the crust. All contain either MSG (621) and/or hydrolysed vegetable protein (HVP), which is a form of MSG. No pies were found without ribonucleotide flavour enhancers (635, 627, 631) and synthetic BHA (320) in fats or vegetable oils. 'No artificial colours or flavours' still means flavour enhancers and synthetic antioxidants.

VARIATION • Mini pies: make pies in muffin pans, bake 5–10 minutes until pastry is cooked. For reduced fat, top with mashed potato instead of extra pastry.

Wade's sausage rolls

This recipe was devised by a Darwin teenager. Kids love to help make them.

500 g low-fat mince
3 chopped shallots
1 clove garlic, crushed (optional)
1 tbsp chopped parsley
commercial puff pastry ready-cut sheets
salt to taste

Preheat oven to 180°C. Mix mince with shallots, garlic, parsley and salt. Cut pastry sheets in half. Place a sausage shape of mince in the middle of the sheet. Roll over, prick top. Cut to required lengths. Bake 20 minutes or until cooked.

Frozen ready-to-use pastries can contain sorbate (202), sulphite (223) and propionate (281), preservatives and synthetic antioxidant BHA 320. Always read the label or check Product Updates on the website because ingredients change frequently.

Cornish pasties, Australian style

According to one story, these were originally called oggies. They were supposedly delivered to their men in the tin mines of Cornwall by wives who signalled that lunch was ready by calling 'Oggie, oggie, oggie, oi, oi, oi'.

1 medium potato

1 medium leek

1 slice of swede (or butternut pumpkin if tolerated)

3 sprigs parsley

250 g low-fat beef mince

2 tbsp peas (glutamates) or green beans

250 g short crust pastry (p. 48)

Preheat oven to 200°C. Finely chop vegetables and parsley. Add mince and peas and mix well. Roll out pastry and cut with saucer to form rounds. Put about 1 tbsp of the mixture on half of each round of pastry. Wet the edges and gently fold over. Using a fork, press around edges and prick tops several times. Brush with milk. Bake on greased oven tray about 30 minutes, until cooked and brown.

VARIATION • authentic Cornish pasties: you'll have to use shallots instead of onion, salt instead of pepper, and preservative-free cottage or cream cheese instead of cheese.

> 'As a Cornishman myself, I make pasties for my family with the pastry as you describe but the meat I use is beef skirt cut into chunks (never mince) and for my vegetarian wife, cheese instead, with chunked up potato, swede and onion seasoned with a little pepper. Having placed a mix of the ingredients in a round of the pastry, I draw its opposite edges up into the mid point, pastry-brush a half moon edge with milk to make the edges stick together, then press them together and crimp the edge to seal it.' Reader, UK

Short crust pastry

You can make your own with this recipe or there are commercial pastry mixes available, including gluten-free. For a sweet pastry, add 4 tbsp sugar.

2 cups self-raising flour (or gluten-free self-raising flour)

¼ tsp salt

1 cup butter or failsafe margarine (p. 183)

cold water to mix

Sift flour and salt. Rub butter into flour with fingertips until mixture resembles breadcrumbs. Mix into a stiff dough with a little water (if too much water is used, pastry will be tough). Turn onto a floured board and knead a little. Do not handle more than necessary. If possible chill in refrigerator for 30 minutes before use. Roll out as required on a floured board. If cooking unfilled, bake at 200°C for about 10 or 15 minutes until golden brown. If filled, bake for about 30 minutes, depending on filling. Freeze left-over pastry.

Creamy chicken pasta

This dish was developed while we were travelling as something we could make with just a hotplate. It can be served hot, warm or cold, travels well and is perfect when you need to take food for socialising.

500 g pasta spirals

1 cup green beans

3 shallots

clove of garlic to taste, crushed

1 tbsp canola oil

3 tbsp preservative-free cream cheese

3 tbsp yoghurt

2 cups cooked diced chicken

salt and citric acid to taste

Cook pasta according to directions. You can add frozen beans (rinsed in tap water) to the cooking pasta. While pasta is cooking, stir-fry shallots and garlic gently in a little canola oil. Drain pasta. While warm, stir through cream cheese, yoghurt, shallots and chicken. You can add chopped celery and carrot when permitted (salicylates) for colour.

School lunches

Preschool alternatives to a plate of fruit

It is not fair for the child to have to eat celery sticks while the others are tucking into strawberries and grapes. Try a fresh peeled pear, a Red Delicious apple when permitted, Saladas plain or buttered, home-made yum balls (p. 158) or muesli bars (p. 159). For birthdays, make a special iced cake at home. Cut it into slices and wrap each piece really well in cling film, with your child's name on it, and keep a few slices in the preschool freezer.

School lunchbox suggestions

Use a lunch box with a frozen drink bottle to keep food fresh • small container of chicken nuggets (HFC, p. 90) • sandwich (p. 40) • chicken drumstick, no skin • rice balls with egg rolls (p. 56) • small container with chopped canned pear • chicken balls (p. 93) • little meat balls (p. 74) • vegetable muffins (p. 161) • buttered tortilla • mini quiche (p. 123) • corn and green bean bake (p. 123) • country vegetable bake muffins (p. 114) • home-made pies or small sausage rolls (p. 46), some tuckshops will heat them up • home-made treats like pear pie (p. 156), muesli bars (p. 159), lunchbox muffins (p. 161), Anzac cookie (p. 168), pear slice (p. 172), slice of cake (p. 161), butterscotch biscuit (p. 168) • vanilla yoghurt or soy yoghurt • stick of celery • hard-boiled egg • water, Soyaccino, magic cordial, soy shake in a spring water bottle with a small amount of water frozen in the bottom • Kettle chips.

School lunches for teenagers

Once peer pressure kicks in, teenagers want to eat junk like everyone else. Our kids would always have a good breakfast then take snack food like lunchbox muffins (p. 161), muesli bars (p. 159), iced finger buns, Kettle chips and home-made soyshakes to school. In her final year, my daughter was amazed when a friend commented 'You are so lucky your mum cooks for you'. After school they would have a nutritious meal like spaghetti with salad, quick fried rice (p. 57), stir-fry on rice, jaffles, eggs on toast or a toasted chicken sandwich with the lot (p. 44). Being hungry teenagers, they would have another nutritious meal at dinnertime.

Children who prefer Vegemite and ham to cakes, biscuits and even fruit are likely to react to MSG, nitrates and amines. They will prefer savoury snacks like Saltine crackers or toast spread with failsafe margarine, pretzels, Kettle chips, hot chips (p. 104) or crunchy potatoes with salt option (p. 53), pies and sausage rolls (p. 46), salty crackers (p. 55), besan bombs (p. 237), chicka-damias (p. 55) and snack rings (p. 56).

How schools can help

Children are more likely to succeed with diet if they have community support. These are ways in which schools can help:
• teachers enforce the no-lunch-swapping rule • teachers praise the child for sticking to his/her diet • teachers give non-food rewards or Pascall's white vanilla marshmallows instead of coloured sweets • day-care centre or preschool provides permitted options instead of plate of fruit • school tuckshops provide some failsafe options (see 'Healthy choice school canteens' factsheet on www.fedup. com.au) • schools provide failsafe alternatives on social occasions, from class parties to sausage sizzles and fetes, e.g. preservative-free sausages on preservative-free bread with permitted mayonnaise and shredded lettuce • school fetes provide colour-free fairy floss • schools encourage an additive-free policy (and are rewarded with more settled behaviour) • school excursions provide picnics instead of going to a fast-food outlet • school camps go additive-free (and notice that children improve).

'I've just returned to teaching after 10 years away. I have been staggered by the changes. I'm just horrified by the level of aggression.' Teacher, Darwin

Schools that throw out their soft-drink vending machines, lollipops, flavoured chips and red licorice see a difference. When Wolney Junior School tuckshop in South London substituted apples, pears and bananas for additive-containing snack foods, their success rate for eleven-year-olds in the national English examinations almost tripled in two years.

'I realise how lucky we are now. Our school parent body bought an oven which is for use by staff and students. In fact the children refer to their lunches as foils – they must be wrapped in alfoil to be heated. We don't have a canteen so this is offered each day for the two coldest terms. A student is responsible for putting lunches in and turning on the oven and a staff member takes them out and puts them in a box to be handed out in the eating area. Admittedly we are a small school – there are advantages!' Parent, South Australia

If you want to help your school canteen go additive-free, perhaps with failsafe options, Additive Education has a newsletter to assist you called Supporting Additive Free Eating (SAFE). They provide a forum for the sharing of support and information, including those in a preschool/childcare setting. See 'Healthy choice school canteens' factsheet at www.fedup.com.au.

WHAT'S IN A HOT DOG?

When we checked, Castlemaine Traditional Aussie Hot Dogs contained preservative 250 (sodium nitrite) and colours 160b (annatto), 160c and 120 cochineal. The roll will probably contain preservative 282 (calcium propionate). Then there's the sauce. These additives, except 160c and 120, are associated with reactions, usually delayed.

Snacks

Quick processor scones

These are popular for afternoon tea, suitable for lunchboxes, and can be quickly freshened in a microwave after freezing.

3 cups self-raising flour (or gluten-free
  if required)

¼ tsp salt

1–2 tbsp butter or failsafe margarine
  (p. 183)

a little more than 1 cup of milk or soymilk

Preheat oven to 230°C. Lightly grease two oven trays. Put flour, salt and butter in food processor and process until blended. Add liquid slowly until dough sticks together in a soft, wet clump and is a bit sticky. Knead on a lightly floured board, roll out, cut into squares or with scone cutters, place on oven tray and bake for 10–15 minutes or until golden brown. The gluten-free variation needs gentler handling. Serve warm wrapped in a clean cloth in a basket or freeze and freshen up in the microwave. Good with butter, golden syrup or pear jam.

Pumpkin scones

Children will be surprised by the colour of these scones. Not suitable for your supervised elimination diet.

2 tbsp butter or failsafe margarine (p. 183)

1½ tbsp sugar

1 cup baked, steamed or microwaved
  butternut pumpkin (salicylates)

1 egg

¼ tsp salt

1 tbsp finely chopped chives

1 tbsp finely chopped parsley

2 cups self-raising flour

milk or milk substitute for glazing

Preheat oven to 220°C. Lightly grease two oven trays. Whiz butter and sugar briefly in food processor to combine. Add pumpkin, egg, salt and chives and whiz briefly. Add flour and whiz again briefly, until just mixed in. Form the dough into a sticky ball and place on oven trays. Flatten to 2 cm thickness and cut into 8 wedges. Brush with a little milk and bake about 15–20 minutes until golden brown. Serve warm with salad. Scones can be frozen and reheated in microwave. These can be used for a light lunch or a hearty afternoon tea.

Pikelets

1 egg
¼ cup sugar
about ¾ cup milk, soymilk or ricemilk
1 cup self-raising flour or gluten-free flour
  (p. 233)
¼ tsp salt
butter or failsafe margarine (p. 183) or failsafe oil (p. 184) for cooking

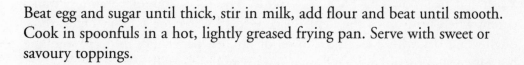

Beat egg and sugar until thick, stir in milk, add flour and beat until smooth. Cook in spoonfuls in a hot, lightly greased frying pan. Serve with sweet or savoury toppings.

Rice flour pikelets (*gluten-free*, p. 236)

Besan bombs (*gluten-free*, p. 237)

Crunchy potatoes

'My children love these as a quick snack after school.' Reader, Melbourne

4 medium potatoes, peeled and cut into
  pieces
2 tbsp failsafe oil (p. 184)
2 tbsp sugar (or salt to taste)

Microwave or steam potatoes. Heat oil in a heavy-based pan. If using sugar, add to oil and stir until sugar is dissolved. Add potatoes and brown on both sides. Serves 4.

Potato wedges

These are low in fat and delicious.

1 large potato per person
1 tsp failsafe oil (p. 184) per person
salt to taste

Preheat oven to 200°C. Peel potatoes and cut into wedges (eighths), storing in a bowl of cold water until finished. Pat dry with a clean tea towel or kitchen paper and toss in a bowl with the oil until coated. Place in a single layer on a lightly oiled oven tray, bake for 20 minutes. Turn, bake a further 20–30 minutes. Sprinkle with salt to serve.

Potato crisps

Wash and peel potatoes. Slice very thinly. The slices should be almost transparent when held up to the light. Place in cold water for 1 hour. Drain thoroughly and dry with a clean tea towel or kitchen paper. Fry in deep, smoking hot oil until crisp and golden brown. Drain and serve with salt.

You would think a packet of chips labelled **'No artificial flavours, no artificial colours, no preservatives'** would be additive-free. Yet some packet snacks with this label include flavour enhancers 621 (MSG) and 635 – which are technically not artificial flavours – and antioxidant (319) – which is used as a preservative, affects people like a preservative, but is technically not called a preservative.

Chickadamias

There's a commercial product called Chic Nuts that's failsafe too.

3 cups cooked chickpeas
1–2 cloves of garlic, crushed
salt to taste

Use canned or precooked chickpeas. (To prepare dried chickpeas, take 1 cup chickpeas, rinse thoroughly, cover with water and soak overnight. Drain and cover well with water. Add ½ tsp sodium bicarbonate. Boil for 1½ to 2 hours. Drain.) Preheat oven to 200°C. Mix chickpeas with garlic and salt and allow to stand 20 minutes. Spread chickpeas on a greased baking tray. Bake for 15 minutes. Turn chickpeas, reduce temperature to 190°C and bake for another 15 minutes. Turn chickpeas. Reduce temperature to 175°C and bake another 30 minutes or until crisp.

Popcorn contains salicylates. It can also contain 'natural butter flavour', colour annatto (160b), artificial colours or BHA.

Water crackers

2 cups plain flour
1 tsp salt
2 tbsp butter or failsafe margarine
   (p. 183)
warm water

Place baking sheet in oven and preheat to 230°C. Combine flour and salt. Rub butter into flour mix, add warm water to form a workable dough. Roll out very thinly on a floured board. Cut into squares or rounds, prick with fork. Place biscuits on very hot baking sheet and bake for 3 minutes.

VARIATIONS • Seeds: sprinkle poppy seeds on biscuits • Cheese: add 50 g of preservative-free cream cheese while mixing dough • Salt: sprinkle 1 tsp salt on top before baking.

Snack rings

1 sheet frozen commercial puff pastry
  sheets
1 clove of garlic, cut
poppy seeds to sprinkle

Rub frozen pastry sheet with cut garlic. As sheet becomes soft enough to cut, sprinkle with poppy seeds and cut into strips 1 cm wide and 2 cm long. Or cut into rounds with a scone cutter then cut out middle with a smaller cutter, leaving a ring. Put on a baking tray and bake at 180°C until pale golden, about 10 minutes.

Rice balls

'I learned this trick from a Japanese friend. They make excellent finger food for children and are good in lunchboxes.' Reader, Alice Springs

white rice
salt

Cook rice according to the absorption method on the side of the packet. When cooked, allow to cool slightly. With clean, wet hands, take a scoop of rice into the palm of your hand and squeeze or roll to make firm. Sprinkle with salt to taste. Kids prefer these really small. Good for afterschool snacks or in the lunchbox with egg rolls (see next recipe).

Egg rolls

1 egg
pinch of salt
pinch of sugar
1 tbsp water

Beat all ingredients to combine. In a medium frying pan cook underside of omelette. When top is starting to get firm, remove from heat, roll up and allow to cool. Slice into thin diagonal rolls and serve with rice balls (above), with a garnish of little celery sticks. Good for lunchboxes.

Arran's fried rice

A quick gluten-free lunch.

2 tbsp failsafe oil (p. 184)
2–3 cups cooked rice
1 tsp finely chopped chives
1 cup cooked chopped failsafe sausages,
   chicken or egg rolls (above)
½ cup frozen beans (or peas when
   permitted)
salt to taste

Preheat frying pan to medium. Heat oil in pan. Add rice and other ingredients. Stir-fry until ingredients are well mixed and cooked. Serves 2.

VARIATION • Fried rice 'pastie': cook a one-egg omelette as for egg rolls (above). Lay the omelette on a plate and place fried rice on one side. Fold omelette in half over the top of the rice. Serve with Birgit's pear ketchup (p. 192).

Butter beans on toast

'My daughter and I love the butter beans on toast for lunch sometimes – a great baked bean substitute.' Reader, Canberra

300 g can of butter beans, or home-
   cooked beans except broad beans
30 g butter
2 tbsp chopped shallots

Drain and rinse butter beans. Heat butter in pan. Add beans and shallots, stir-fry quickly. Serve on toast or rice. Serves 2.

Popples

'These dairy-free, gluten-free snacks have a kind of commercial taste which gluten-free kids are often deprived of. They have the thumbs up from our hungry teenager, who likes them as a dry snack rather than with milk on.' Reader, NZ

150 g packet of plain puffed cereal (e.g. rice, millet, etc.)

1 cup sugar

¼ cup syrup (golden, rice or pure maple)

¼ cup failsafe oil (p. 184)

½ teaspoon salt

¼ cup water

Pre-heat oven to 180°C. Place puffed cereal in baking dish. Make syrup mixture with sugar, syrup, oil, salt and water, boiling 2–3 minutes (brings mixture to very soft toffee state). Pour syrup mixture over puffed cereal and mix till evenly coated. Place in oven for approximately 5 minutes, stirring cereal at least once during that time. Take care not to burn; it's done when the mixture just starts to brown very slightly.

Other snack suggestions

Anything from the breakfast and lunch sections • fresh peeled pear or canned pear (limit 2 whole pears per day) • rice cakes, wheat-based crackers like Saladas with failsafe margarine or with spreads like cashew paste, preservative-free cream cheese, golden syrup or pear jam • yoghurt, soy yoghurt (no 160b) • cashew nuts, raw (limit 10 per day) • Kettle chips • add citric acid to a packet of Kettle chips and toss for a salt and vinegar flavour • pretzels • plain sweet biscuits like shortbreads, see Shopping List • fresh bread rolls with butter or garlic butter (p. 185) • preservative-free toast with butter and golden syrup • preservative-free crumpets, if you can find them • celery sticks with preservative-free cream cheese • plate of raw salad vegetables (p. 118) with dip (p. 188) • carob milkshake or soyshake (p. 62) • water, soda water or magic cordial (p. 63) • icypoles (p. 66) • jelly cups (p. 153) • sago cups (p. 152) • custard cups (p. 152) • home-made muesli bars and yum balls (p. 158) • muffins, cakes and biscuits (p. 158) • home-made snack rings (p. 56) • some additive-free commercial croissants or plain Sara Lee vanilla pound cake (not suitable for dairy-free diets) • left-overs, like a slice of quiche, pizza, cold sausage (p. 75) or a hard-boiled egg from the fridge • Red Soup • egg on toast • plate of pasta with butter and salt (p. 128) or mince topping (p. 76) • Peters Dixie cup ice-creams • white iced finger buns without sprinkles or coconut from Brumby's hot bread shops. These can be frozen in separate bags and used either cut in half or sliced and buttered in school lunchboxes.

Finger food for babies and toddlers

'The best way to get babies to eat is to make everything into crumbed finger-shaped patties so they can hang on to it.' Mother of a toddler, failsafe since 14 months, Perth

Babies with suspected food issues should be closely supervised by a dietitian experienced in food intolerance. Your dietitian will advise you when to introduce foods like eggs, wheat, dairy foods, nuts and seafood (usually not until 12 months at the earliest).

Suggestions from mothers include • rusks – bake wedges or fingers of bread, rye bread, gluten-free bread in a slow oven for 2 hours or until very hard – good for teething • pureed baby pears or stewed pear • bananas if tolerated (amines) • fingers of steamed cooked potato, swede, celery, butternut pumpkin, sweet potato and carrots when permitted • permitted vegetables: steamed and mashed, formed into a finger shape or different shapes, rolled in breadcrumbs (p. 194), baked in a moderate oven for 10–15 minutes or until crispy on the outside • bubble and squeak (p. 109), crumbed and cooked as above • chicken fingers: finger-shaped patties of minced chicken, made up with cornflour, oats if permitted and a pinch of salt, bake for 20 minutes or panfry in a little failsafe oil for a real treat • fish fingers: flaked white fish fillets, mixed with mashed potato and dipped in cornflour, egg, failsafe breadcrumbs (p. 194) • when permitted, strips of egg (egg rolls, p. 57) • failsafe muffins, shortbread biscuits, Anzac biscuits, Milk Arrowroot biscuits (reduced sugar is a good idea) • mini sausage rolls (p. 46), mini pasties (p. 47), mini pies (p. 44) • home-made icypoles.

Drinks

Water is the best drink.

A 2006 study at Boston Children's Hospital monitored the weight of over 100 teenagers, while letting half of them consume sugary drinks. They concluded that a single 330 ml can a day of sweetened drinks could lead teens to put on half a kg a month, 6 kgs a year. A can of commercial soft drink can contain 10 teaspoons of sugar compared to one or two in the drinks below, but, even with these, save sugary drinks for treats.

Tastes change when processed commercial products are reduced. Children who won't drink water because 'I don't like it' can try the following options.

- filtered water with a home filter
- spring water
- mineral water
- soda water
- plain home-made water icecups

Fruit juice

Fruit juice is perceived as a healthy drink despite concerns from doctors' groups since 1978 that overconsumption of fruit juice has been associated with toddler diarrhoea, short stature and obesity in preschool-aged children. All fruit juices, whether commercial or home-made, are high in salicylates, except orange juice, which is very high in salicylates and amines. Tomato and vegetable juices contain salicylates, amines and sometimes natural glutamates as well. Even pear juice is not permitted because commercial pear juice contains salicylates in pear peel.

Pear juice is a common reason for failure on this diet (p. 256). Make a juice drink using diluted pear syrup from canned pears, but remember that pears are limited to two per day from all sources.

Pear smoothies

1 pear half (fresh, soft or canned in syrup)
1 cup milk, A2 milk, soy, or rice milk

Blend until frothy.

VARIATIONS • Add 1 tbsp home-made yoghurt • Use instead of pear: 1 tsp of carob powder and 1–2 tsp sugar • 1 raw egg for extra nutrition (not recommended in the USA where raw eggs often carry salmonella: egg powder may be safer) • salicylate fruits when permitted (canned, fresh or frozen mango, stewed rhubarb, fresh tamarillo or persimmon pulp with added sugar if needed) • amine fruits when permitted (banana, and yellow – not red – paw paw, also called papaya).

Salicylate and amine options are not suitable for your supervised elimination diet. These can be used after challenges when you know what you can tolerate.

Octopus

'This is a family treat. On a hot day we get a big batch going, with ice everywhere and everyone lending a hand.' Reader, Darwin

The quantities are per blender load, about two serves. You will need a bag of crushed ice.

1 cup crushed ice
1 cup or more of tinned pears
dash of pear syrup from canned pears
dash of cold water
½ tsp citric acid
2–3 tsp sugar

Whiz in blender. Adjust quantities to suit individual tastes.

Carob milkshake

¾ cup milk, soymilk or ricemilk
2 tsp sugar (more or less to taste)
1 tsp carob powder

Blend until frothy. Children who are used to chocolate drinks may need more sugar at first.

Commercial flavoured milks can contain artificial colours or annatto, e.g. banana (160b annatto), chocolate (133 brilliant blue and 155 brown). Milkshake syrup contains benzoates (210–213).

Caramel milkshake

2–3 tsp golden syrup
1 tsp butter or failsafe margarine
   (p. 183)
⅔ cup milk or soymilk

Put syrup and butter in a mug, microwave for 30 seconds, add milk and blend with a wand blender until frothy.

'Strawberry' milkshake

Your kids probably won't know that there are no strawberries in this! Not suitable for your supervised elimination diet.

2 tbsp rhubarb (salicylates) stewed with
   sugar
⅔ cup milk or soymilk
extra sugar to taste

Put in mug, blend until frothy with a wand blender.

Indian yoghurt drink

Called lassi, this is one of the few drinks, other than water, that is drunk with meals in India. It is also used as a snack. It can be sweet or salty.

½ cup plain yoghurt

1¼ cups ice-cold water

sugar to taste or ¼ tsp salt

Blend until creamy. Serve with ice.

Magic cordial

Our grandmothers called this 'poor man's lemonade'. A failsafe three-year-old calls it magic because it looks like water and tastes like lemon cordial. The following recipe is for the syrup, which can then be diluted to taste. Like all sweetened drinks, this should be limited.

1 cup sugar

1 cup boiling water

½–1 tsp citric acid

Place water and sugar in a two-cup jug and stir until sugar is dissolved. Add citric acid. Store in the refrigerator in a glass bottle such as a tonic-water bottle. Dilute to taste with water before drinking.

VARIATION • for failsafe lemonade drizzle a small amount of the sugar syrup above into a glass and top with plain soda water or mineral water. Even small quantities of preservative-free commercial lemonade can affect sensitive children.

'For the most part water is their main source of fluids, lemonade for treats and now, even better, magic cordial. The best thing is I can sneak a magic cordial and everyone thinks I'm drinking water. Vodka, magic cordial and soda water is not a bad treat either for social occasions for Mum.' Reader, Darwin

Cordials, sports drinks, soft drinks and even natural mineral water with 5 per cent fruit juice can contain up to five additives: e.g. tropical cordial contains tartrazine (102 yellow) and sunset yellow (110) as well as preservatives sodium benzoate (211) and sodium metabisulphite (223), plus 'flavour'.

Commercial soft drinks

• Soda water • Preservative-free tonic (e.g. Schweppes) • Preservative-free lemonade (e.g. Schweppes in bottles limited to less than 1 small glass a week, because there are some salicylates and amines in natural lemon flavour).

Hot lemon drink

A soothing drink for cold and flu (p. 224).

Hot carob drink

1 cup water	Boil water or heat in microwave.
1 tsp carob powder	Add carob powder and stir well.
sugar to taste	Add sugar and milk to taste.
milk or soymilk	

VARIATIONS • Cold: dissolve sugar and carob powder in a small amount of hot water. Top up with ice-cold water and serve over ice cubes • Milk: use all milk or soymilk instead of water • Mocha: use half decaffeinated coffee powder, half carob powder.

> Some readers report that more than 1–2 cups per day of decaffeinated coffee can cause problems.

Iced coffee

If you want the taste of commercial iced coffee, you have to use very large amounts of sugar and coffee, so, like all other sweetened drinks, this is best limited to one or two per day.

2 tsp sugar or more to taste	Dissolve sugar and coffee powder in
1 tsp or more instant decaffeinated coffee powder	boiling water. Top up with ice-cold milk and serve over ice cubes. Makes
2 tbsp boiling water	1 cup.
milk, A2 milk, soymilk, ricemilk	

Alcohol

Gin and preservative-free tonic, whisky and soda, and unflavoured vodka are permitted, for drinking and flavour in cooking (most alcohol evaporates during cooking). All other spirits, beers and wines are not suitable. Some readers who like a bottle of wine on the table for special occasions drink persimmon wine – see Product Updates on www.fedup.com.au – but it is not suitable for your supervised elimination diet.

Failsafe Irish Cream (for the over 18s, contains dairy products)

'This is better than Bailey's,' wrote a twenty-something reader.

1 cup whisky

1 can sweetened condensed milk (400 g)

3 eggs

1½ tsp carob powder or Nestlé Choc Bits (amines)

½ tsp butter

milk or soymilk, extra

Blend whisky, condensed milk and eggs together. Melt butter and add carob, or Choc Bits if used, add to whisky mixture and blend for 2 minutes. Dilute to taste with milk or soymilk. Keeps in the refrigerator for a week.

Kefir drink (contains dairy foods)

Kefir is a probiotic, fermented milk that increases levels of beneficial gut bacteria and decreases levels of potentially harmful gut bacteria. It is cultured from living organisms called kefir grains that will multiply and produce kefir indefinitely if properly handled, or it can be made from commercial kefir-starters that only produce a limited number of batches. Since kefir grains contain many more microorganisms than commercial kefir starters or yoghurt, I bought my grains from http://users.sa.chariot.net.au/~dna/Makekefir.html.

2 cups fresh milk or A2 milk or goats' milk

2–3 tbsp kefir grains

Pour 2 cups fresh milk into a clean jar and add kefir grains. Cover with a non-airtight lid and stand for about 24 hours at room temperature in a dark place such as a cupboard. Stir with a clean spoon at least once during the last 12 hours of fermentation. To harvest, stir kefir milk gently and strain into a jug, then repeat the process with a clean jar. Since kefir is a fermented product, I first made sure I could tolerate kefir by carrying out a challenge – drinking at least one cup per day every day for a week while sticking to my diet otherwise and watching for amine symptoms. Milder tasting kefir can be produced by using a higher milk-to-grain ratio, shorter culturing time and/or cooler temperatures, using refrigeration to slow fermentation if necessary. Kefir can be made with soymilk but may require an occasional dose of cows' milk.

Icypoles and icecups

You will need your own icypole moulds or plastic cups. Adjust dilutions to suit individual tastes. More water makes the icypole harder, more sugar makes it softer. Some schools sell plain water icecups, quick, cheap and healthy, for 10 cents each.

VARIATIONS • Plain water • Magic cordial (p. 63) • pear syrup diluted with equal quantities of water (limit of 2 whole pears or equivalent per day) • canned pears, blended without syrup • yoghurt or home-made iced decaf with extra sugar • A2 milk, soymilk or ricemilk with maple syrup and/or carob powder • Pear smoothie (p. 61).

> Icypoles from shops can contain up to ten of the following unacceptable additives: 102, 110, 122–129, 132, 133, 142, 151, 155, 160b, preservatives 200–203, 210–213, 220–228, and artificial flavours. There are currently no commercial icypoles that we recommend.

Carob icypoles

600 ml milk, soymilk or ricemilk

½ cup sugar

1 egg

4 tbsp water

2 tbsp failsafe margarine (p. 183)

½ cup arrowroot

2 tsp carob powder (cocoa if amines are tolerated)

Heat milk in a large saucepan on the stove. While milk is heating, beat sugar, egg, water, margarine, arrowroot and carob powder in a bowl. When milk reaches simmering point, pour in the egg mixture and continue to beat over the heat until mixture boils and thickens. Remove from heat. Allow to cool a little then pour into icypole moulds or icecup containers.

VARIATION • Ice-cream on a stick: use 1 tbsp pure maple syrup, 2 tsp Birgit's pear jam (p. 186) or ½ banana (amines) instead of carob powder.

Peters Chocolate Billabong is an example of what globalisation does to our food. Since Peters was acquired by food giant Nestlé, this 'ice confection' now contains eight yellow, red and blue artificial colours as well as artificial flavours. Before that it was a 'low fat ice-cream' containing basic ingredients: skim milk concentrate and/or whey solids, sugar, cream, cocoa, gelatine, egg yolk, vegetable gum and water.

Frozen yoghurt iceblocks

½ tsp gelatine or agar agar (see box on
   p. 68)

1 tbsp water

200 ml vanilla yoghurt or soy yoghurt

2 tbsp pure maple syrup

1 ripe pear, mashed

Sprinkle gelatine over water in a cup, microwave until gelatine is dissolved and boils to drive off sulphites. Allow to cool slightly. Combine yoghurt, syrup and pear in a bowl. Stir in gelatine mixture. Pour mixture into icypole moulds. Freeze until set. Makes 12.

Magic jelly cups

½ cup sugar dissolved in ½ cup warm
   water

½ tsp citric acid

300 ml cold water

3–4 tsp gelatine dissolved in ½ cup
   boiling water

Combine ingredients in order.
Refrigerate until set.

GELATINE AND AGAR AGAR

A relatively high level of sulphur dioxide (750 mg/kg) is permitted in *gelatine,*
although it is largely driven off by heat, storage and by boiling. When two
samples of commercial gelatine were tested for sulphite preservative 220 by a
state health department, one sample contained 370 mg/kg of sulphur dioxide
while the other contained none. *Agar agar* is a preservative-free alternative for
asthmatics and others who know they are extra-sensitive to sulphites. Also
known as kanten, agar agar is a white powder made from seaweed. It is available from health-food stores, but gels with a different texture.

Vitamin icypoles

See shopping list for recommended multivitamin and mineral supplements free
of nasty additives, flavours, salicylates or amines. Many parents have found the
easiest way to get these into children is to dissolve the tablet in any of the icypole
mixtures above, stir well, and spread over at least two icypoles, since the dose for
children is half a tablet per day. Children like the orange colour, which is the
natural colour of vitamin B1. The cold of the ice numbs the tastebuds and
makes medicine easier to take.

I hate being forced to ingest artificial colouring with medications, so if I really
have to take medications such as antibiotics, I ask for colour-free generic
capsules, or, if they are coloured, empty the powder out. It is easiest to take
mixed with 1 tbsp ice-cream.

Main Meals

In the first few weeks, during withdrawal symptoms and food cravings, your child will probably want to eat a lot of foods like HFC (p. 90) and chips (p. 104).

In the longer term, many parents find that soups and stews such as Darani's amazing chicken noodle stew (p. 71) are nutritious, easy to make in bulk, and freeze well for cook's nights off.

Soups and stews

Noodle soup

1 tbsp butter

½ medium leek, chopped

8 cups home-made chicken stock (p. 96)

¼ small cabbage, shredded

½ cup green peas (glutamates)

½ cup green beans, chopped

2 blocks colour-free two-minute noodles
   (or rice noodles if gluten-free)

salt to taste

Melt butter in large pan and stir-fry leek on low heat until soft. Add chicken stock, cabbage, peas and beans, stir though and bring to the boil. Add broken noodles and simmer until noodles are cooked. Season to taste. Serves 10.

VARIATION • Add 2 lightly beaten eggs to soup just before serving.

> Although health authorities advise against adding salt in home-cooked recipes, that doesn't apply to us because we have to avoid so many salt-containing foods, from yellow cheeses to processed foods such as takeaways, packet snacks and most processed cereals. Health authorities now recommend the use of iodised salt.

Red Soup

'I've always hated Brussels sprouts but I've just discovered I've been eating them for the last six months, thanks to Sue's Red Soup recipe.' Father, Darwin

1 cup (half a 375 g packet) of red lentils – these cook much more quickly than brown lentils
2 tbsp white rice
10 cups water or home-made chicken stock (p. 96)
2 swedes, peeled and cubed
1 cup celery, chopped
1 cup leeks or shallots, sliced
2 cups chopped cabbage
8 Brussels sprouts, sliced

Rinse lentils. Place lentils and rice in water and bring to the boil. Prepare and add vegetables. Reduce heat and simmer gently until cooked, about 40 minutes.

For vegetable haters, blend with a wand blender just before serving. Keeps in fridge for 3 days, or freezes well.

> My children learned to eat vegetables with Red Soup. At first I made it without swedes and sprouts and served it thoroughly blended. Every night for two weeks I offered a small reward if they ate more soup than the previous night, starting with less than a teaspoonful. After that, daily vegetable soup – including Brussels sprouts – became a habit that, to my surprise, they have continued at university.

Andra's quick chicken noodle soup (p. 43)

Darani's amazing chicken noodle stew

Three-year-old Ethan ate this nearly every day during his elimination diet and nutritionists were surprised by how much it met or exceeded recommended daily intakes for essential nutrients.

1 whole free-range chicken
1 leek (halved lengthways)
1 tsp salt
1 cup red lentils
12 Brussels sprouts or ½ cabbage
1 swede
4–6 sticks celery
4–6 shallots
1 cup frozen green beans
375 g pkt Orgran rice and corn spaghetti
    noodles or Fantastic rice noodles

Place chicken in pot with leek and enough water to cover, add salt, bring to the boil and simmer until cooked through, about 45 minutes. Remove chicken and allow to cool a little. Strain stock, return to pot and add red lentils then washed and finely chopped vegetables. Gently simmer until well cooked, about one hour. Meanwhile, remove skin and bones from chicken, finely chop or process and return to pot with vegetables. Add noodles and cook for a further 10–15 minutes. This usually makes enough to fill about 8 rectangular take-away containers (2 serves in each), which can then be frozen and used as needed. This stew can be watered down to a soup if preferred. It can also be blended for fussy eaters.

Irish stew (p. 85)

Nana's chicken soup

For this recipe use the shortest possible cooking time to minimise amines.

1 large or 2 small chickens with as much skin peeled off as possible (to reduce amine content)

1–2 stalks celery, finely chopped

1 swede, peeled and grated

1 leek, chopped

⅓ cup pearl barley, rinsed (contains gluten), or brown lentils (gluten-free)

salt to taste

Place all ingredients in a large saucepan and add enough water to almost cover the chicken. Bring to the boil and simmer for about 1 hour or until chicken and vegetables are tender. At end of cooking, lift chicken onto chopping board, cut off meat and add pieces to soup. Freezes well.

Commercial chicken soups usually contain MSG labelled as hydrolysed vegetable protein, plus often the ribonucleotide flavour enhancer 635, which is a mixture of 627 and 631 and is associated with itchy skin rashes.

Kerry's vegetable-hater soup

Kerry says, 'I've never liked vegetables, but when they're cooked like this they don't taste like vegetables.'

½ cup barley (contains gluten) or rice (if gluten-free)

3 cups water

1 leek

2 Brussels sprouts

1/8 cabbage

1 cup green beans

1 medium potato

Put barley and water in a saucepan and bring to the boil. Simmer for 30 minutes. Chop all vegetables in food processor. Add to soup. Simmer until tender. Add more water if necessary. Serves 4.

Meat

Fresh beef, lamb, veal and rabbit are permitted, but cooking and storing methods can increase amines. It is best to buy meat fresh, cook it that day, or freeze and use within four weeks. A father in the USA whose children are exceptionally amine sensitive explains:

> 'Turns out, I've been giving my kids meats with lots of amines for the past two years, including the last two months, when I was trying to be failsafe. We bought meats the day they arrived at our store, right off the truck, but when I investigated, some of them came from 1000 miles away, in cartons that were refrigerated, not frozen. You can't believe (well, actually, I suppose you could) how much better my kids are now that we buy all our meats from a local butcher.'

Failsafe rissoles

Cooking rissoles and sausages on the barbecue is a good way to get fathers to share the cooking, but make sure the meat is not charred as this increases amine content.

The quickest way to cook rissoles is to simply shape fresh mince into patties and cook. This recipe takes a little more time but tastes better.

600 g of preservative-free mince
3 shallots or 1 large leek, finely chopped
1 clove of garlic, crushed (optional)
3 stalks of celery, chopped
salt to taste
1 egg, beaten

Mix all ingredients in a large bowl. Shape into patties and grill or fry. Serve with mashed potato or chips and permitted vegetables (p. 102).

VARIATION • for extra vegetables try this tip from a Queensland reader:

> 'Is anyone else having trouble with getting their kiddies to eat these YUK veggies (as my kids put it)? Try camouflage. Rissoles are a great host for finely – and I mean finely – chopped Brussels sprouts, cabbage, leeks, green beans. An

extra egg and a tablespoon of flour holds them together. Try not to turn them too often as they will fall apart. Rosti potato cakes [p. 104] are another great hiding place for vegetables.'

Burgers from fast food outlets may contain bread preservative (282) in buns, preservatives (202 and 211) and HVP in pickles or sauces, antioxidants from the range 310–312, 319–321 in oils used for frying, preservative (200) and colour (160b) in cheese slices. You can make your own, completely additive-free.

Failsafe burgers

Assemble burgers using your choice of the following:
• failsafe rissoles (see recipe above) • toasted preservative-free burger bun or crusty bread slices • butter or failsafe margarine (p. 183), preservative-free cream cheese or lentil spread (p. 189) • lettuce, mung sprouts, fried leeks, fried egg • Mighty Mayo (p. 190), pear puree (p. 247) • salicylate options: beetroot, snowpea sprouts, fancy lettuce.

'Non-failsafe family members can add whatever they like – tomato, cheese, sauce – which means that everyone is happy.' Reader, Sydney

Birgit's glazed meatballs

500 g minced beef or lamb
2 cloves of garlic, chopped
2 shallots, chopped
½ cup peas (contains glutamates)
parsley, chopped
salt to taste
1 egg
1½ cups failsafe crumbs (p. 194)
2 tbsp failsafe oil (p. 184), butter or
    failsafe margarine (p. 183)
2 tbsp home-made pear jam (p. 186) or
    golden syrup

Combine mince, garlic, shallots, peas, parsley, salt, egg and crumbs and roll into walnut-size balls. Shallow fry in hot oil. Remove meatballs from frying pan. Reduce heat and put pear jam in pan, stirring until it caramelises (be careful not to burn it), put meat balls back in pan and glaze gently with jam (again being careful not to burn).

Freshness is the key for avoiding amines, so the new method of meat distribution in our supermarkets is a problem for amine responders. All supermarket meat is now vacuum packed, shipped, then cut and repacked as fresh, which means it can be up to ten weeks old when you eat it. Vacuum packing can inhibit the growth of bacteria but does nothing to retard the development of amines. People who are sensitive to amines – like me – need to approach any possible amine-containing foods with caution.

Failsafe sausages

Sausages often have a high fat content and are best saved for special occasions, or you can ask for sausages lower in fat, but you will have to pay extra for the extra meat you are getting. Make sure that the meat is fresh. A growing number of butchers are selling frozen failsafe sausages (see www.fedup.com.au). Check ingredients, however – sausages labelled 'preservative and gluten-free' are not failsafe because they usually contain herbs and spices and may contain MSG.

A recipe for your butcher for 10 kg sausages

650 g brown rice flour (2 kg for 30 kg)

3 leeks (10 leeks for 30 kg)

3 cloves of garlic (10 for 30 kg) or less
   to taste

½ cup salt (1½ cups for 30 kg)

Make up to 10 kg with fresh minced beef or chicken (no skin).

Commercial sausages are permitted to contain high levels of sodium metabisulphite (223), a major contributor to childhood asthma.

Sausages in foil

If you can't get your butcher to make failsafe sausages, use the recipe below. Or make your own with a sausage attachment for your mincer or food processor.

600 g of preservative-free minced beef or chicken

3 shallots or 1 leek, finely chopped

1 clove of garlic, crushed (optional)

1 finely chopped stalk of celery

1 tsp finely chopped parsley

salt to taste

1 egg, beaten

Have ready a long strip of foil. Mix all ingredients in a large bowl. Shape into little sausage-sized patties and lie end to end on the foil. Then roll up and twist the foil between them to make links. Cook (still in foil) in a medium-hot frying pan. Serve with pear puree, leek sauce (p. 192), fried leeks, mushy peas (p. 112) or Birgit's pear ketchup (p. 192).

Failsafe mince topping

This recipe can be used as a topping on pasta, pizza, rice, toast, and mashed potato (as a quick cottage pie), or in jaffles and pies.

2 shallots or 1 leek, finely chopped

1 clove or more of garlic, crushed

1 tbsp failsafe oil (p. 184)

500 g preservative-free low-fat beef or lamb mince

salt to taste

1 tsp chopped parsley

2 tbsp cornflour dissolved in 2 cups of water or home-made chicken stock

1 can (420 g) red kidney beans (optional)

In a heavy-based frying pan or large saucepan stir-fry chopped shallots and garlic in failsafe oil, then remove from heat. Add mince to pan, stir until cooked. Drain fat if necessary. Add shallots, garlic, parsley, salt and cornflour mixture, stir until thickened. Suitable to make a double batch and freeze in small containers if used within four weeks.

If amines are a problem you can cook mince in the microwave, but mix it well as it starts to cook or it will form large lumps.

VARIATIONS • Beef and beans: add kidney beans drained, or blended for vegetable haters. Blending makes a thicker topping and works well with young children. Use a wand blender straight in the can • Beef and lentils: after mince is cooked, cover with water or home-made chicken stock (p. 96) and add 1 cup of rinsed red lentils, salt and permitted vegetables (celery, swede, Brussels sprouts, finely chopped). Cook for about 30 to 40 minutes, thicken with cornflour if necessary. The veggies are not obvious. When reheating, mix in microwave dish with ¼ cup finely chopped cabbage for chow mein effect. This makes a different meal as the cabbage is still crunchy.

Mountain burritos

Use Mountain Bread flat sheets (ingredients: flour, water, salt) available from supermarkets as tortillas or make tortillas (p. 78). Choose from the following fillings, avoiding salicylate and amine options while on your supervised elimination diet:

failsafe beef and beans (above) or lentil mash (p. 107)

Howard's bean paste (p. 106)

shredded lettuce

mashed sweet potato (salicylates)

preservative-free cream cheese (contains dairy) or sour cream

grated cheddar cheese (amines)

Spoon the beef mixture onto the tortillas. Add selected toppings and roll up, burrito style, to keep the filling from spilling out as you eat.

VARIATIONS • *Dairy-free*: use soy cream cheese instead of cheese or sour cream • *Gluten-free*: use gluten-free flatbread or make your own buckwheat pancake (p. 36) as a wrap • *Vegetarian*: use lentil mash (p. 107) instead of mince.

A common brand of commercial tortillas contains sorbic acid (200), potassium sorbate (202), calcium propionate (282), TBHQ (319) and BHA (320).

Tortillas

'My boys love to take these to school/kinder with just butter, especially on excursions.' Reader, Victoria

4 cups flour
½ tsp salt
2 tsp failsafe baking powder
4 tbsp butter
water

Combine dry ingredients in a bowl and rub in butter. Add water a small amount at a time and work mixture into a dough. Knead dough until smooth, cover and set aside for 10 minutes. Form dough into balls the size of an egg. Roll each ball into a circle approx 12 cm in diameter. Heat frying pan on medium to high heat. Place tortilla in pan and cook about 1 minute each side until lightly speckled. Eat plain, with butter or as burritos with garlic meat topping (p. 125), lettuce, and carrot and cheese if permitted.

Spring rolls

2 tsp failsafe oil
300 g minced beef, chicken or lamb
any of the following vegetables finely diced: garlic, celery, beans, leek, shallots, Brussels sprouts; plus perhaps bok choy or other Chinese greens, carrot, corn kernels (salicylates), peas (glutamates) from your allowance
½ cup cooked rice or rice noodles
1 tbsp preservative-free cream cheese (optional)
2 teaspoons golden syrup (optional)
failsafe spring-roll wrappers
salt to taste
milk or water for sealing wrappers
failsafe oil (p. 184) for frying

Stir-fry meat until browned, add vegetables and cook until tender. Add rice and optional ingredients. Allow mixture to cool. Separate spring-roll wrappers into individual sheets. Place 1 or 2 tbsp of mixture at the top of each sheet, fold left and right sides into the middle. Moisten all over the wrapper and then roll from the top. Shallow-fry in oil or bake at 180°C for 15 minutes. The filling mix, with a small amount of sweet potato or butternut pumpkin (salicylates) to help bind the mixture together, can also be used to make mini pies in a muffin pan.

Pies (p. 44)

Cornish pasties (p. 47)

Jaffles (p. 44)

Cottage pie

This is a traditional recipe. For a quick version you can simply serve the meat on the mashed potato.

500 g failsafe mince (p. 76)
2 cups mashed potato
butter or failsafe margarine (p. 183)
1 tsp finely chopped parsley

Spoon failsafe mince into a pie dish. Top with mashed potato, dotted with butter. Bake at 180°C until top is golden, approximately 20 minutes. Garnish with parsley. Serve with cooked permitted vegetables.

Sammy's steak and pea mini-pies

'I add blitzed butter beans to the potato, sneaky mum!' Reader, Alice Springs

1 kg chuck/stewing steak, diced small
½ cup plain flour
4 tbsp of failsafe oil
½ leek, finely chopped
2 tbsp chives, chopped
8 cloves of garlic
1 swede, diced small
salt to taste
3 cups of peas (glutamates)
commercial puff pastry
10 cups cold mashed potato
water

Toss steak in the flour to coat, fry in a large pan with the oil until brown, then remove and set aside. Gently fry the leek, chives and garlic. Add swede and steak to the pan.

Cover with water and cook covered on a low heat until meat is tender (1–2 hours). Add peas and cook for a further 20 minutes. Cut pastry sheets into four, grease a muffin tin and push the pastry into the muffin tins to form the shell of the pies.

Fill the pies with the cooled meat filling then top with mash or more pastry. Bake at 180°C for 25–30 min or until pastry is golden. Freezes well as a lucky dip for Mum's night off.

Beef and leek pie (p. 45)

Stir-fries

A stir-fry served on steamed rice is a nutritious meal relatively high in vegetables and grains, and low in meat and fats. Some restaurants will prepare a failsafe stir-fry if given advance notice.

During your supervised elimination diet, use permitted vegetables such as garlic, green beans, cabbage, shallots, leeks and mung sprouts. Later you might be able to use limited amounts of vegetables like carrots, snow peas and Chinese vegetables like bok choy. Diced chicken or beef is cooked in failsafe oil and thickened with a water/cornflour blend. Salt, garlic, citric acid and pear syrup (from canned pears) can be used to add flavour. Avoid soy sauce because even natural soy sauce is very high in natural MSG, but cooked golden syrup has a similar flavour.

> At a Mongolian restaurant we chose ingredients for our stir-fry from a selection of seemingly fresh, natural meat and vegetables, so we were surprised that we all reacted to the meal. A few weeks afterwards, my husband met the waiter socially and discovered that all the meat contained MSG and the 'fresh' vegetables contained sodium metabisulphite (223).

Basic beef stir-fry

400 g of lean beef, cut into long thin strips

4 cups permitted vegetables cut into same-size pieces

1 tbsp golden syrup

1 tbsp cornflour or arrowroot dissolved in 1 cup water (optional)

salt to taste

Place a small amount of failsafe oil (p. 184) in a frying pan and fry the meat. Remove meat from pan and wipe pan clean with paper towel. Put another small amount of oil in pan and stir-fry vegetables until cooked but still crunchy. Add meat, stir in golden syrup. Thicken with the arrowroot or cornflour mixture if you want. Add salt to taste. Serve on a bed of noodles or rice. Serves 4.

Egg and vegetable stir-fry (p. 122)

Chicken and leek stir-fry (p. 97)

> In 2004, Food Intolerance Network members equipped with sulphite test strips tested mince in butchers' shops in Australia, New Zealand and Sweden. Although it is illegal to add sulphites to mince, they found that 43 per cent of mince beef contained sulphites. A subsequent NSW Food Authority survey in Sydney found an even higher rate of 58%. The Australian Veterinarians Association warns that pets can die from eating too much sulphited pet meat. Ask your butcher for no sulphites or test the mince you buy with sulphite test strips available from www.fedup.com.au at cost.

Meat loaf

500 g minced beef or lamb

1 large stalk finely chopped celery

½ grated Red Delicious apple (salicylates, optional)

1–2 tsp salt or to taste

1 clove of garlic, crushed, or to taste

1 cup brown rice flour or preservative-free breadcrumbs

1 leek, finely chopped and stir-fried

1 egg, beaten

Mix all ingredients, put in loaf tin, spread top with Birgit's pear ketchup (p. 192, optional). Bake 40 minutes at 180°C. Serve with pear puree, pear ketchup or leek sauce (p. 192). Leftovers can be sliced and frozen for use in sandwiches and jaffles.

Mince and potato casserole

This is an excellent recipe and you can hide vegetables in it too.

2 tbsp failsafe oil (p. 184)

500 g lean beef mince

1 small leek, sliced

1 cup finely chopped cabbage

1 clove of garlic, crushed (optional)

salt to taste

4 medium potatoes, sliced

butter or failsafe margarine (p. 183)

Fry mince in oil until browned. Add leek, cabbage, garlic and salt. Place one third of mixture on the bottom of a greased casserole, cover with half the potato slices. Add remaining meat and cover with remaining potatoes, dotted with butter. Cook uncovered at 180°C for about 1 hour.

VARIATION • People who don't react to dairy foods or amines can sprinkle with mozzarella or mild cheese instead of butter.

Alison's crumbed cutlets

This recipe uses a quick and easy method of crumbing, which can also be used for chicken nuggets (p. 90), schnitzel (p. 93) and fish (p. 100). Kids love crumbed food, which is higher in fat than usual and can ease the pain of avoiding take-aways.

1 cup milk, soymilk or ricemilk

2 tbsp flour or cornflour

2 cutlets per person

1 cup failsafe breadcrumbs (p. 194)

failsafe oil (p. 184) for frying

Pour milk into a large jug and add flour. Mix until smooth with the consistency of cream. Dip cutlets into mixture then roll in crumbs to coat. Cook in frying pan in about 2 mm of oil, being careful not to overheat oil. When cooked, drain cutlets on paper towels. Serve with mashed potato, citric lemon juice (p. 194) and permitted vegetables.

Grilled meat and three veg

Lamb chops are a Harry Potter favourite. Other meats suitable for grilling include beef or lamb steak or chops, chicken breasts cut into strips or halved widthways to make thinner (these are good for sandwich fillings too) or failsafe sausages, see above. Serve with lashings of mashed potato, with or without mashed swede and other vegetables – see Mum's Mash (p. 110) – green beans and stir-fried cabbage.

good quality beef steaks, lamb steaks, lamb chops, chicken breasts (no skin)

Preheat griller or barbecue to medium. Cook steak or chops until just tender, turning only once. Generally, cook the second side for half the time of the first side. Top each piece with a thin slice of garlic butter (p. 185) if liked.

As an amine responder I have to be careful with meat: the fresher the better. I always cook my meat the day I buy it or freeze it and use it within a month. Browning meat, charring or grilling will increase amine content so I aim for medium rare. Extremely sensitive amine responders may need to steam or microwave their meat. Delicious-tasting meat juices and even home-made gravy made from meat juices are high in amines. Marinades must be made of failsafe ingredients. Any commercial marinade, sauce or gravy is very high in salicylates, amines and MSG. Meat from supermarkets that has been vacuum-packed can be high in amines and has caused me some nasty migraines. I now shop at my local butcher and ask whether meat is fresh or vacuum packed. I've also checked his mince myself with a sulphite test strip.

Birgit's pear-glazed steak

1 tbsp butter, failsafe margarine (p. 183)
  or failsafe oil (p. 184)
200 g per person of beef steak, e.g.
  rump, sirloin, porterhouse
salt
1 tbsp Birgit's pear jam (p. 186)
crushed garlic (half clove per person)
1 shallot, chopped
1 tsp chopped parsley
¼ cup water
½ cup cream (optional)
gin for flavour (optional)

Preheat pan to medium. Heat butter in pan and add steaks. Sprinkle salt on top and put pear jam in pan to caramelise. Wait until the first side is brown before turning. When the second side is brown, test meat by cutting into the side to see if it is done. Remove and add crushed garlic, shallots and parsley to the pan. Add water, cream and gin and stir to make gravy. Serve with microwaved vegetables or steamed rice and salad.

VARIATION • *Dairy-free*: mix 1 tsp cornflour with water, place in pan and stir to thicken.

> A home-cooked meal using the most expensive cut of meat such as fillet steak is cheaper than buying a fast-food meal for the whole family when you include the costs of transport, extras and drinks.

Kebabs

1 kg rump steak or diced lamb
⅔ cup failsafe oil (p. 184)

Trim steak and cut meat into 2 cm cubes. Moisten with oil. Thread meat cubes onto skewers. Grill, turning and basting for about 5 minutes. Makes 16–20. Serve with lettuce, chopped shallots and cooked green beans with hummus (p. 189) or plain yoghurt wrapped in failsafe pita or Lebanese bread.

VARIATIONS • Thread alternate meat cubes and chunks of leek on skewers • Brush kebabs with a mixture of oil and golden syrup for a soy sauce flavour.

Quality Lebanese Bread is fully failsafe (ingredients: wheat flour, water, sugar, yeast, salt) and good for pocket-bread sandwiches, pizza bases and kebabs.

Irish stew

This is the easiest main meal in the book!

500 g diced lamb

water

salt to taste

4 potatoes, peeled

1 large leek

1 carrot (optional, salicylates) or other permitted vegetables

1 cup green beans, sliced

Put meat into a medium saucepan. Add enough water to cover the meat. Sprinkle salt over. Cut potatoes, leek and carrot into thick slices and arrange on top of meat. Vegetables do not have to be covered by liquid as they will steam. Bring to the boil and simmer gently until meat is tender or for 1 hour. Add beans in last 10 minutes. Serve on steamed rice or cous-cous (contains gluten).

VARIATIONS • Fry chopped leek in 1 tbsp failsafe oil (p. 184) until tender and remove from pan. Stir-fry lamb in extra oil until browned, add remaining ingredients including leek and cook until meat is tender (contains some amines) • Just before serving, blend 1 tbsp cornflour with a small amount of water, mix well with extra liquid from stew then add back into stew, stirring until thickened • Try thickening with ½ cup of brown lentils added at the start • Also an excellent recipe using boned rabbit.

Cooking increases amines (p. 12). Reduce amine levels by using good-quality meat, which requires less cooking than tougher cheap cuts. Amine responders can avoid meat juices in this stew.

Indian style lamb with leeks and potatoes

The owner of a popular Indian restaurant in Sydney says the secret of a good curry is plenty of onions, salt and oil. This failsafe version of a traditional curry uses leeks.

800 g diced lamb

1 tsp finely crushed garlic

½ cup failsafe oil (p. 184)

1 tbsp sugar

1 large leek, cut into fine rings

2 large potatoes, peeled and quartered

1½–2 tsp salt

2 cups water

Put lamb in a bowl. Add garlic, mix well, cover and set aside for 2–3 hours. Heat the oil in a medium-high frying pan until hot. Scatter in the sugar and immediately add the leeks. Stir and fry the leeks until they are a rich brownish colour. Add the meat. Stir and fry the meat for about 10 minutes or until it browns lightly. Now add the potatoes and stir-fry for about 5 minutes. Add salt and water. Bring to the boil, then lower the heat, cover and simmer for about 1 hour or until lamb is tender. Stir gently once or twice during cooking. Serve with steamed rice, green beans, Birgit's pear ketchup (p. 192) and plain pappadums (not pepper or spicy) which can be microwaved. Serves 4.

'My partner loves curry and does not appear to be sensitive to foods. We simply add it to certain recipes at the end of the cooking after we have served the kids. That way everyone is happy.' Reader, Victoria

Quick beef stroganoff

2 tsp failsafe oil (p. 184)

375 g lean boneless sirloin or fillet steak, trimmed and cut into strips

⅓ cup chopped leek or shallots

1 clove of garlic, crushed

½ cup home-made chicken stock

125 g wide colour-free egg noodles

¼ cup light sour cream

¼ cup natural reduced-fat yoghurt

1 tbsp chopped fresh chives or parsley

Heat water in saucepan for cooking noodles. Heat oil over medium heat in a large heavy-based frying pan. Add beef strips, fry until browned, about 2 minutes. Remove from pan. Stir leek and garlic in frying pan until tender, add stock and simmer for 2 minutes. Cook noodles according to directions on packet. In a small bowl, combine sour cream and yoghurt. Return the beef and meat juices to frying pan, add sour cream mixture, stirring gently over low heat. Serve on noodles, sprinkled with chives or parsley. Serves 4.

> People who are very sensitive to amines may react to sour cream.

Roasts

Roasts are easy and popular with children. We do chicken, lamb and beef roasts but pork is too high in amines to be acceptable. Gravy is not failsafe even if the ingredients in the premix sound okay or you make it yourself, because of amines in the meat juices.

Roast lamb or beef

'My son loves the leek sauce [p. 192] instead of gravy.' Reader, Darwin

1 leg of lamb or roast of beef
potatoes, peeled and halved
leeks, washed, trimmed, cut into lengths
   and wrapped in a foil parcel
chokos, peeled, quartered and sprinkled
   with salt
extra vegetables (see variation)

Preheat oven to 180–200°C. Trim excess fat and put meat in a lightly oiled roasting pan. Allow cooking time of 30–35 minutes per 500 g of meat. Prepare vegetables. Allow 1 hour for vegetables, turning once during cooking. When the meat is cooked, it will be easier to carve if you allow it to stand for 15 minutes, keeping warm on a serving dish. Vegetables can be drained on kitchen paper and kept warm in the oven with the door open. Serve with leek sauce (p. 192), pear puree or Brussels sprout puree (p. 110), green beans or green peas if tolerated (p. 111).

VARIATION • Extra vegetables: butternut pumpkin, sweet potatoes and parsnips all bake well but contain salicylates so are not suitable for your supervised elimination diet. Peel pumpkin and sweet potatoes and cut into similar size pieces. Peel parsnips, trim both ends and cut into halves lengthwise. Wrap in a foil parcel with a small knob of butter to bake.

To delay amine build-up, left-over meat should be frozen the day of cooking and eaten within four weeks from date of purchase. To freeze for sandwiches, see instructions for free-flow chicken (p. 95).

Yorkshire pudding

The secret to this traditional recipe is in heating the oil.

¾ cup plain flour
¼ tsp salt
1 large egg
1 cup milk
failsafe oil (p. 184)

Beat all well together until bubbles appear. The mixture can be left to stand for an hour but this is not essential. Heat a little oil in small muffin tins. Remove from heat. Half-fill with batter. Cook at 200°C for 20–30 minutes.

Rabbit provençal

Rabbit can be obtained in many places by asking your butcher. It can be dry so it is best stewed, pot-roasted or casseroled.

1 large leek, sliced into rings
2 tbsp failsafe oil
1 rabbit, about 2 kg, boned
¼ cup flour or gluten-free flour
salt
2 cups milk or soymilk or cream if
   preferred
1 small carrot (salicylates), chopped
1 stick celery, chopped
1 tsp chopped parsley

Fry leeks in oil until translucent and set aside. Roll rabbit joints in the flour and fry until some browning is visible, turning. Place in casserole. Add leek, salt, milk, carrot and celery and stir. Cover and place in oven for 1.5–2 hours at 160°C. Garnish with parsley and serve with mashed potatoes and green beans.

Herbed rack of lamb

2 racks of lamb with 6 cutlets in each
2 tbsp chopped chives and parsley
4 tsp of failsafe oil (p. 184)
2 tbsp of pear syrup (from canned pears)
⅛ tsp of citric acid dissolved in ¼ cup water

Preheat oven to 190°C. Trim fat from the racks of lamb, leaving a thin layer to prevent drying out. Combine parsley, chives, pear syrup and citric-acid mix in a large dish. Place racks of lamb, meat side down, in the marinade and brush exposed parts of racks with marinade. Cover and marinate in the refrigerator for 30 minutes. In a roasting pan, stand the racks of lamb upright with trimmed sides on the outside, and interlace the bones to form an arch. You might have to tie together with white kitchen string, which is removed before serving. Roast for 1 hour, brushing occasionally with marinade. Serve with roast potatoes and butternut pumpkin (salicylates, when permitted) and green beans. Carve down between the bones to serve. Serves 4.

Teach your children to cook. Psychologist Steve Biddulph recommends that a boy of 10 should be able to prepare an entire evening meal for the family. At a Darwin sleepover, the birthday boy aged 12 cooked breakfast of omelette and toast for his guests. Responsible teenagers can put on a roast with vegetables so that working parents come home to the delicious smell of nearly cooked dinner.

Chicken

Fresh chicken is one of the safest foods, except for the skin, which contains amines. Plain takeaway BBQ or rotisseried chicken used to be failsafe but most are now pre-seasoned and stuffed. Avoiding the stuffing and seasoning does not help because chemicals permeate the meat and cause reactions. Unless you can find a plain chicken, you will have to cook your own.

HFC (Halliwell Fried Chicken)

'My kids just love this recipe.' Deborah Halliwell, Darwin

500 g chicken breasts or thighs, cut into nugget shapes
1 clove of garlic, crushed
salt to taste
plain flour or gluten-free mix of cornflour and brown rice flour for coating
failsafe oil (p. 184)

Mix chicken with garlic and salt and let it stand for about 30 minutes. Roll chicken pieces in flour until all are coated then freeze for 15 minutes to make flour stick better. Deep fry. This takes only minutes. Do in batches and drain on paper towels when done. Serve with French-fried potato chips (p. 104).

VARIATIONS • Crunchy chicken: place chicken pieces in a bowl and stir with salt and flour until well coated. Then stir with enough oil to make sure all pieces are coated. Bake in a preheated 180°C oven for 1 hour • Coat as directed and shallow fry in failsafe oil (p. 184) until crisp and golden brown. Serve with chips, vegetables or on hamburger buns with lettuce and mayonnaise.

Fast-food chicken will probably contain MSG, antioxidants from the 310–312, 319–321 range and/or spices.

Shaker nuggets

'Extra easy chicken nuggets. My niece and nephew (who live on processed food) prefer these to the ones their mother buys.' Reader, email

2 chicken breasts, diced (about 500 g)
½ cup rice crumbs (see Shopping List)
salt to taste

Put rice crumbs in a freezer bag, add chicken and shake until evenly coated. Place on a lightly oiled baking tray and bake at 180°C for 10–15 minutes or shallow fry for a more golden appearance.

Commercial chicken nuggets may contain nasty additives such as sulphites and flavour enhancers.

Rebecca's panfried chicken

Sugar-glazed chicken turns a beautiful brown.

600 g chicken breast fillets, cut into
   nugget shapes
2 tbsp failsafe oil
1 tbsp white sugar (optional), or salt to
   taste

Preheat frying pan to medium. Add oil and wait until hot, then add sugar and stir to dissolve. Place chicken pieces in oil mixture and cook until first side is golden brown and sides of chicken pieces are cooked. Turn and cook until second side is brown. Serve with mashed potato and other tolerated vegetables. Serves 4.

Golden chicken

My favourite chicken recipe. There is a tantalising smell during cooking.

600 g chicken breasts, skinned
MARINADE
2 tbsp failsafe oil (p. 184)
3 tbsp golden syrup
2 shallots, finely chopped
1 clove of garlic, crushed (optional)
1 pinch citric acid (optional)
salt to taste

Cut chicken into strips or nugget shapes. Add chicken to marinade and coat well. Cover and marinate for 30 minutes if possible. Preheat grill or barbecue. Cook until browned on first side. Turn chicken and cook until done. Test the chicken with a skewer. The juices should be clear when the chicken is cooked. To prevent the marinade burning, keep chicken pieces touching. Serve with mashed potato and other permitted vegetables, or on rice or fried rice with chopped swedes, bean shoots, green beans, shallots, garlic and salt.

Chicken balls

500 g minced chicken

1 tsp chopped parsley (optional)

1 clove minced garlic (optional)

1 egg

1 cup crushed Rice Bubbles or gluten-free
   rice crumbs

salt to taste

failsafe oil (p. 184) for frying

Form chicken, garlic and parsley into balls, dip in egg and coat in crushed rice bubbles with salt. Shallow fry in failsafe oil until cooked through.

Chicken schnitzel

Children love crumbed food. You can use this method for fish, crumbed cutlets and veal schnitzel. These are good hot or cold and can be used in lunchboxes. Commercial breadcrumbs all contain preservative (282) and possibly spices or flavour enhancers.

500 g chicken breasts, cut into thin
   slices

flour or gluten-free flour

½ tsp salt

1 egg, beaten

home-made bread crumbs or rice crumbs
   (p. 194)

failsafe oil for frying

Cut chicken into thin slices or nugget shapes. Season flour with salt, then coat chicken slices. Dip into beaten egg and cover with crumbs. Fry gently in shallow oil until golden brown on both sides. Drain on paper towels. Garnish with parsley and serve with mashed potato, vegetables and citric lemon juice (p. 194).

VARIATIONS • Fish fingers: use the same method above with flaked white fish fillets mixed with mashed potato and dipped in cornflour, egg, rice crumbs. Fish has to be very fresh not freshly thawed. You are unlikely to find fresh enough fish at a supermarket; we always find a fish shop with personal service and ask for the freshest white fish • Sao chicken: use crushed Sao biscuits for crunchier crumbs.

Chicken casserole

This is a delicious recipe, good for family or dinner guests, or when you need to take a hot dish.

500–900 g cooked chicken, diced (e.g. microwaved, or leftover from stock, p. 96)

2 tbsp butter or failsafe margarine (p. 183)

1 or 2 leeks, finely chopped

1 clove garlic or more, crushed (optional)

2 tbsp cornflour or arrowroot

1 cup or more milk, soymilk or ricemilk

salt to taste

2 medium potatoes, cooked and mashed

extra butter or failsafe margarine for topping

Preheat oven to 200°C. Stir-fry leek and garlic in butter until transparent. Add cornflour and cook for about one minute, stirring. Add milk and salt and reduce heat. Cook, stirring, over a low heat until thickened. Put chicken in a medium-size casserole dish, pour leek sauce over, top with mashed potato and dot with butter. Bake for about 30 minutes until brown and crispy. Serve with steamed cabbage and green beans.

VARIATIONS • With pasta: stir through cooked pasta or gluten-free pasta • Chicken and leek topping: follow recipe for leek sauce and pour over chicken, use as topping for noodles or pasta • Family pie: top pie with one sheet of commercial puff pastry instead of mashed potato • Asparagus: stir through fresh or drained canned asparagus (if tolerated, salicylates).

Roast chicken

Roasts are easy and delicious. Leftovers should be frozen and can be used as sandwich fillings (see p. 96 to make chicken stock from your roast).

1 chicken

potatoes, peeled

1 large leek, washed and cut into 8 cm chunks, wrapped in a foil parcel

STUFFING

cooked rice

chopped shallots

salt to taste

Preheat oven to 180°C. Trim excess fat off chicken, stuff cavity with stuffing mixture and put in a lightly oiled roasting pan. Allow 30 minutes cooking time per 500 g of chicken. Peel vegetables, cut into similar size pieces and pat dry to stop them sticking to the pan. Add them to the baking dish when there is a good hour of cooking time left. When the chicken is cooked, it will be easier to carve if you allow it to stand for 15 minutes, keeping warm on a serving dish. Vegetables can be drained on kitchen paper and kept warm in the oven with the door open. Serve with green beans or other tolerated green vegetables and permitted gravy (p. 191), pear puree or Brussels sprout puree (p. 110). Left-over chicken should be frozen the day of cooking.

VARIATION • Use butternut pumpkin, sweet potato and parsnip (salicylates) when tolerated. Peel all vegetables thickly. Include pumpkin and sweet potato with potatoes. Slice parsnips in halves lengthwise, wrap in foil parcels with a dob of butter and put in oven beside baking dish.

FREE-FLOW CHICKEN

You can slice leftover or microwaved chicken into small pieces, spread in a thin layer on a sheet of foil and cover with another sheet of foil. Frozen chicken pieces can be used on sandwiches, without thawing. They are also useful for stir-fries, fried rice, jaffle or pie fillings.

Chicken risotto

This recipe is useful the day after a roast chicken dinner, when stock and cooked chicken are on hand.

1 tbsp failsafe oil (p. 184)

2 shallots, finely chopped

1 clove of garlic, crushed

1 cup diced potato

1½ cups short grain white rice

4 cups boiling chicken stock (p. 96)

½ cup boiling water

2 cups frozen beans (or green peas if tolerated, p. 111)

1 cup cooked diced chicken

1 tsp finely chopped parsley

salt to taste

Heat oil in a large saucepan and stir-fry onion, garlic and potato for 2–3 minutes. Add the rice and stir with a wooden spoon until all the grains are coated with oil and the rice is very lightly toasted. Gradually pour in boiling chicken stock, stirring constantly. Cover and simmer for ten minutes, stirring occasionally. Add boiling water if needed. Stir through frozen beans or peas and diced chicken and simmer for 5 minutes. Add parsley and salt to taste. Serve immediately. Serves 4.

Chicken stock

There are two ways of preparing chicken stock. To reduce amine build-up, cook for the shortest time you can and do not include the skin.

- When you have finished with your roast chicken, you can put the bones and neck in a saucepan with water, leek, parsley, celery and salt, and simmer for one hour. Strain, cool and skim off fat. Store in refrigerator or freezer.
- Another way of making stock gives you more concentrated stock and leaves you with a cooked chicken. In a large saucepan, cover the skinned chicken with water and add a chunk of leek, celery, parsley and salt. Simmer for one to two hours, depending on the size, then strain off the juice. When it cools you have a bowl of good stock and a pleasantly moist chicken suitable to eat cold, in salads, to slice and freeze for school lunches, or for recipes requiring cooked, diced chicken such as the chicken fried rice, below.

Birgit's Indonesian-style fried rice

2 tbsp butter or failsafe margarine
  (p. 183) or oil (p. 184)
2 eggs
salt to taste
1 clove of garlic, crushed
½ cup celery, finely chopped
½ cup cabbage, finely shredded
½ cup finely diced carrots or corn kernels
  (when permitted, p. 112)

2 cups cooked rice, white or brown
1 cup cooked chopped meat: e.g.
  chicken, beef, lamb, sausages
1 shallot, finely chopped
1 tsp parsley
1 tsp golden syrup mixed in 2 tbsp water
  (optional)

Preheat frying pan to medium. Put butter in pan. Beat eggs in a cup with salt and add to pan. Stir until cooked like very dry scrambled egg. Add garlic and fry briefly. Add celery, cabbage and carrots and stir-fry vegetables for 1–2 minutes. Then add rice. Stir-fry until ingredients are well mixed. Add cooked meat, chopped shallots and parsley. Just before serving, stir through golden syrup mixture, which tastes like soy sauce. Serve with salad or as a side dish. Serves 2 as a main course.

Chicken satay

Arrange cubes of chicken (no skin) on satay sticks, brush with golden marinade (p. 195) and grill. Serve on a bed of rice with mock-peanut sauce.

MOCK-PEANUT SAUCE

1 tbsp butter

1 clove of garlic, crushed

salt to taste

1 tbsp golden syrup

2 tbsp Freedom Foods soy butter (may not suitable for your supervised elimination diet, p. 188)

Melt butter in saucepan over low heat, and stir in other ingredients until mixed. Just before serving, brush over satay sticks with a pastry brush and pour remaining sauce over rice.

Chicken and leek stir-fry

250 g diced, cooked chicken

4 cups chopped leeks, garlic, green beans, cabbage, shallots, mung bean sprouts or salicylate-containing vegetables like carrots, snow peas, corn kernels and Chinese greens when tolerated

1 tbsp cornflour or arrowroot dissolved in 1 cup water or chicken stock (optional)

Place a small amount of failsafe oil (p. 184) in a frying pan. Add all ingredients to pan and stir-fry until vegetables are cooked but still crunchy. Thicken with arrowroot or cornflour mixture and flavour with salt, citric acid, pear syrup, or golden syrup if liked. Serve on a bed of noodles or rice. Serves 4.

Darani's amazing chicken noodle stew (p. 71)

Chicken noodle frittata

1 cup water or home-made chicken stock
    (p. 96)
1 packet colour-free 2-minute noodles or
    rice noodles (about 60 g)
2 eggs, lightly beaten
2 tbsp water
1 tsp finely chopped parsley
garlic, crushed (optional)
1 cup cooked chicken, chopped
salt (optional)

Boil noodles in water or stock for two minutes, drain. Mix together eggs, extra water, parsley and garlic. Add chicken and noodles. Pour into a preheated, oiled 20 cm frying pan and cook for 5 minutes without stirring. Brown under a hot grill.

VARIATION • Chicken frittata – add cooked diced chicken to frittata for vegetable haters (p. 115).

Chicken in yoghurt sauce

500 g chicken fillets, cut into pieces
1 cup fresh natural yoghurt
1–2 tbsp failsafe oil (p. 184)
1–2 cloves of garlic, crushed
chopped chives

Place chicken fillets in a casserole dish. Combine remaining ingredients, spoon over chicken. Bake at 180°C for about 30 minutes. Turn halfway through cooking. Serves 4.

Chicken parcels

⅓ cup pear puree
1 tbsp yoghurt
2 shallots, finely chopped
2 sheets preservative-free puff pastry
4 chicken breast fillets

Put pear puree, yoghurt and shallots into a bowl and mix well. Cut pastry sheets in half and place a chicken fillet on each piece. Spoon a quarter of the pear mixture onto each chicken fillet and roll pastry around chicken to form a parcel. Arrange parcels on a tray and bake at 180°C for 20 minutes or until golden.

Chicken and chickpeas

A highly nutritious, delicious and easy meal that freezes well.

750 g chicken thighs, chopped

½ large leek, chopped

½ cup peeled chopped potatoes

1 tin (420 g) chickpeas, drained

½ cup red lentils

garlic, crushed, to taste

salt to taste

water as required

Arrange chicken in a heavy-based saucepan, add remaining ingredients and cover all with water. Bring to the boil and simmer until cooked, about 45 minutes. The lentils will make a satisfying thick sauce. Serve with rice or cous-cous plus other permitted vegetables. Freeze leftovers in big containers as extra meals.

VARIATIONS • Use as filling in failsafe puff pastry triangles by mashing lightly when cooked • Use jointed or boned rabbit instead of chicken.

Seafood

Fresh seafood can be okay if eaten within 12 hours of being caught – 24 hours at most – or frozen within 12 hours and eaten within two weeks (one week for people who are extra sensitive). Fish must be white fleshed, not pink like salmon, tuna or trout, and prawns are always high in amines no matter how fresh they are. Other seafood like calamari, lobsters, oysters, mussels, scallops, crab and marron (freshwater crayfish farmed in Western Australia) are permitted when fresh. Amines develop with age, freezing, and processing such as canning and smoking.

Fish and chips

A quick method of cooking fish and chips and kids love it.

1 cup milk or soymilk

2 tbsp flour or cornflour

1 fresh white fish fillet per person

1 cup failsafe breadcrumbs (p. 194)

failsafe oil (p. 184) for frying

Pour milk into a large jug and add flour. Mix until smooth with the consistency of cream. Cut fish fillets into even-sized pieces and dip pieces into mixture. Roll in breadcrumbs to coat. Cook in frying pan in about 2 mm of failsafe oil (p. 184) but don't overheat the oil. When cooked, drain fillets on paper towels. Serve with oven fries (p. 103), citric lemon juice (p. 194) and salad.

Even if takeaway fish is fresh, crumb and batter mixes may contain colours so grilled fish is the safest. Fried fish and hot chips will be cooked in oil containing synthetic antioxidants such as BHT or BHA, which can cause problems, usually the next day. Even frozen potato wedges and oven-roast potatoes may contain flavour enhancer 635 or natural colour 160b – read the label.

'We asked "Is there any colour in the batter?" "Only a little bit of this", she said, holding up a jar of bright orange powder, sunset yellow (110).' In a Queensland cafe

Panfried fish

fresh white fish fillets
cornflour or rice flour to coat
failsafe oil (p. 184) for frying
salt to taste
citric lemon juice (p. 194)
parsley

Dust fillets with cornflour. Heat oil in frying pan until medium hot, fry fish gently on each side until flesh flakes away from the bone when tested with a fork. Serve with salt, citric lemon juice and decorated with parsley, accompanied by chips or mashed potato and salad.

Due to mercury contamination, Food Standards Australia New Zealand (FSANZ) advise pregnant women, women planning pregnancy and young children to limit their intake of shark (flake), broadbill, marlin and swordfish to no more than one serve per fortnight, with no other fish to be consumed during that fortnight. For orange roughy (also sold as sea perch) and catfish, the advice is to consume no more than one serve per week, with no other fish being consumed during that week (www.foodstandards.gov.au).

Oysters natural

Oysters are an outstanding source of zinc, an essential nutrient. Half a dozen contain 27 mg of zinc, compared to the next closest foods: steak, at 7 mg a serve, and lentils, at 3 mg. They also contain the same amount of calcium as half a cup of milk. Oysters from registered oyster growers go through a special flushing process to rid them of toxic microflora.

½ dozen fresh oysters per person
small jug citric lemon juice (p. 194)

Serve with crusty fresh preservative-free bread or toasted pita bread, or gluten-free bread. Decorate with parsley.

Spanish paella with mussels and scallops

2 tbsp failsafe oil (p. 184)
2 chicken fillets, cut into 4 cm pieces
1 leek, finely chopped
2 shallots, finely chopped
1 clove garlic, crushed
1½ cups white short-grain rice
1½ cups home-made chicken stock
  (p. 96)
1 tsp salt
250 g fresh scallops
250 g fresh mussels
1 cup green peas if tolerated, or green
  beans

In a large saucepan, heat oil and fry chicken pieces until browned. Remove chicken, add leek, shallots and garlic and cook lightly. Add rice to pan, cook 3 minutes. Pour in chicken stock and salt. Bring to the boil, return chicken to pan, cover and steam over a very low heat for 25 minutes. Do not remove lid. Lightly fork through seafood and peas. Steam a further 10 minutes until rice has absorbed all the liquid. Serve with a tossed salad.

The fish is not okay when the sign 'fresh' in a fish shop means 'thawed this morning for your convenience' or 'has been on ice for 14 days'.

Mussels with sauce

8 fresh mussels in half shell

2 shallots, finely chopped

2 tbsp citric lemon juice (p. 194)

3 tbsp gin or home-made chicken stock
  (p. 96)

1 clove of garlic, crushed

½ cup (100 ml) cream or yoghurt

½ tsp salt

1 tsp parsley, finely chopped

Put mussels, shallots, citric lemon juice, gin, garlic and cream in small saucepan and simmer gently until mussels are cooked. Remove mussels and put in shells. Simmer sauce until reduced by half. Pour over mussels and garnish with parsley.

Vegetables and vegetarian meals

Vegetables are the key to health. They contain fibre and natural chemicals that protect against cancer and heart disease. During your supervised elimination diet the only permitted vegetables are potatoes, celery, cabbage, red cabbage, green beans, Brussels sprouts, leeks, shallots, chives, garlic, iceberg lettuce, swedes, chokos, mung bean sprouts, bamboo shoots and dried or canned beans, chickpeas and lentils. Even if you fail your challenges, the following vegetables may be tolerated in limited quantities: green peas, asparagus, beetroot, carrot, Chinese greens, corn, other lettuce, marrow, parsnip, butternut pumpkin, snow peas, snow pea sprouts, sweet potato and turnip (p. 250).

Research suggests it takes eight to ten attempts before children will accept new foods, but more than half of Australian parents give up offering a food after two or three attempts. Do persevere – it'll work eventually! The best way to get vegetables into kids is to hide them.

'My son likes meat and is not a great vegetable eater. Generally I put the available allowed veggies in the food processor and chop them so finely that he doesn't know what is what. That way he will eat them, as long as there is some meat with them as well.' Reader, Singapore

Vegetarians should be aware that some vegetable sources of protein may not have the complete range of essential amino acids, so people who don't eat meat, fish, poultry, eggs or dairy products need to eat a variety of protein-containing foods every day. Dried beans and nuts are excellent sources of protein for vegetarians.

Potatoes

Potatoes contain significant amounts of Vitamin C, as well as potassium and fibre. Large white potatoes are low in salicylates when peeled thickly. Small new potatoes or potatoes with red skins contain salicylates. Green and sprouted potatoes contain poisonous chemicals including solanine. Even small amounts of solanine can cause migraines, fatigue and stomach aches in sensitive people, so any potato with green patches should be discarded. Potatoes can be microwaved, steamed, roasted, boiled and mashed. Boiling leads to losses of Vitamin C. Reduce this by using just enough water to cover the potatoes, simmer gently with the lid on until just done, drain slightly and mash in the cooking water, with a dob of butter or failsafe margarine (p. 183).

Oven fries

large white potatoes or swedes, peeled
   thickly
canola or failsafe oil for frying (p. 184)
salt

Microwave potatoes until nearly soft. Allow them to cool enough to handle, then cut into chip shapes. Coat in failsafe oil by putting them in a plastic bag with the oil and gently rolling around. Spread in a single layer on an oven tray. Bake for 20–25 minutes at 180°C. Serve sprinkled with salt. Oiled, unbaked chips can be frozen for later use.

Frozen oven fries usually contain synthetic antioxidants (310–312, 319–321) in the oil, not necessarily listed on the label, and may contain colours, including 160b.

French-fried potato chips

large white potatoes
canola or sunflower oil for frying (p. 184)
salt

Wash and peel potatoes thickly. Cut into chip shapes. Soak in cold water for 1 hour, then drain thoroughly and dry with a cloth. Fry in deep, hot oil until crisp and golden brown. Drain well and serve sprinkled with salt.

Commercial hot chips are almost always cooked in oil containing at least one synthetic antioxidant from the 310–312, 319–321 range. They may also contain colours like 160b. Beer-battered chips also contain gluten, salicylates and amines.

Crunchy potatoes (p. 53)

Potato wedges (p. 54)

Potato crisps (p. 54)

Mary's potato bake

4 potatoes, peeled and thickly sliced
3 cloves of garlic, peeled and crushed
¼ cup chopped leeks and/or shallots
3 cups (600 ml) cream, milk or soymilk

Place potato slices in a casserole dish. Stir garlic and chopped leeks or shallots into cream. Pour the mixture over the potatoes and stir lightly. Bake at 180°C for 1 hour or until the potatoes are soft. Serves 4.

Rosti potato cakes

3 medium potatoes, peeled and grated
½ cup of finely chopped shallots or leeks
2–3 tbsp butter or failsafe margarine (p. 183), soft

Mix all ingredients together, form into cakes and fry in hot failsafe oil (p. 184).

VARIATION • These are another way of camouflaging very finely chopped or grated vegetables such as Brussels sprouts, cabbage, leeks and green beans for fussy eaters. An egg and a tablespoon of flour or gluten-free cornflour will help to hold them together.

Baked potatoes

4 large potatoes
TOPPING
2 shallots, chopped
½ cup preservative-free cottage cheese
  or ricotta
4 tsp yoghurt (optional)
parsley garnish

Peel potatoes thickly. Bake foil-wrapped for 50 minutes in a 200°C oven. Remove foil. With a sharp knife, cut a cross on the top of each potato, and gently squeeze until the top opens out. Brush with failsafe oil (p. 184) and return to oven for 10 minutes. Top with topping mixture and serve immediately.

VARIATION • Microwave for 3–4 minutes per potato until tender. Cut each potato in half and dress with topping mixture.

Tex Mex potatoes

1 tbsp butter, failsafe margarine (p. 183)
  or failsafe oil (p. 184)
1 cup sliced leek
4 large baked potatoes
1 can 3 bean mix (440 g, no spices)
½ cup yoghurt

Heat butter or oil and stir-fry leek. Add bean mix and heat through. Cut a deep cross into potatoes and open out. Top with bean mixture and yoghurt.

Legumes – chickpeas, lentils and dried beans

Fruits and vegetables contain beneficial natural antioxidants that can neutralise free radicals known to cause cancer. When researchers from the US Department of Agriculture rated 130 common foods for their antioxidant power, most of the top twenty were dried beans, nuts or berries, and three of the top five were dried beans. All dried peas, beans and lentils are permitted except broad beans. Red kidney beans are exceptionally good value, coming in at number three, and as the only dried beans that don't cause wind, they contained more than three times the antioxidant power of apples.

Studies have shown that people who eat legumes at least four times a week have less heart disease and live longer. Antioxidants in supplements do not have the same beneficial properties as they do when eaten in whole foods so nutritionists now recommend that we learn to include dried beans in our diet.

Rating	Food	Antioxidant capacity in tocopherol equivalents
1	pecan nuts	not failsafe
2	mexican red beans	14,920 failsafe
3	red kidney beans	14,412 failsafe
5	pinto beans	12,358 failsafe
11	black beans	8,040 failsafe
17	black-eyed peas	4,342 failsafe
18	Red Delicious apples	4,257 if tolerated

Legumes can be eaten in the form of failsafe hummus (p. 189), roasted chickpeas (Chickadamias p. 55), trail mix (p. 217), chicken and chickpeas (p. 99), chickpea-fortified ricemilk, lentil pie (p. 117), lentil mash (p. 107), red lentil soup (p. 70), Howard's bean paste (below), failsafe mince with kidney beans (p. 76), pizza topping (p. 126), kidney or butter beans on toast (great tossed with 1 tbsp of Birgit's pear ketchup) and bean mix in salads and stews, canned or home-cooked. A popular way to eat kidney beans: take a whole tin of cooked kidney beans, blend with a wand blender and add to soups, stews or failsafe mince.

Howard's bean paste

Soak dried beans overnight in twice their volume of water. Rinse and discard water, cover with water and add a little oil to stop foaming. Pressure-cook for 12 minutes or simmer for 60 minutes. Drain. Or use red kidney beans from a can, drained and rinsed.

1 cup cooked red kidney beans

2 tsp failsafe oil

pinch salt

¼ tsp citric acid

crushed clove of garlic (optional)

2 tbsp water

Mix in blender to a thick paste, adding a little water if too thick. Keep in fridge. Great in sandwiches, wraps, as a dip, a salad dressing, and on pizza.

VARIATION • For a quicker, wetter version, simply open a can of kidney beans and blend with 1 tbsp failsafe oil and 1 clove of garlic to taste – add to failsafe mince, soups and stews.

Kidney beans are less likely to cause flatulence than other dried beans because they contain only low levels of oligosaccharides. A certain amount of flatulence is healthy and oligosaccharides are considered beneficial for the immune system. To reduce flatulence caused by other beans, soak the beans and discard the soaking water.

Lentil mash

Use as a delicious pie filling, toast topping or vegetable side-dish.

1 cup brown or green lentils

3 cups water

2 medium potatoes, peeled and
  quartered

2 tbsp failsafe oil (p. 184)

½ cup chopped leek or shallots

½ cup chopped celery

1 cup other chopped vegetables
  (Brussels sprouts, cabbage)

dob butter or failsafe margarine (p. 183)

2 tbsp chopped parsley

salt to taste

Soak the lentils in the water for at least three hours in a medium saucepan. Add potatoes, cover and simmer gently until soft, about 20 minutes. If you don't pre-soak the lentils then the cooking time is about 50 minutes and more water is required. Separately stir-fry leek, celery and vegetables until translucent. Set aside. Mash or puree cooked lentils and potato with wand blender to a consistency like mashed potatoes, adding extra water if needed. Add butter or Nuttelex. Combine mash with vegetables and parsley.

People with allergies to nuts or soy may have cross-reactivity problems with legumes. Consult your dietitian or allergist.

Shallots

In this book, shallots refer to the member of the onion family which are like thin leeks, with an unformed bulb, as in the rat's left hand. Sometimes they are called spring or green onions, but spring onions, which have a rounded bulb like an onion, are not allowed. Shallots, leeks, chives and garlic are all members of the onion family and appear to be linked with the prevention of cancer and heart disease.

Leeks

A member of the onion family, leeks have a mild, sweet flavour and are a good source of folate and potassium. Thin slices of leek, fried in butter and oil, make a good accompaniment to sausages, burgers and other grilled meats.

Cabbage

The white varieties of cabbage are particularly rich in Vitamins C and K and are a good source of vitamin E and potassium as well as beta carotene, fibre, folate and thiamine. As well, cabbage contains a number of compounds thought to protect against cancer. Red cabbage has a slightly higher salicylate content than white cabbage but is still considered low in salicylates.

Traditionally, shredded cabbage was boiled until tender and tossed with butter and salt before serving. See also soup (p. 69), mince and potato casserole (p. 82), and stir-fry (p. 80). Red cabbage served raw in very thin slices adds colour to the meal and appeals to children. Raw cabbage can cause wind and stomach discomfort so is better cooked for some people.

Cabbage on the side

1 cup of cabbage per person, sliced very finely

½ tbsp butter or failsafe oil (p. 184) per person

In frying pan or saucepan, stir over low heat until cooked to taste, either crunchy or soft. The more slowly it is cooked the sweeter it will taste. Reduce fat by substituting 1 tbsp water per person instead of butter or oil and cooking covered.

Bubble and squeak

Mix leftover mashed potato and leftover cabbage together. Fry in oil on both sides until brown. Top with chopped chives or parsley.

Birgit's cabbage rolls

In this traditional German recipe, the sweetness of the cabbage and the flavours of the mince mix together.

4 large cabbage leaves

400 g of failsafe beef or lamb mince (p. 73)

approximately 1 cup home-made chicken stock (p. 96)

Cut out the thick centre stalk from the base of each cabbage leaf. Wash leaves, pour boiling water over and drain, or microwave until soft. Place one quarter of mince mixture on each leaf and roll up, tucking in the sides to form a parcel. Put in a greased casserole. Pour over enough chicken stock to come halfway up the sides of the rolls. Bake for 1 hour at 180°C.

Brussels sprouts

These are one of the most nutritious of all leafy green vegetables, rich in iron, fibre, protein, beta carotene, Vitamin C and folate. They contain a number of chemicals that protect against cancer.

Eat steamed or microwaved until tender with a dob of butter (p. 183). Hide them in soups (p. 69), pies (p. 44), frittatas (p. 115), or puree (following).

Mum's mash

'Brussels sprouts were a problem in the beginning but I knew my children loved mashed potatoes. I was not giving up on Brussels sprouts or swedes as veggie options so first of all I mashed the potatoes and swede together. No one seemed to notice and ate it all up. Next I added Brussels sprouts, which I cooked separately then added to the potato and swede, mashing it all together with the stab blender, a bit of milk and butter with a bit of salt to taste on serving. No one noticed at first until my son said one night, "What's in this mashed potato? It's really nice." I answered, "I call it Mum's mash. If I tell you will you keep eating it?" "Yeah!!!" he answered. "It's great!!!" Perseverance paid off, as it often does.' Reader, Canberra

Brussels sprouts with sauce

1 cup white sauce (p. 192)
4 Brussels sprouts, steamed or
  microwaved

Pour white sauce over. Dot with butter or failsafe margarine (p. 183) and cook under a hot griller or in the oven until golden brown.

Brussels sprouts puree

This sauce is a traditional accompaniment to game, but it is just as good with chicken, roast beef and lamb. Cook sprouts in a pot with a tight-fitting lid with a little water and butter or failsafe margarine (p. 183) until soft right through. Puree the sprouts in a blender or food processor. Add salt and cream (or dairy or soymilk, preservative-free cream cheese or yoghurt) to taste.

Swedes

Swedes are pale golden turnip-shaped root vegetables, called rutabagas in the USA. Like cabbages and Brussels sprouts, they are cruciferous vegetables, which contain compounds thought to prevent cancers. These chemicals can cause an iodine deficiency if you do not get much of this mineral in your diet. Iodine is found in seafood, fruit, vegetables, cereals and daily multivitamin and mineral supplements. Ask your dietitian if iodine deficiency is a problem in your area (some soils in which vegetables are grown are low in iodine). Swedes are a useful source of Vitamin C. Serve raw in sticks or grated, mashed alone, with potato or as oven fries (p. 103).

Chokos

Originally from Latin America, chokos are green vegetables with the crispness of apples. Like any new vegetable, they should be tried ten times to get used to the new taste. Some children like them raw, cut into sticks like carrots. Try them quartered, peeled thickly, steamed and served with butter and salt, even cold. They can also be stewed like pears with sugar, or used to substitute for pears – with extra sugar – in any recipe.

> Parents who say 'I don't have to worry about vegetables because my children eat so much fruit' need to know that many natural chemicals thought to protect against cancer occur in vegetables but not in fruit. Nutrition gurus now recommend five serves of vegetables and two serves of fruit a day. One serve is half a cup. A failsafe seven-a-day could be a tinned pear with cereal for breakfast, a chunk of lettuce and a stick of celery with lunch, fresh peeled pear for afternoon tea, a mug of Red Soup (which is 2 serves), potato and green beans with the main meal.

Green peas

Peas are low in salicylates and amines but contain some natural glutamates so are not permitted during your supervised elimination diet. A single serve of cooked peas supplies almost half the Vitamin C and a quarter of the thiamine that an adult requires daily. They also supply folate, fibre and phosphorus. If peas are one of the few vegetables your child likes, you might like to do a green-pea challenge first. Vegetable haters may prefer peas served frozen, the kind of gimmick that appeals to kids. Nutritionally this is not a bad idea because vitamins are lost during cooking.

Mushy peas

An old English recipe, which makes a surprisingly colourful sauce.

½ tsp butter or failsafe margarine (p. 183) 1 shallot, finely chopped 1 cup fresh shelled peas or frozen peas ½ cup home-made chicken stock or water salt to taste	Melt butter in a small saucepan and stir-fry shallot. Add peas and stock and bring to the boil. Cover and simmer for 10 minutes. Add salt, puree peas in blender.

Snow peas and snow-pea sprouts

Eat when tolerated (salicylates). One serve of snow peas contains more than the daily requirement for vitamin C, as well as being a good source of beta carotene, potassium and fibre. Serve raw or in stir-fries.

Carrots

Carrots (salicylates) are an important vegetable to use after your supervised elimination diet. They are exceptionally high in beta carotene, a nutrient found in all red, orange and green vegetables. In the body, beta carotene is converted to Vitamin A, which is essential for health. One medium-cooked carrot will contribute enough vitamin A for about 3 days. Other failsafe sources of Vitamin A include eggs, margarine, butter, milk and some fortified soy products and vegetables. Beta carotene is colouring agent 160a and is permitted. Absorption of beta carotene from raw vegetables with tough-walled cells like carrots is increased about four or five times when they are cooked and mashed.

Pumpkin

Butternut pumpkins (salicylates) are a good source of beta carotene, and also contain Vitamin E. See roast pumpkin (p. 88) and pumpkin scones (p. 52). One of my favourite spreads on rice cakes is mashed leftover roast pumpkin.

Beetroot

Beetroot (salicylates) is rich in potassium, a good source of folate and contains some Vitamin C. Eat raw, grated in salads, freshly boiled, or as canned beetroot, e.g. in hamburgers (p. 74) and sandwiches (p. 40).

Beetroot dip (p. 188)

Traditional Scottish Potato Salad (p. 119)

Some brands of canned beetroot contain spices, high in salicylates.

Asparagus

Asparagus (salicylates) is rich in folate and a useful source of Vitamin C, beta carotene and potassium. Eat fresh as a steamed vegetable, in salads, in dips (p. 188) or in sandwiches.

Tofu

Tofu is a vegetarian, non-dairy cheese. Firm tofu can be used as a meat substitute, which is why an old Chinese name for it is 'meat without bones'. You can use it in any dish where you would usually add slices of chicken breast, including salads, stir-fries, pasta, soups, stews and sandwiches. Silken tofu is smooth and creamy. It can be used in desserts and dressing (p. 190). Once opened, tofu should be refrigerated. Cover it with cold water and change the water daily. To use, drain the water and pat tofu dry. Cut into strips if needed.

Japanese-style tofu in sauce

300 g firm tofu
flour for coating
1 egg, beaten
2 shallots, finely chopped
SAUCE
2 cm of gin in a glass (a bit less than ¼ cup)
1–2 tbsp golden syrup
¼ cup home-made chicken or vegetable stock
pinch salt

Cut tofu into cubes, dip in flour, dip in egg, dip in flour again. Shallow-fry in failsafe oil (p. 184). Drain excess oil. Sprinkle in shallots. Mix together the ingredients for the sauce and pour into pan, stir gently until sauce caramelises and serve.

Tofu stir-fry

1 tbsp failsafe oil (p. 184)
300 g firm tofu, cubed
1 cup chopped leeks
1 cup chopped celery
1 cup very finely chopped swedes
2 bunches baby bok choy (salicylates, when tolerated), ends trimmed, leaves separated and washed
1 tbsp home-made chicken or vegetable stock or water
1 tbsp golden syrup

Heat oil in wok, add tofu and toss until golden. Remove and set aside. Add a small amount of oil and stir-fry leek, celery and swedes. Add tofu, bok-choy, stock and golden syrup and toss to combine. Cook 1 minute or until the bok choy is slightly wilted. Serve on noodles or rice.

Country vegetable bake muffins

1 leek, chopped and washed
1 cup finely shredded cabbage
1 cup diced celery or ½ cup diced celery and ½ cup shredded red cabbage
1 cup finely chopped shallots
½ cup mung bean sprouts (optional)
½ cup blended tofu (optional)
½ cup self-raising flour or gluten-free flour (p. 233)
¼ cup failsafe oil
4 eggs
salt to taste
poppy seeds

Preheat oven to 180°C. Combine all ingredients. Spoon mixture into muffin pots that have been well greased and lightly dusted with preservative-free breadcrumbs. Sprinkle with poppy seeds. Bake for 25–30 minutes or until set. Freeze muffins for school lunches. Mixture can also be baked in a 20 cm round springform cake tin for 35–40 minutes.

Annette's Spanish omelette (p. 122)

Frittata for vegetable haters

This recipe is a particularly ingenious version of 'hide the vegetables'. The frittata is good hot or cold, and goes well in the school lunchbox.

2 cups raw vegetables chopped small
  (e.g. small potato, 2 Brussels sprouts,
  celery, shallot)
small garlic clove or to taste
fresh chives, chopped
salt to taste
4 eggs
¼ cup cream, milk, soymilk or ricemilk
1 tbsp failsafe oil for frying pan

Place vegetables, garlic, chives and salt in the food processor (not blender), add eggs and milk and process all together. The mixture will be fine and fluffy so there is no need to cook the vegetables first. Pour the mixture into oiled, preheated 25 cm frying pan and cook on very low heat with the lid on (takes about 20 minutes). There is no need to flip the frittata as with the lid on the top it will cook, but keep heat low or the bottom will burn. Finish under the grill if necessary. Serves 4.

Quick vegetable and bean stir-fry

4 cups permitted vegetables cut into
  same-size pieces
failsafe oil (p. 184) for frying
1 can (300 g) kidney or other beans,
  drained
salt to taste

Put small amount of oil in pan and stir-fry vegetables such as leeks, shallots, garlic, mung bean sprouts, green beans and other vegetables as tolerated (p. 102). Add kidney beans and salt. Serve on a bed of noodles or rice. Serves 4.

VARIATIONS • Pour a lightly beaten egg into a clearing in the pan. When nearly cooked, scrape off pan with egg slice and mix with other ingredients • Top with grated cheese (contains dairy products and amines, tasty cheese contains natural MSG) if tolerated • As a sauce, top with Howard's bean paste (p. 106).

Vegetable parcels

4 cups permitted vegetables cut into
  same-size pieces
4 sheets commercial puff pastry

Preheat oven to 200°C. Place vegetables in the middle of pastry sheet. Wrap into parcel. Bake 15–20 minutes. Serve with salad and leek sauce (p. 192).

Frozen ready-to-use pastries can contain sorbate (202), sulphite (223) and propionate (281) preservatives and synthetic antioxidant BHA 320. Always read the label or check Product Updates on the website because ingredients change frequently.

Barley vegetable casserole

⅔ cup pearl barley (contains gluten)
2½ cups home-made chicken stock
  (p. 96) or water
1 tbsp failsafe oil (p. 184)
1 clove of garlic, crushed
2 sticks celery, chopped
2 Brussels sprouts or carrots
  (salicylates), chopped
1 cup green beans or peas (glutamates)

Soak barley overnight in stock. Bring to boil and simmer 1 hour. Drain barley and reserve liquid. Fry garlic and vegetables in the oil over low heat for 8 minutes, stirring so they won't burn. Add stock from cooked barley and simmer for 20 minutes or until vegetables are tender and liquid has almost evaporated. Add the barley and reheat. Serves 4.

Creamy vegetable casserole

'This is a lovely creamy textured veg-casserole. I never use cheese, instead I add a tsp of salt to a white sauce, thickened with cornflour, and everyone is completely fooled, thinking that I make the best cheese sauces in the world! This trick goes way back to my non-dairy days.' Reader, Darwin

4 large potatoes, peeled thickly and
  sliced thin
1 clove of garlic chopped
1 sliced leek
¼ cabbage, diced
2 cups white sauce (p. 192)

Cover the base with a layer of
potato, then half of the garlic and
leek and half the cabbage. Repeat
the layering and cover with two cups
of white sauce. Cook uncovered at
180°C for one hour.

Vegetable pie

1½ cups cooked rice (can be frozen and
  thawed)
1 tbsp butter or failsafe margarine (p. 183)
2 eggs
1 cup grated mozzarella (if tolerated
  – dairy food, high in amines)
½ cup sliced leek
1 cup chopped celery
1 tbsp failsafe oil (p. 184)
1 cup cabbage, shredded finely
1 cup thinly sliced potato or corn kernels
  (salicylates)
½ cup yoghurt and cottage cheese,
  combined to creamy consistency (or soy
  yoghurt and tofu for dairy-free)
2 eggs, extra
salt to taste
failsafe breadcrumbs (p. 194)
butter or failsafe margarine (p. 183) extra

Preheat oven to 190°C. Add butter
and lightly beaten eggs to rice
while still hot. Press into 23 cm
pie plate and sprinkle with half
the grated cheese. Fry onion and
celery in oil until tender. Place in
pie, sprinkle with remaining cheese.
Layer cabbage and potato into pie.
Combine yoghurt mix, eggs and salt
and pour into pie. Top with crumbs
dotted with butter. Bake for
40 minutes or until pie is set.

Lentil pie

lentil mash (p. 107)
short-crust pastry (p. 48)
butter
rice crumbs (see Shopping List)

Prepare lentil mash. Prepare pastry.
Preheat oven to 200°C. Press pastry
into 20 cm flan dish, fill with lentil
mash. Dob with butter and sprinkle
with rice crumbs. Bake for
25 minutes or until brown.

Salads

Plate of salad vegetables

Celery sticks, raw choko sticks, chunks of iceberg lettuce, mung bean sprouts, finely sliced red or green cabbage, with dip (p. 188). If you can tolerate some salicylates, you can choose from carrot and beetroot sticks (or grated), asparagus, snow peas and snow pea sprouts, fancy lettuce (not greens like rocket) and Chinese greens. Other salad additions can include cold cooked potato, green beans, Brussels sprouts, swede, beetroot and beans, as well as raw cashews, pasta twists, chopped chicken, preservative-free cream cheese and slices of hard boiled egg.

Coleslaw

¼ cabbage, shredded

¼ red cabbage, shredded

2–4 celery stalks, chopped

1 fresh pear, peeled and chopped

¼ cup raw cashews, chopped

2 tbsp chopped shallots or chives

1 carrot, grated (when tolerated, salicylates)

Toss ingredients together in a salad bowl and moisten with a dressing of your choice (p. 190). Coleslaw improves if made 2 hours before serving.

Tossed salad

1 lettuce, torn into pieces

3 cups chopped vegetables such as celery, parsley, chives, mung bean sprouts, cold cooked green beans. Choose 1 cup from asparagus, beetroot, carrot, Chinese greens, lettuce other than iceberg, snow peas and snow pea sprouts if tolerated (p. 102).

1 clove of garlic

salt to taste

¼ cup salad dressing (p. 191)

Rub salad bowl with cut garlic. Add salad vegetables, pour over salad dressing and toss until coated lightly.

Supermarket bagged salads are convenient but not nutritious. Researchers tested blood samples from healthy volunteers after eating fresh lettuce and the same lettuce after three days in MAP (modified atmosphere packaging) storage. Levels of healthful antioxidants such as Vitamin C and beta carotene rose significantly after ingestion of fresh lettuce but there was no change after eating MAP stored lettuce.

Potato salad

2 large potatoes, about 500 g

1 cup Mighty Mayo (p. 190)

salt to taste

1 stick celery, finely chopped

1 tbsp shallots or chives, finely chopped

1 tbsp chopped parsley

1–2 hard-boiled eggs, finely sliced
(optional)

Peel potatoes and cook until tender. Cut into cubes and while still warm, mix in mayonnaise, taking care not to break potatoes. When cool, add other ingredients and chill well.

Traditional Scottish potato salad

10 medium waxy potatoes, peeled and
diced

1 cup green beans or peas (contain
glutamates)

1 cup cooked beetroot, diced

2 shallots, chopped

1 tbsp parsley, chopped

salt to taste

4 tbsp Mighty Mayo (p. 190)

parsley to garnish

Boil the potatoes in salted water for 10 minutes or until tender. Drain and pat dry. Cook the beans or peas separately about 5 minutes until tender. Drain. While the vegetables are still warm, mix together and stir in the chopped shallot, parsley and salt to taste. Fold in mayonnaise and garnish with sprigs of fresh parsley.

Whole green bean salad

½ cup salad dressing (p. 191)
4 cups cooked green beans
3 shallots, chopped
4 hard-boiled eggs, chopped
3 tbsp mayonnaise (p. 190)

Pour salad dressing over beans and shallots and leave to marinate for several hours. Just before serving, mix together eggs and mayonnaise and spoon over the beans. Serves 4–6.

Rice salad

¼ cup Mighty Mayo (p. 190)
1 cup rice cooked in 2½ cups of home-
    made chicken stock (p. 96)
2 hard-boiled eggs, sliced
1 cup celery, sliced
1 shallot, chopped
1 lettuce

Pour dressing over hot rice, toss and set aside to cool. Add remaining ingredients, toss gently and chill. Serve on a bed of shredded lettuce.

Mixed bean salad

½ cup red kidney beans
½ cup black-eyed peas
½ cup chickpeas
½ cup butter beans
½ tsp sodium bicarbonate
Mighty Mayo (p. 190)

Wash beans and peas in cold water. Soak overnight in 3 times the volume of water. Discard the soaking water. Place beans in pot, cover with water and add bicarbonate, bring to the boil and simmer until tender, at least 1 hour. Drain beans, rinse and cool. Pour dressing over cold beans and mix well. Sprinkle with chopped parsley.

Eggs

Eggs are a highly nutritious package of vitamins, minerals and essential amino acids and an important failsafe source of Vitamin A. Expert recommendations vary between three and seven eggs a week, including those used in cooking. For a skinny, food-intolerant child this limit does not apply. Check with your dietitian. One suggested that up to 4 eggs a day would be reasonable in such a case.

Fresh eggs cook better and are low in amines. Test a whole egg in water. If it's fresh it sinks. An egg should never stand on its end in water, let alone float. The thicker the white, the fresher the egg.

IT'S OFF!!

Eggs scrambled and omelette (p. 37)

Cracked egg pies

6 slices bread
1 tbsp butter or failsafe margarine
  (p. 183)
6 eggs
1 shallot, chopped

Remove crusts from bread and flatten each slice with a rolling pin. Spread both sides of bread with butter and press into muffin tins. Crack an egg in the centre of each bread case. Sprinkle with chopped shallots and bake at 180°C for 20 minutes or until egg has set. Makes 6 pies.

BOILED AND POACHED EGGS

An automatic egg cooker makes an excellent gift for a food intolerant family or university student. You just add as many eggs as you want (1–7), fill with water to the hard or soft fill line and walk away.

Annette's Spanish omelette

This is like a frittata. It is served cut into wedges and can be eaten hot or cold.

1 tbsp failsafe oil (p. 184)

1 large leek, finely chopped

1 clove of garlic, crushed (optional)

1 cup cabbage, finely chopped

2 medium potatoes, cooked and diced
  (roast leftovers are easy)

5 eggs

½ cup soymilk

1 tbsp finely chopped parsley

salt to taste

Preheat frying pan to medium. Put oil in pan and heat. Stir-fry leek, garlic and cabbage until transparent. Add potatoes and stir until coated with oil. Mix together eggs, soymilk, parsley and salt. Pour over leek mixture in frying pan, cover and cook over moderate heat until set.

Chicken noodle frittata (p. 98)

Egg Foo Yung

5 eggs, well beaten

½ cup finely diced cooked chicken

1 cup finely chopped leek or shallots

1 cup mung bean shoots

½ cup diced celery

failsafe oil (p. 184) for frying

Combine all ingredients, divide into 4 portions and fry one at a time in hot oil. Serves 4.

Egg and vegetable stir-fry

4 cups permitted vegetables cut into same-size pieces

failsafe oil (p. 184) for frying

3 eggs

salt to taste

Put small amount of oil in pan and stir-fry vegetables such as leeks, shallots, garlic, mung bean sprouts, green beans and other vegetables as tolerated (p. 102). Whisk eggs and add to a clearing in the pan when the vegetables are nearly cooked. Allow to nearly set then scrape off with egg slice, turn until all cooked. Mix cooked eggs through vegetables. Serve on a bed of noodles or rice. Great with a spoonful of Birgit's pear ketchup (p. 192). Good cold and handy for a lunchbox.

Quick quiche

CRUST

1 sheet of commercial puff pastry or short-crust pastry (p. 48) or gluten-free pastry (p. 48)

FILLING

2 cups of raw vegetables, e.g. cabbage, leek, shallots, peas and carrots (if permitted), finely chopped

1 tbsp failsafe oil (p. 184)

4 eggs

salt to taste

1 cup milk or soymilk or ricemilk

¼ cup yoghurt or soy yoghurt (optional)

1 tsp finely chopped parsley

Preheat oven to 200°C. Stir-fry vegetables until transparent. Set aside. Beat eggs with a fork until light and fluffy. Add salt, milk, yoghurt and parsley and mix thoroughly. Spray 22 cm quiche pan with failsafe canola oil spray and line with pastry. Arrange vegetables over base. Spoon egg mixture gently into dish. Bake for 30 minutes or until golden brown.

VARIATIONS • Add 1 cup of chopped, cooked chicken or one small (285 g) can of asparagus tips (salicylates), drained • Mini quiche: use patty pans, bake for 10–15 minutes.

Corn and green bean bake

This bake is not suitable for your supervised elimination diet.

4 cups (500 g) frozen green beans and corn kernels (salicylates)

1 medium leek, finely chopped

½ cup self-raising flour or gluten-free self-raising flour (p. 233)

1 can (440 g) creamed corn (salicylates)

4 eggs

salt to taste

Cook frozen vegetables according to directions on pack. Drain and allow to cool. Combine leek, sifted flour, corn and lightly beaten eggs. Season with salt. Add cooked vegetables and mix well. Spoon mixture into a greased and lined 20 cm round deep cake tin. Bake at 180°C for 50–55 minutes. Allow to stand in tin for 10 minutes, cut into slices to serve. Serves 4–6. Good cold in lunchboxes.

Pizza and pasta

When pizzas originated in Naples a few hundred years ago, they were thin flexible breads that could be folded. The art was in the dough, and the topping was simple: a smear of oil, a few slices of fresh tomato, and a sprinkle of salt and herbs like oregano.

> 'My son thought he could never eat a pizza again without tomatoes and cheese so I avoided pizzas for a while until we got used to a diet. The first time we had failsafe pizza he was thrilled to bits and didn't worry at all about the lack of tomatoes and cheese. He particularly loves the garlic meat topping.' Reader, Canberra

Commercial pizza bases usually contain BHA 320, not on the label. Quality Lebanese bread (ingredients: wheat flour, water, sugar, yeast, salt) or the tortilla recipe (p. 78) make good pizza bases.

Yeasted pizza base

1 tsp active dried yeast
1 cup water
½ tsp sugar
1 tbsp failsafe oil (p. 184)
½ tsp salt
2½ cups plain flour (see following for gluten-free)

Throw all ingredients in your breadmaker and press DOUGH, or dissolve the yeast in the water with the sugar. Mix with oil, salt and flours in a large bowl. Blend well and knead until smooth and elastic on a floured board. Let rise in a bowl in a warm place until doubled in volume (about 1½ hours). Punch down and knead again for a few minutes to make dough easy to handle. To make two 30 cm pizzas, divide the dough in half, stretch out to about a 15 cm circle by hand, then roll out to 30 cm. Place on a greased pizza pan and cook at 220°C for 15 minutes.

Quick pizza dough (yeastless)

2 cups self-raising flour or gluten-free
   flour (p. 233)
pinch of salt
2 tbsp butter or failsafe margarine (p.
   183)
enough milk or soymilk to make a
   workable dough (about ¾ cup)
failsafe oil (p. 184)

Sift the flour and salt into a mixing bowl. Rub in the butter. Add the milk gradually, mixing to a soft dough. Roll out to form a circle and place on a well-oiled oven tray. Brush with oil and bake at 220°C for 15 minutes. Remove from the oven. Cover with topping. Bake until golden, about 15 minutes.

Tomato paste, parmesan cheese, olives, pepperoni, anchovies, mushrooms, ham and pineapple all contain various combinations of very high salicylates, amines and natural MSG. Ham contains nitrates (249–252). Meat toppings on commercial pizzas usually contain added MSG and/or ribonucleotide flavour enhancers.

Garlic meat topping

2 cloves of garlic, crushed
chopped shallots
500 g low-fat mince
2 tbsp cornflour dissolved in 1½ cups water
failsafe oil (p. 184)
salt to taste

Stir-fry garlic and shallots in a little oil, remove from pan. Fry mince in a little oil, stirring until cooked. Add garlic and shallots to mince with cornflour mixture, reduce heat and stir until thickened. Spoon over pizza base. Sprinkle with salt.

Cheese topping

Spread pizza base thickly with preservative-free cream cheese. Next, spread a layer of meat or vegetarian topping. If you do not react to amines, you can sprinkle over grated mozzarella cheese.

Vegetarian topping

Spread a layer of preservative-free cream cheese or soy cream cheese on base. In a food processor or blender, combine two tins of partially drained red kidney beans with garlic to form a smooth paste. Spread on pizza. Other options: permitted cooked vegetables, scrambled eggs (p. 37), mozzarella (amines).

Potato and garlic topping

Roast or microwave 4 cloves of garlic. Spread over base. Arrange slices of cooked potato over pizza. Drizzle over failsafe oil (p. 184) and sprinkle with salt. Serve with mushy peas (p. 112).

Beef and leek pie filling (p. 45)

Chicken topping

Spread base with thick layer of preservative-free cream cheese. Spread with chopped cooked chicken (microwave or leftover roast), sliced canned pear or mango (salicylates), and a sprinkle of finely chopped parsley.

Sunday roast topping

Spread with leek sauce (p. 192) and top with pieces of leftover roast chicken, lamb or beef and roast vegetables. Sprinkle with salt.

Supermarket tomatoes advertised as vine-ripened have been picked at the 'breaker stage' – meaning they are a good size and should be *ready* to turn colour – then ripened artificially with ethylene gas.

Margarita topping

Supermarket tomatoes have no place in your supervised elimination diet. They are very high in salicylates, amines and natural glutamates, particularly when concentrated in sauce and paste. If you can access some homegrown heirloom tomatoes (see failsafe gardening, p. 218) you can make this light margarita topping as an occasional treat.

2–3 slices of ripe homegrown tomato per person
cheese (fresh white Italian mozzarella made from buffalo milk if you can get it, or
    supermarket mozzarella if you can tolerate amines, or preservative-free cream
    cheese)
parsley and chives, finely chopped
salt to taste
rice bran oil (optional)

Arrange tomato slices over pizza base. Sprinkle with parsley, chives and salt. Top with grated mozzarella cheese or spoonfuls of cream cheese, and drizzle a little rice bran oil over. Bake at 200°C.

In the twentieth century, plant-breeding programs to develop a pest-resistant firm tomato that could be easily transported probably increased the salicylate content of tomatoes.

Garlic bread

garlic butter (p. 185)
1 loaf of failsafe French bread (p. 40)

Preheat oven to 180°C. Cut each loaf crosswise into diagonal slices, without cutting all the way through. Soften garlic butter and spread each side of slices.

Wrap loaf tightly in foil and bake on baking tray about 20 minutes, until heated through. Serve immediately.

> Commercial garlic bread can contain calcium propionate (282) in the bread, colours (102, 110 or 160b) and preservatives (200, 202, 320, 321) in the garlic margarine.

Pasta

Apart from takeaways, spaghetti bolognaise is the meal that most often causes children's behaviour problems the next day, but that doesn't mean you have to give up pasta. There are toppings other than tomato-based sauces and tasty cheese. Wheat or gluten-free pasta is available in health food sections of supermarkets.

Three-minute spaghetti

Great as a quick meal (or snack) served with salad.

1 cup (100 g) uncooked three-minute
    spaghetti
knob butter or failsafe margarine (p. 183)
preservative-free cream cheese
garlic salt

Cook and drain spaghetti. Add butter, cream cheese and garlic salt and stir through. Serve hot.
Serves 1.

'This meal is extremely popular with my children and just fantastic for the nights when I really want something quick with as little effort as possible. Or something Grandma can do without any problems for lunch or dinner when the children are visiting. I add free flow chicken [p. 95] to it as well if I have some in the freezer.' Reader, Canberra

Creamy chicken pasta (p. 48)

Garlic pasta

2 tbsp preservative-free failsafe oil
 (p. 184) or butter or failsafe margarine
 (p. 183)
2 cloves of garlic, crushed
2½ cups (250 g) pasta (regular or wheat-
 free)
1 tsp finely chopped parsley
pinch of salt

Stir-fry the garlic in the oil until the garlic is slightly brown. Discard the garlic. Cook and drain the pasta. Pour the warm oil over the pasta, sprinkle with parsley and salt and toss it thoroughly to mix all the ingredients. Serves 4.

Check processed garlic for additives, garlic salt for MSG and crushed garlic for vegetable oil, which may contain unlabelled antioxidants like BHA (320). It is quick to use fresh garlic crushed, or simply rub a cut clove over the bowl or plate.

Spaghetti Caesar

6 eggs
4 tbsp cream or natural yoghurt
salt to taste
2 cups cooked spaghetti
1 tbsp finely chopped parsley

Blend together eggs, cream and salt. Pour egg mixture over spaghetti and cook over low heat until egg mixture is slightly set and clinging to spaghetti. Add parsley and gently stir through. Top with chopped chives. Serves 4.

Birgit's cheese pasta sauce

1 tbsp butter or failsafe oil (p. 184)
2 cloves of garlic, crushed
125 g preservative-free cream cheese
½ cup carrots finely diced (salicylates)
½ cup celery finely diced
½ cup cream (optional)

½ cup chopped shallots
1 tsp finely chopped parsley
1 cup cooked chicken cut into cubes
salt to taste
1 tbsp gin (optional)
small quantity of water

Preheat frying pan to medium. Put garlic in with butter and cream cheese. Stir to melt cheese. Add carrots and celery. Add cream. Simmer until vegetables are soft. Add shallots, parsley and chicken. Season with salt. Add gin. If sauce is too thick, thin with water. Serve with spaghetti, gluten-free pasta or mashed potato.

VARIATION • *Dairy-free*: use 1½ cups white sauce (p. 192) instead of cream and preservative-free cream cheese.

Chicken lasagne

double quantity of Birgit's cheese pasta
   sauce (p. 129)
1 cup home-made chicken stock (p. 96)
2 cups cooked diced chicken
instant lasagne sheets
1½ cups white sauce (p. 192) for topping
grated mozzarella cheese for topping (if
   amines tolerated, p. 12)

Thin cheese pasta sauce with chicken stock. In a casserole dish spread a layer of chicken, then sauce, and top with instant lasagne sheets. Repeat layers if needed. Spread white sauce for topping and sprinkle with grated mozzarella cheese or dot with butter. Bake at 180°C for 45 minutes.

VARIATIONS • Use 2 cups of garlic meat topping (p. 125) instead of cooked chicken • For vegetarian lasagne, substitute 2 cups cooked kidney beans, processed with 2 cloves garlic.

Special occasion lasagne
A reader in her twenties uses this rich recipe as her standard 'special occasion' dinner when entertaining friends (contains dairy).

MEAT SAUCE
1 tablespoon failsafe oil
1 leek, chopped
1 clove of garlic, crushed
500 g minced lean beef
1½ tsp chives, finely chopped

2 × 425 g tins peeled pears, undrained and diced

1 tsp salt

1 tsp sugar

3 tbsp pear puree

CHEESE SAUCE

2 tbsp butter or failsafe margarine (p. 183)

3 tbsp plain flour

2 cups milk or soymilk

salt to taste

125 g preservative-free cream cheese

OTHER INGREDIENTS

1 packet large instant curly lasagne

½ cup sour cream and yoghurt

Preheat oven to 200°C. **MEAT SAUCE**: heat oil in medium saucepan, gently fry leek and garlic for 5 minutes. Add mince and chives. Fry on medium heat, stirring regularly until meat is brown. Thoroughly mix pears with syrup, salt, sugar and pear puree, cover and simmer slowly for 30 minutes, stirring occasionally. **CHEESE SAUCE**: melt butter in medium saucepan and stir in flour. On medium heat, gradually stir in milk. Mix in salt and cream cheese. Stir constantly until mixture thickens and starts to bubble. To assemble, pour half of hot meat sauce in the base of the baking dish. Cover with two lasagne sheets. Pour ⅓ cup of the remaining meat sauce over the lasagne sheets, followed by ⅓ of the cheese sauce. Repeat with lasagne, meat and cheese sauces until lasagne is used up, finishing with the cheese sauce. Bake for 30–35 minutes. Remove from oven and gently pour cream over top of the lasagne. Lower heat to 150°C and cook for a further 10 minutes. Let stand 5–10 minutes before serving. Serves 4–6.

VARIATIONS • If amines are okay, add 1 cup grated cheddar cheese to white sauce, sprinkle top with grated mozzarella cheese.

Something Sweet

'You should call your next book *1001 ways to cook a pear* – only joking!' Reader, Darwin

Desserts

Fruit for desserts

Pears are the only permitted fruit. For amine responders who don't react to salicylates, lucky you – many fruits like cherries, melons and strawberries are safe for you, but be careful: don't assume that *all* fruit and vegetables are now permitted. Common fruit, including pineapples, citrus, grapes, dates, raspberries and sultanas, contain both amines and salicylates and some contain natural MSG as well (see p. 2). For salicylate responders who don't react to amines, you can eat any dessert recipes containing bananas – or chocolate – and buy additive-free desserts like Sara Lee Chocolate Bavarian.

Sulphites in desserts

Gelatine and glucose syrup usually contain sulphur dioxide. Although most can be driven off by boiling, the small amounts that remain can affect extra-sensitive people with asthma, irritable bowel symptoms, headaches or behaviour problems. Avoid desserts that contain these ingredients if you are sensitive to sulphites.

People who can tolerate salicylates, amines and natural glutamates but not additives can eat fresh fruit, but must avoid dried fruits that contain sulphur dioxide (220).

Pear mousse

2 cups stewed or canned pears, pureed in
    blender
¼ cup caster sugar
1 tsp citric acid dissolved in 1 tbsp water
1 tbsp gelatine, dissolved in 4 tbsp water
1–2 egg whites, beaten until stiff
⅔ cup (150 ml) cream, whipped

Combine ingredients in order above,
and refrigerate.

VARIATION • When tolerated, use Golden or Red Delicious apples, mango,
rhubarb (salicylates) or pawpaw (amines).

Baked pears

½ cup golden syrup or rice malt
½ cup water
2 tbsp citric lemon juice (p. 194)
4 pears

Combine golden syrup, water and
citric lemon juice. Peel pears and
arrange them whole in an ovenproof
dish. Pour syrup over them and bake
at 180°C for about 40 minutes or
until tender.

Pears are a good source of dietary fibre and
vitamin C. They are the only fruit low in salicylates. They should be ripe and peeled, but don't
eat more than a couple a day. If canned, they
must be in syrup, not natural juice, because peel
is used in the juice. Hard canned pears should
be given to less sensitive family members. Pears
ripen from the inside out and will ripen more quickly if placed in a paper bag.
Pears that feel slightly soft or have a small bruise are already ripe.

Caramel pears

4–5 pears
½ cup sugar
1 tbsp golden syrup
1 tbsp butter or failsafe margarine (p. 183)
1 tbsp flour or rice flour
1 cup boiling water

Peel, core and quarter pears. Put in flat buttered ovenproof dish. Combine sugar, golden syrup, butter, flour and water and bake uncovered at 180°C for about 1 hour.

VARIATION • Use Red or Golden Delicious apples (salicylates) instead of pears.

One Red Delicious apple contains as much antioxidant as 1.5 kg of Vitamin C, according to researchers at Cornell University. The secret is that the apple contains not only vitamin C, but about 100 other antioxidant compounds as well.

Pear fool

For a simple dessert, mix equal quantities of pears or other sweetened pureed fruit with thick cream, or creamy yoghurt.

Golden pears or apples

1 pear or Golden Delicious apple
   (salicylates) per person
golden syrup

Peel and core pears or apples. Microwave on high for 2 minutes per piece of fruit. Place in a bowl with juices from cooking. Drizzle with golden syrup. Serve with Narni's custard (p. 153), ice-cream or yoghurt.

Golden banana

1 banana (amines) per person
pure maple syrup

Peel and slice banana. Microwave for 1 minute. Pour over maple syrup. Serve with yoghurt or Narni's custard (p. 153) or ice-cream.

Howard's pear crumble

One of the most used recipes in our house.

3–4 cups of stewed, fresh or canned
  pears, peeled and diced

TOPPING

¼ cup butter or failsafe margarine (p.
  183)

1½ cups rolled oats (see next recipe for
  gluten-free option)

¼ cup brown sugar

Preheat oven to 180°C. Drain juice, sweeten if necessary, and place fruit in the bottom of a pie dish. To make the topping, melt the butter in a pan, then stir in oats and sugar. Spread over fruit. Bake for 30 minutes or until topping is golden.

VARIATION • Use Golden Delicious apple and/or stewed rhubarb (salicylates).

Pear crumble 2

1 cup flour (gluten-free if required)

1 cup sugar

2 tbsp butter or failsafe margarine (p.
  183)

1 can pears (800 g) in syrup

Preheat oven to 180°C. Mix flour and sugar and then rub butter in with your fingertips. Sprinkle crumble mixture over pears and bake for 15 minutes or until topping is cooked.

Alison's lunchbox pear or apple pies

These are nice hot with Narni's custard (p. 153), ice-cream (p. 146) or cream, but better cold and go well in lunchboxes.

5 ripe pears or Golden Delicious apples (salicylates)

¼ cup sugar or to taste

½ tsp citric acid

3 tsp cornflour

8 small (10 cm) pie dishes or muffin tins

2 sheets of commercial puff pastry or gluten-free sweet pastry (p. 48)

Thickly peel and slice pears or apples. Add sugar and citric acid. Cook on stovetop or in microwave until soft, then mash. Mix cornflour with a little cold water and then add some of the cooked fruit. Add this back into the fruit and cook on the stove until thickened. Remove from heat and cool. Slightly defrost two sheets of commercial puff pastry and cut into quarters. Place each quarter into pie dish and shape to fit leaving corners hanging over the edge of the dish. Place about one tablespoon of fruit in each pie dish. Fold over the edges of the pastry into the middle to cover the fruit. Bake at 200°C for 15 to 20 minutes.

VANILLA

Limit per day of vanilla essence is 2 drops. Vanilla has been omitted from most of the recipes in this book because many sensitive children are affected by it. Until you know whether your child is one of these, it is easier to avoid vanilla in home cooking and minimise your child's exposure to vanilla in commercial products.

Pear shortcake squares

SHORTCAKE

2 cups self-raising flour

6 tbsp (125 g) butter or failsafe margarine (p. 183)

½ cup sugar

1 egg, beaten

1–2 tsp milk or soymilk or ricemilk

brown sugar sprinkle

icing sugar sprinkle

FILLING

1 can (800 g) pears, drained and blended, or 3 ripe pears peeled, sliced and stewed with 1 tbsp sugar

Sift flour into bowl. Rub in butter until it resembles breadcrumbs. Mix in sugar and egg. Add enough milk to form a firm dough. Knead until smooth. Divide into two sections and put in freezer for about 15 minutes. Prepare filling. Take one section of dough out of freezer and roll out on a cornfloured board. Pick up very carefully with an egg slice and press into slab tin (or baking tray). Spread pear mixture on top. Sprinkle with brown sugar. Roll out second piece of dough and place on top of shortcake. Bake at 180°C for 25 minutes. Cut into squares and sprinkle with icing sugar.

VARIATIONS • Apple shortcake: use Golden Delicious apples (salicylates) instead of pears, or 2 pears, 1 apple to reduce salicylates but retain the apple flavour • *Gluten-free*: 2 cups self-raising gluten-free flour mix instead of self-raising flour.

Stewed rhubarb

Rhubarb contains salicylates, so is not suitable for your supervised elimination diet. Don't use aluminium cookware with rhubarb as natural chemicals in the rhubarb can react with the metal to release harmful aluminium oxide.

1 kg rhubarb (salicylates)
1 cup of sugar or golden syrup (or less to taste)
¼ cup water

Wash stalks, discard the leaves, which are very poisonous, and chop rhubarb into small pieces. Add sugar and water and simmer on the lowest heat until tender. Serve on cereal, or with Narni's custard (p. 153), ice-cream (p. 146), yoghurt or pavlova (p. 139) for dessert. Freezes well.

In the last five years, rhubarb has become the number one vegetable in terms of sales in Britain due to its health effects. With high-quality fibre and a low glycaemic index, rhubarb has a natural laxative effect and is used by Chinese doctors to promote gastrointestinal health. It is not suitable for people with gout because of its high oxalic acid content.

Rhubarb stirabout

Rhubarb (salicylates) is not suitable for your supervised elimination diet. Pears can be used if rhubarb is not tolerated.

4 tbsp butter or failsafe margarine (p. 183)

1 cup self-raising flour (or gluten-free flour)

4 tbsp caster sugar

1 egg or equivalent egg-replacer

100 ml milk

3 cups raw rhubarb, cut into 1 cm pieces

golden syrup to taste

Rub butter into flour until it resembles bread crumbs. Add sugar. Beat egg and add. Add as much milk as necessary to make a stiff batter. Add the rhubarb. Pour into a greased pie dish. Bake at 220°C for 30 minutes. Cut into pieces and serve with golden syrup on top.

Mangoes (salicylates, not suitable for supervised elimination diet)

Mangoes contain both Vitamin C and beta carotene, the latter of which the body can convert to vitamin A.

½ cup fresh mango cubes per person

1 cup low-fat yoghurt or soy yoghurt

¼ cup light sour cream (optional)

permitted ice-cream (p. 146)

With a sharp knife, carefully cut both cheeks off an unpeeled ripe mango. Score mango flesh into squares, then turn mango peel inside out. You can now pick out the mango cubes with a fork. Eat fresh or serve with ice-cream, or layer in tall glasses with yoghurt and ice-cream. Frozen mango pulp is good in smoothies and home-made ice-cream.

Fresh persimmons (salicylates, not suitable for supervised elimination diet)

The national fruit of Japan, persimmons look like orange tomatoes and are an excellent source of Vitamin C. Most are ready to eat only when they are soft and squashy all over, although some varieties remain firm. Remove the stem, cut in half and scoop the flesh out with a spoon. Persimmons also make a delicious smoothie. In Japan, you can buy dried persimmons – for a price.

Fresh tamarilloes (salicylates, not suitable for supervised elimination diet)
The 'lost food of the Incas', tamarilloes are shiny red or yellow egg-shaped fruits
with colourful flesh and edible black seeds. They are an excellent source of vitamins C and E. Eat when soft and ripe. Cut in half and scoop out the flesh with
a spoon, or peel and add to salads or fruit salads. Tamarilloes can also be used
to decorate cheesecakes, pavlovas (see below) or ice-cream (p. 146). Or stew
gently with sugar and serve with yoghurt, or blend with water and sugar as a
drink.

Mini pavs
A luxurious and easy dessert that can be gluten-free and dairy-free. I like these
with stewed rhubarb.

2 egg whites

6 tbsp caster sugar

1 pinch citric acid

Preheat oven to 180°C. Combine all ingredients. Beat for 10 minutes until glossy then spoon onto a greased oven tray in 4 rounds. Put in oven and turn oven down to 120°C. Cook for 15 minutes. Allow to cool in oven. Topping suggestions are sliced or pureed pears; salicylate fruits like sliced or pulped tamarillo, stewed rhubarb, mango; banana (amines); cream and ice-cream, dairy-free custard (p. 153) or yoghurt (p. 35). Serves 4.

Contrary to popular belief, sugar doesn't cause hyperactivity. Over-the-top
behaviour at parties is more likely to be related to additives and salicylates.
There does seem to be a connection between salicylates and sugar – a child
who seems addicted to sugar is probably a salicylate responder. A word of
warning, though: sugar lacks essential nutrients, contributes to obesity and is
bad for teeth, so it is best limited and eaten as part of a balanced meal. Save
lollies for special treats.

Macaroons

2 egg whites
1 cup caster sugar or ½ cup caster sugar
   plus ½ cup brown sugar
½ cup white rice flour
½ cup cornflour

Preheat oven to 180°C. Line 2 baking trays with nonstick baking paper. Combine all ingredients in a mixing bowl and beat for 5 minutes. Place tablespoons of the mixture 2 cm apart on the trays. Bake in preheated oven for 10–15 minutes or until lightly browned. Stand on trays for 5 minutes before cooling on a wire rack.

VARIATION • Serve plain or with Narni's custard (p. 153) and ice-cream, or with caramel sauce using leftover egg yolks (p. 186).

Classic pavlova

Crisp on the outside, soft like marshmallow on the inside.

4 egg whites
pinch salt
¼ level teaspoon cream of tartar
1 pinch citric acid
1 cup caster sugar
1 tbsp cornflour (gluten-free if necessary)
   or arrowroot

Grease a baking tray and sprinkle with cornflour to prevent pavlova sticking to tray. Preheat the oven to 130°C. Place egg whites, salt, cream of tartar and citric acid in a bowl and beat strongly for 10 minutes until glossy. Gradually beat in two-thirds of the sugar, a tablespoon at a time. Gently stir in remaining sugar and cornflour. Bake for 1¼ hours. Allow to cool in oven.

Grandma's caramel tart filling

My favourite dessert when I was a child. Serve as a tart in a precooked sweet-pastry case (p. 48) or gluten-free (p. 48).

1 egg yolk

3 tbsp water

1 cup milk or soymilk

1 cup brown sugar

1 tbsp cornflour (gluten-free if necessary)

1 egg white, beaten

Beat egg yolk and water. Boil milk and add egg-yolk mixture. Mix brown sugar and cornflour, add to mixture and stir constantly while bringing to the boil. Cook for 1 minute. Fold through beaten egg white when mixture has cooled a little. Pour into prepared pastry shell.

English toffee pie

This recipe is more time-consuming than most but is exceptionally delicious.

CRUMB CRUST

125 g plain sweet biscuit crumbs, e.g. Milk Coffee

3 tbsp butter or failsafe margarine (p. 183)

for gluten-free crust use half of Butterscotch biscuits recipe with gluten-free option
  (p. 168)

FILLING

½ cup sugar

¼ cup water

3 eggs, separated

½ cup extra sugar

3 tsp gelatine

1 tbsp of boiling water

1 tbsp whisky

1 cup cream

CRUMB CRUST

Process together biscuits and butter. Press into base and sides of a lightly greased 20 cm pie plate. Refrigerate while filling is prepared. The gluten-free crust requires baking for 10 minutes.

FILLING

Put sugar and water in small saucepan and stir over low heat until sugar is dissolved. Increase heat and boil without stirring until toffee turns a light golden brown. Beat egg-yolks and extra sugar until light and creamy. Cook in top of double saucepan over simmering water until sugar has dissolved and mixture is thick and creamy. Pour toffee mixture into hot egg yolk mixture, stirring constantly. Continue stirring over hot water until mixture is smooth and toffee has combined evenly. Remove from heat. Sprinkle gelatine over boiling water, stir to dissolve. Microwave 20 seconds until boiling to drive off preservative. Add to hot toffee mixture with whisky. Allow to cool. Fold in whipped cream and softly beaten egg whites, spoon evenly into crust and refrigerate until set. Serve with whipped cream or Narni's custard (p. 153), ice-cream (p. 146) and permitted fruit. Refrigerate. Tastes even better the next day!

Pear clafoutis

Pears are covered with a light, not-quite-cake topping in this remarkable dessert, which is very easy to make and looks stunning.

1 large can (800 g) pears in syrup
1 cup self-raising flour
3 eggs
½–1 cup caster sugar (to taste)
½ cup milk or soymilk or ricemilk
1 tbsp sifted icing sugar

Preheat oven to 180°C. Drain pears and reserve syrup. Arrange pears, cut side down, in a lightly greased 25 cm flan dish. Sift flour into a bowl and make a well in the centre. Break eggs into the well, add sugar and milk and mix to form a smooth batter. Pour batter over pears. Bake for 45 minutes or until firm and golden. Serve hot or cold with pear syrup and yoghurt or Narni's custard (p. 153) or ice-cream (p. 146). Serves 6.

Butterscotch meringue pudding

½ cup golden syrup

2 tbsp of butter or failsafe margarine
  (p. 183)

2½ cups of soymilk

2 tbsp cornflour (gluten-free if necessary)

1 egg, separated

MERINGUE TOPPING

2 egg whites

½ cup caster sugar

Heat the golden syrup and butter in a saucepan over low heat until golden brown. Slowly add 2 cups of the soymilk and stir over low heat until mixed. Blend the cornflour with the remaining milk, add to the mixture and bring to the boil, stirring constantly. Add the egg yolk and beat thoroughly. Remove the saucepan from the heat and allow the mixture to cool. Just before serving, whisk egg whites until stiff. Fold in half the caster sugar and continue to whisk until meringue is glossy. Fold in remaining sugar. Pile the meringue on top of the butterscotch and brown it under a hot grill for about 5 minutes or until lightly browned. Serves 4.

Lemon meringue pie

A classic dinner-party dessert, always very popular.

Short-crust pastry (p. 48)

FILLING

1 cup water

⅔ cup sugar

2 tsp citric acid

1 cup water extra

5 tbsp cornflour

1 tsp gelatine

1 tbsp butter or failsafe margarine (p. 183)

3 egg yolks

MERINGUE

3 egg whites

½ cup caster sugar

pinch salt

1 tsp cornflour

Preheat oven to 200°C. Make pastry, adding 1 tbsp sugar if preferred sweet, and press into 25 cm shallow pie dish. Bake about 10–15 minutes until just golden, then cool. Combine water, sugar and citric in a saucepan, bring to boil. Mix extra water, cornflour and gelatine and add to saucepan, stirring continuously until it thickens. Take off heat and stir in butter and yolks. Cool a little and pour into baked pie-crust. Beat whites to a soft peak, add sugar-salt-cornflour mixture a little at time, beating to a glossy texture. Spread meringue on pie with a broad spatula, then bake about 10 minutes at 180°C until browned. Delicious with yoghurt or cream.

> Avoid high omega-3 eggs as the fish oil fed to the chickens leaves a very fishy taste in recipes like that above.

Self-saucing microwave golden syrup pudding

This quick and easy winter dessert will be a hit with the whole family.

4 tbsp butter or failsafe margarine (p. 183)
¾ cup milk or soymilk or ricemilk
1½ cups self-raising flour (wheat or gluten-free)
1 cup caster sugar
SAUCE
1 cup boiling water
½ cup golden syrup

In a medium-size microwave bowl, melt butter thoroughly then stir in milk. In a second microwave bowl, mix flour and sugar together. Beat in butter and milk. Using first bowl, mix together sauce. Pour over top of pudding. Cover and cook in microwave oven for 10 minutes. Eat straight away.

Rice pudding

Popular in many countries in the world, individual containers of rice pudding are sold at takeaway street stalls in Egypt.

600 ml milk or A2 milk or soymilk
3 tbsp short or medium-grain rice
1 tbsp butter or failsafe margarine (p. 183) (optional)
1–2 tbsp white sugar (or brown, or more to taste)
¼ tsp salt or to taste
1 tsp pure maple syrup

Place milk, rice and butter in a medium saucepan and bring to the boil. Reduce heat, cover and simmer gently until rice is tender, about 35 minutes. Add remaining ingredients and simmer for an extra 15–20 minutes. The pudding will thicken towards the end of the cooking time. Serve hot or cold. Serves 4.

Lemon mousse

1 tbsp gelatine

1 cup water

3 eggs, separated

¾ cup sugar

1 tsp citric acid dissolved in 2 tbsp water

1 cup cream

Dissolve gelatine in boiling water. Beat egg yolks, add sugar and citric acid mix and beat again. Add dissolved gelatine and stir quickly. Whip cream lightly and stir in. Beat egg whites stiffly and stir in lightly. Pour into serving bowl and chill.

Wedding whip

300 ml thickened cream (whippable)

1 tbsp icing sugar

1½ cups vanilla yoghurt

100 g white marshmallows

½ cup canned pears (or fresh tamarilloes or mangos, salicylates), diced

Beat cream until firm and peaks form. Fold in other ingredients, cover and refrigerate for 30 minutes. Spoon into 6 serving glasses.

Secret pancakes

'These have become a weekend favourite in our house. My 9-year-old son loves to do this, a night off for me! We cook up a big batch of pancakes, with soymilk of course, and then devour them with great enthusiasm. We top them with golden syrup, or "citric water" and sugar, a substitute for lemon juice and sugar. To make the citric water – or secret water, as my 5-year-old calls it – we just add citric acid to water to taste.' Reader, Victoria

1 cup plain flour

pinch salt

1 egg

1¼ cups milk or milk substitute (e.g. soymilk)

Sift flour and salt, break egg and add to a well in the middle of the flour. Stir
in flour gradually from the sides, adding milk a little at a time. When half
the milk is used, all the flour must be moistened. Beat well to remove all the
lumps and make it light. When quite smooth, add the remainder of the milk
gradually. Let mixture stand for 30 minutes. Melt a little butter in a pan, wipe
dry with kitchen paper, melt another little piece of butter in the pan. Pour
about 2 tablespoons of the batter into the pan, and allow it to spread evenly
by moving the pan about. Cook quickly until set and underside is slightly
brown. Toss or turn the pancake with a spatula and cook on other side till
brown. Drain on absorbent paper.

Ice-cream

Commercial vanilla ice-creams can be failsafe if free of colours including annatto
(160b). Although there are a number of safe brands (see Shopping List) there
are also many shops without a single failsafe ice-cream. When I talk to the over-
seventies about what they ate as kids, they always remark that ice-cream was
something their mothers made for special occasions.

Gelatine is permitted to contain a very high 750 ppm of sulphite preservatives. In practice this varies from none to high levels, but sulphites are
driven off by heat so boiling is ideal in gelatine recipes. If you know you are
extremely sensitive to sulphites, avoid anything with gelatine and use agar
agar instead (p. 68).

Pear ice-cream with dairy-free option (7 per cent fat)

¾ cup sugar

1 egg

¾ cup water

1 cup canned pears in syrup (drained and blended)

200 ml light cream (20 per cent fat)

Mix together according to ice-cream maker's instructions. This is a surprisingly delicious ice-cream. We also make it with mango, which tastes wonderful but is not okay for your supervised elimination diet.

VARIATION • For an A2 milk or dairy-free low-fat ice-cream, use 1 cup sugar, 1 egg, 1 cup canned pears in syrup (drained and blended), 1½ cups A2 milk or soymilk or rice milk.

Toppings: permitted fruit, pear puree, pure maple syrup, caramel topping (p. 186), Nestlé caramel Top 'n' Fill, carob topping (p. 194).

> Maple-flavoured topping contains preservative 202. As well as preservative, raspberry topping contains two artificial red colours, and caramel topping – which looks natural – contains three artificial colours.

Anne's easy ice-cream (13 per cent fat)

There's no need for an ice-cream maker with this super easy ice-cream recipe. If you make it with full cream and full fat milk the fat content is 30 per cent.

600 ml light thickened cream (20 per cent fat)
400 g tin skim sweetened condensed milk

Whip cream to soft peaks, about 5 minutes, beat in condensed milk, freeze. To make a softer, fluffier ice-cream, beat again when half frozen.

VARIATIONS • Stir through chopped honeycomb or carob-coated honeycomb before freezing • Chopped carob or white chocolate (lower in amines than regular chocolate but not suitable for your supervised elimination diet) can be added to make a choc-chip version • Bavarian: pour half the mixture into container to freeze, then add carob powder and pour gently on top.

Commercial ice-creams usually contain artificial yellow colour or natural but nasty annatto (160b), especially if labelled 'all natural, no artificial colours, flavours and preservatives' or 'light'. Ice-creams with caramel or butterscotch pieces, which could be failsafe, usually contain colours. The fat and additive content of ice-cream has crept up over the years and reduced-fat products usually contain nasty additives such as annatto to make them look creamier.

Home-made dairy ice-cream (15 per cent fat)
This is a traditional recipe that uses simple wholesome ingredients.

1 cup milk
1 egg
2 egg yolks
4 tbsp sugar
½ cup cream (35 per cent fat)

Boil milk. In a bowl, whisk egg, egg yolks and sugar into a froth, pour the milk on top and stir mixture over a low flame until it is reduced to a thick consistency. Whip cream with a beater and gently stir into the mixture, pour into a bowl and freeze. Lightly beat and freeze once more before serving to give it a soft creamy texture.

Ice-cream maker ice-cream (10 per cent fat)
I have a Breville scoop factory ice-cream maker. This is an easy recipe and not too rich.

1 egg
1 cup milk
¾ cup sugar
1 cup light cream (20 per cent fat)

Blend egg, milk and sugar until sugar dissolves. Add cream and blend until just combined. Refrigerate for one hour before using in ice-cream maker. With machine running, pour in the cream mixture. Process for 15 minutes until mixture reaches desired consistency. If frozen, remove from freezer 15 minutes before serving to soften.

Ice-cream confections can be extremely high in fat. If you eat ice-cream frequently, compare nutrition labels. For example:

Product	grams fat per 100 g	saturated fat per 100 g
Streets Magnum minis	22	15 includes chocolate
Sara Lee	13	9
Peters Original vanilla	7	5
Fruccio frozen soy	2	2 no longer manufactured!

Non-dairy ice-creams

The following four non-dairy frozen desserts are acceptable ice-cream substitutes, in my order of preference. They all keep like commercial ice-cream. For best results, remove from the freezer 15 minutes before serving to soften. When introducing these to a child, serve with a topping, e.g. pure maple syrup.

Syrup ice-cream (3 per cent fat)

The eggs give this frozen dessert a lovely creamy colour. We make it in an ice-cream maker but the traditional beat-freeze until partially frozen then re-beat and re-freeze method works too.

½ cup white sugar

4 tbsp water

2 egg yolks

2 tsp gelatine

2 tbsp warm water

2 cups soymilk or ricemilk

Make syrup by heating sugar and water in saucepan until sugar is dissolved. In a bowl, whisk the egg yolks until pale and frothy. Gradually add syrup, continue to beat until mixture cools slightly. Sprinkle gelatine over warm water, microwave 20 seconds to drive off preservative. Stir gelatine mixture into egg mixture. Add soymilk to mixture and beat well. If using an ice-cream maker, refrigerate mixture for at least one hour before processing.

VARIATIONS • For different flavours, use 1 tbsp pure maple syrup, 1 tbsp whisky, 3 tbsp mango pulp (salicylates) or 3 tbsp mashed ripe banana (amines). The last two contain chemicals but each serve of ice-cream contains very little.

Soy ice-cream (6 per cent fat)

Made with agar agar, this is the favourite recipe of a little girl who is extra-sensitive to sulphites.

½ cup water

1 cup sugar

2 tsp gelatine or agar agar

3 cups soymilk

¼ cup failsafe oil (p. 184)

1 tsp xanthan gum

¼ cup golden syrup, pure maple syrup, rice malt or mango pulp (salicylates) for flavour

Put cold water in a saucepan. Sprinkle in sugar and gelatine, stir, and boil gently for a few minutes. Put soymilk, oil, gum and flavour into a large mixing bowl, add the gelatine mixture and whip well. Chill until nearly set then pour into ice-cream maker if you have one. Otherwise, freeze in shallow tray till very cold and starting to freeze. Whip really well and freeze again. Whip again when half-frozen. This time it should be really thick. The mixture should be very cold and starting to set for the last whip. The gum gives it a creamy texture.

Carob dixie cups (4 per cent fat)

'I found it took several weeks, perhaps months, of eating soy or rice milk as ice-cream, custard, etc., before my boys would consider drinking it.' Reader, Melbourne

2½ cups (600 ml) of milk or soymilk or ricemilk

½ cup sugar

1 egg

4 tbsp water

1½ tbsp (30 g) failsafe margarine (p. 183)

½ cup of arrowroot

2 tsp carob powder (cocoa if amines are tolerated)

Heat milk in a large saucepan on the stove. While milk is heating, beat sugar, egg, water, margarine and arrowroot in a bowl. When milk reaches simmering point pour in the egg mixture and continue to beat over the heat until mixture boils and thickens. Remove from heat. Allow to cool a little then pour into icecup containers with lids.

Icey ricey ice-cream (2 per cent fat)

This is a surprisingly good rice-based ice-cream substitute free from dairy, egg, gelatine and soy. Although vanilla has been omitted from most of the recipes in this book (p. 136) it may be necessary in this recipe.

2 cups cold rice milk (Vitasoy Rice Milk works well and tastes best)

½ cup caster sugar

1 tbsn pure maple syrup or 4 drops pure vanilla essence

1 tsp xanthan gum

1 egg or 2 tsp egg replacer

Blend all ingredients together in a food processor or blender, or alternatively beat well with a whisk or mixmaster. Pour mixture into ice-cream machine, leave till thickened and icy, approximately 15 minutes. Spoon into container and place in freezer till set, usually a few hours. If you don't have an ice-cream machine, pour mixture into a container and freeze for 1–2 hours. Remove, beat mixture well, and return to freezer for another 1–2 hours. Repeat another two times, then leave till set. Can be served in 'milkshake' with a spoonful of carob powder, drizzled with carob sauce, or with a little pear.

Pear sorbet

½ cup sugar
1½ cups (400 ml) chilled water
1 cup pear puree, frozen
2 egg whites

Dissolve sugar in water. Blend frozen pear puree into sugar water. Beat egg whites until stiff and gently stir into pear mixture. Pour into ice-cream maker while it is running and process for 20 minutes. Best frozen before serving. Serves 8.

VARIATION • Mango sorbet: use one cup of frozen mango puree (salicylates) instead of the pear puree. Spread between 8 people, it isn't very much and tastes better than the pear.

Pure fruit ice-cream

Make pure fruit ice-creams from pear puree (or, when tolerated, from bananas or mangoes), frozen and then beaten until smooth in a food processor.

Lemon sago cups

Of course, there are no lemons in this low-fat popular dessert.

½ cup sago
2½ cups (600 ml) water
2 tbsp water extra
½ tsp citric acid
4 tbsp golden syrup
4 tbsp sugar

Soak sago for one hour or more in water until soft. Add salt to taste. Boil until transparent. Add extra water, citric acid, golden syrup and sugar. Pour into moulds or cups to set.

Sago milk pudding cups

I love this traditional recipe when made with A2 milk.

½ cup sago
2 cups milk or A2 milk or soymilk or ricemilk
½ cup sugar

Soak sago in milk for two hours. Bring to the boil slowly and simmer about 10–15 minutes until transparent, stirring occasionally. Add sugar to taste. Mix well, pour into moulds or cups and leave to set. Heavenly served with pure maple syrup.

Narni's custard

This is an easy-to-make low-fat alternative to ice-cream.

1 egg

2 tbsp cornflour (extra for thicker custard)

2–4 tbsp sugar (to taste)

3 cups milk or A2 milk or soymilk or ricemilk

1 tbsp maple syrup

In a large microwavable jug, beat ingredients together until sugar dissolves. Microwave for 5 minutes. Stir. Repeat in 1-minute intervals until thickened, making sure it doesn't boil over. Thickens further as it cools.

Commercial custard powders contain either artificial yellow colours 102 and 110, or natural annatto 160b, which also affects people. 'Flavour' may also be a problem.

Jelly cups

3 tsp gelatine (1 extra in the tropics)

½ cup pear syrup or magic cordial (p. 63)

1½ cups extra liquid

Dissolve gelatine in liquid and boil gently for a few minutes. Add the extra liquid, stir well. Pour into tumblers or similar individual serving containers and allow to cool.

Commercial jelly crystals contain artificial colours.

Golden dumplings

A traditional recipe for a winter dessert.

SAUCE

1 cup water

½ cup sugar

1 tbsp golden syrup

1 tbsp butter or failsafe margarine (p. 183)

DUMPLINGS

1 cup self-raising flour

1 tbsp butter or failsafe margarine (p. 183)

1 egg, lightly beaten

cold milk

Place sauce ingredients in pan and heat. For dumplings, rub butter into flour, stir in egg and enough milk to make a fairly stiff dough. Roll into little balls and drop into the boiling syrup for about 5–10 minutes.

Dominion pudding (p. 202)

Bread and butter pudding

6–8 slices preservative-free bread

1½ tbsp (30 g) butter or failsafe margarine (p. 183)

3 eggs, lightly beaten

2¼ cups milk or soymilk

¼ cup pure maple syrup

2 tsp caster sugar

Spread bread slices with butter. Arrange slices with butter side up over base of lightly greased 23 cm ovenproof dish. Combine eggs, milk, syrup and sugar in a large bowl, pour mixture over bread. Press bread gently into egg mixture with spoon. Bake at 180°C for 30 minutes or until just set. Stand 10 minutes before serving. Serve warm or cold with cream or ice-cream.

VARIATION • Place ½ cup diced canned pears on bread layer before adding egg mixture.

Baked custard

2½ cups (600 ml) milk or soymilk

2 eggs

2 tbsp sugar

½ cup powdered milk or soymilk

¼ tsp salt

Whiz all ingredients in blender until smooth. Place in a casserole dish and stand in a tray of water. Bake at 180°C approximately 1½ hours or stir over a low flame until it thickens.

VARIATIONS • Add 1 tbsp instant decaffeinated coffee • Line the casserole with caramel, made by boiling 1 cup sugar and ½ cup water until a light caramel colour. Do not stir.

Easy rice pudding

For very young children who are extra sensitive, this recipe can be made with Neocate hypoallergenic formula (only available with prescription).

⅓ cup rice

2½ cups (600 ml) ricemilk or soymilk or
  cows' milk

1–2 tbsp of sugar

Mix in ovenproof container, bake for 3 hours at 100°C. Serve with rice milk ice-cream (p. 151) on the top.

Black rice pudding with butterscotch sauce

This version of a Balinese dish is my family's favourite gluten-free, dairy-free dessert. You can buy black sticky or glutinous rice in Asian specialty shops.

PUDDING

1⅓ cups (300 g) black sticky rice, rinsed

3½ cups water

800 g can of pears in syrup, drained

1 cup sugar

BUTTERSCOTCH SAUCE

2 tbsp golden syrup

2½ tbsp (50 g) butter or failsafe margarine (p. 183)

½ cup milk or soymilk

Put black rice and water in a small saucepan and bring to the boil. Simmer gently for 30–40 minutes until all the water is absorbed. While the rice is cooking, dice pears and mix with sugar. When rice is cooked, thoroughly stir through pear mixture. Spoon into individual serving dishes, pat down and allow to cool. These will keep in the refrigerator, covered for 2 days. To make sauce, place golden syrup, butter and milk in a small pan, heat but don't boil, stirring until butter is melted. When sauce is hot, pour over pudding and serve immediately. Good with ice-cream, too.

Pear ricotta pie

1 frozen butter puff pastry sheet or pre-
    cooked short-crust pastry shell (p. 48)
    or gluten-free (p. 48)
250 g ricotta cheese
drained, canned or fresh pears
1 egg, separated
3–4 tbsp caster sugar
1 tsp whisky (optional)
150 ml whipped cream

Cook frozen pastry sheet as a pie shell according to instructions on packet. Beat ricotta cheese until smooth, add remaining ingredients except egg white. Beat egg white until stiff and gently stir into mixture. Pour straight into pie shell or put slices of fruit in bottom of shell and spoon topping over.

VARIATION • Use a crumb shell as below or omit shell altogether.

No-bake cheesecake

Easy and popular, this recipe contains dairy products. See following recipe for a dairy-free cheesecake.

CRUMB CRUST
180 g plain sweet biscuits (see p. 168 for gluten-free)
125 g melted butter or failsafe margarine (p. 183)
FILLING
3 tsp gelatine
2 tbsp water
250 g preservative-free cream cheese
1 can sweetened condensed milk (400 g)

¼ cup citric lemon juice (p. 194)
½ cup cream
carob powder for topping

Process biscuits and butter, press into the base and sides of 20 cm springform pan and refrigerate. Sprinkle gelatine over warm water, boil in microwave until nearly boiling over (about 30 seconds). Beat cream cheese until smooth, add condensed milk, beat until well combined. Add citric lemon juice and cream, beat well. Add gelatine in water, beat well. Spoon mixture into prepared crust, sprinkle with carob powder and refrigerate until set.

Caroline's classic baked cheesecake with dairy-free option

This old recipe makes a very flat cheesecake compared to modern standards, so you may want to double the filling.

CRUST
gluten-free crust (p. 168) OR
125 g plain sweet biscuits
60 g butter or failsafe margarine (p. 183)
FILLING
250 g preservative-free cream cheese or
   Kingland soy cream cheese (dairy-free)
⅓ to ½ cup sugar
2 eggs
2 tbsp citric lemon juice (p. 194)

CRUST
Process biscuits and butter. Press into base of 20 cm springform pan.
FILLING
Combine cream cheese and sugar in basin, and beat until smooth and well blended. Add the eggs one at a time, beating well after each addition. Stir in citric lemon juice. Pour into prepared crust. Bake at 180°C for about 20 minutes. Allow to cool in oven.

VARIATION • Top with magic spread (p. 185).

Muesli bars, muffins, cakes, biscuits and slices

The recipes in this section are essentially different combinations of flour, sugars, eggs and butter with flavours like golden syrup, citric acid and fruit. You can adapt recipes from any recipe book by sticking to failsafe ingredients. Children like to know that they can have treats, but it is best to keep sugary snacks to a minimum. See Ethan's menu, p. 39, for an example of a balanced diet.

Yum balls

These sweet and crunchy no-bake balls are best made with a small chewy type of puffed rice like Healthy Life or Happy Human than big soft brands.

½ cup rice malt

1 tbsp pure maple syrup

2 cups Rice Bubbles (contain gluten) or gluten-free puffed rice

Combine rice malt and maple syrup in a large microwave container. Cook on high for 1 minute, stir, then cook again for 2 minutes. Stir puffed rice into rice malt mixture and press down firmly. Cook a further 2 minutes, remove from microwave. Roll into balls as soon as the mixture cools enough to touch, working quickly before it sets. Don't burn your hands.

VARIATIONS • Use a large microwave container suitable for slices. Cook as above, but instead of making into balls, press firmly down and cut into bars • Use a total of 2 cups of any of the following ingredients: wheat flakes or gluten-free rolled rice flakes, rolled soy flakes, puffed rice, puffed amaranth, puffed millet and/or chopped raw cashews.

Pear muesli bars (1580 kJ/100 g)

These look and taste like commercial muesli bars.

⅓ cup glucose syrup

2 tsp failsafe oil (p. 184)

1 tbsp white sugar

1 tbsp lecithin granules

2 tbsp Birgit's pear jam (p. 186)

4 cups rolled oats

2 cups Rice Bubbles

Combine first five ingredients in a large saucepan. Heat gently, stirring, until sugar is dissolved and sulphur dioxide is driven off the glucose syrup. Add remaining ingredients and stir well to mix. Press very firmly into a greased baking tray using greaseproof paper to avoid stickiness. While they can be cut into bar shapes after cooling, without cooking, they are best baked 5–10 minutes at 180°C (depending on desired crispness) before cooling and slicing. Store in an airtight container.

VARIATIONS • Wheat and nuts: ½ cup rolled wheat flakes (Weet-Bix) and ½ cup raw cashew nuts, finely chopped in place of 1 cup rolled oats • *Gluten-free*: Use a total of 6 cups of rolled rice flakes, rolled soy flakes, puffed rice, puffed amaranth, puffed millet and/or chopped raw cashews. Best baked 5 mins at 180°C • Caramel choc chip: use brown sugar instead of white sugar, add ¼ cup unflavoured carob buttons or choc chips if amines are tolerated.

Despite 'healthy' names, commercial muesli bars can be laden with fats, sugars and even trans fats. As well, what appears to be dried fruit can be a mixture of maltodextrin, glucose, fructose, humectants, vegetable fat, modified maize starch, flavours, colours, vegetable gum, food acids, firming agents and emulsifiers. Look at these energy levels (kJ/100 g):

Mars Bar (for comparison)	1920
Home Brand honeycomb & nut choc-coated	1960
Nice & Natural nut & cereal muesli bar	1895
Day Dawn apricot & yoghurt	1752
Kelloggs K-time cereal bar, fruit & flakes	1743

Birgit's baked muesli bars

200 g butter or failsafe margarine (p. 183)
4 tbsp sugar
½ cup Birgit's pear jam (p. 186)
2 eggs
2½ cups rolled oats (gluten)
⅔ cup cornflour

Put butter, sugar and pear jam in a large bowl, mix well with an electric mixer, add eggs and mix again. Work oats and cornflour into mix. Press into slice tin. Bake at 180°C for 20–30 minutes. Cut into bars. Allow to cool. Store in an airtight container.

Rolled oat bars

For gluten-free option, see gluten-free slice (p. 239).

1 cup wholemeal self-raising flour
2 cups rolled oats
150 g butter or failsafe margarine (p. 183)
½ cup sugar
1 tbsp golden syrup

Combine flour, oats and sugar in a bowl. Melt butter, add golden syrup and mix into dry ingredients. Press into slice tray and bake for 15–20 minutes at 160°C until brown. Cut into bars while still hot. Leave to cool before removing from tray. Makes 20.

Rice puffs

Contain dairy foods (butter), and gluten (malt in Rice Bubbles).

½ cup brown sugar
½ cup golden syrup
125 g butter or failsafe margarine (p. 183)
6 cups Rice Bubbles

Combine sugar, syrup and butter in a pot and simmer gently for 2–3 minutes, stirring constantly. Remove from heat and allow to cool for a minute. Add Rice Bubbles and mix thoroughly. Press into greased tin 23 × 23 cm (or equivalent), using back of spoon. Refrigerate, then cut into squares.

Margie's lunchbox muffins

A very easy and popular recipe.

1½ cups self-raising flour
½ cup sugar
1 egg, lightly beaten
⅔ cup milk or soymilk
¼ cup failsafe oil (p. 184)
½ cup canned or fresh pear, diced

Sift flour into a bowl and add remaining ingredients, stirring with a fork until mixed. Lightly grease a 12-cup muffin pan with failsafe margarine or brush with failsafe oil and use an ice-cream scoop or spoon to three-quarter-fill cups. Bake at 180°C for 15–20 minutes.

VARIATIONS • Carob chip: add ½ cup carob chips, no added flavour • Pear muffins: add ½ cup chopped fresh or canned pear and use pear syrup instead of milk • 'Pear' muffins: add chopped cooked choko and a little more sugar; the result tastes just like pear • Apple muffins: add 1 chopped Golden Delicious apple (salicylates) and 1 tbsp extra sugar • Iced: ice with white or lemon-flavoured icing (p. 196) • High fibre: add ¼ cup rice bran, increase milk to 1 cup • *Gluten-free*: use self-raising gluten-free flour (p. 233) instead of self-raising flour • Vegetable muffins: use ½ tsp salt instead of the sugar and add finely diced safe vegetables such as chokos, Brussels sprouts, potato and green beans as another good way of getting vegetables into children.

Fete cake

This cake, and Cool cupcakes – formerly known as the basic plain cake – are always well-received and go like proverbial hot cakes. They make a good plate to take to a party or a school fete.

2 cups self-raising flour or gluten-free flour (p. 233)
¼ tsp salt
125 g butter or failsafe margarine (p. 183)
½ cup sugar
2 eggs, well beaten
½ cup milk

Grease a cake tin. Preheat oven to 180°C. Sift flour and salt. Cream butter and sugar. Add beaten eggs gradually. Add flour and salt alternately with milk. Put in tin and bake 40–45 minutes. Ice with white or other icing (p. 196).

VARIATION • Cool cup cakes: As for cake, but use paper patty cases. Makes 24. Bake for 12–15 minutes. Ice with pink or white icing (p. 196).

> Research shows that consumers eat more if a chicken dish is called 'spicy' whether or not it contains spices. Use names based on favourite characters that will appeal to your children, or ask them to make up names – such as 'memolade' for failsafe lemonade.

Jane's pear dessert cake

Everyone loves this soft, moist cake.

2 cups self-raising flour or gluten-free flour (p. 233)

4 tbsp cornflour (gluten-free if necessary)

4 large eggs

1 cup pear syrup from 800 g can of pears

2 cups sugar

8 tbsp soft butter or failsafe margarine (p. 183)

sliced canned pears for topping

Sift dry ingredients. Add eggs, syrup, sugar and butter, beat until well mixed. Pour into a large greased and lined cake tin (32 × 20 × 5 cm). Place sliced pears on top. Bake at 180°C for 1 hour. Serve warm. Leftovers can be used for school lunches.

Carrot cake

3 cups grated raw carrot (salicylates)

¾ cup chopped pears

½ cup raw cashews, chopped

3 eggs

½ cup canola or rice bran oil

2 cups self-raising flour (or self-raising gluten-free flour)

1 tsp sodium bicarbonate (2 tsp if gluten-free)

1 cup sugar

ICING

125 g preservative-free cream cheese

1 cup icing sugar, sifted

3 tbsp butter or failsafe margarine (p. 183)

Pre-heat oven to 180°C. Grease a square 20 cm tin. Prepare carrot, pears and cashews. Beat eggs until thick and stir in oil. Sift dry ingredients together and combine. Fold in remaining ingredients. Bake 50 minutes (10 minutes longer for gluten-free). Delicious without icing and can be served for dessert, or beat together icing and spread on top.

VARIATION • This recipe also makes excellent carrot muffins – bake 15–20 minutes.

Poko cake

This pear and choko cake is very moist, works well gluten-free, and is best eaten the day after baking.

3 cups grated raw choko (two large chokos)

½ cup chopped pears

½ cup raw cashews, chopped (optional)

3 eggs

½ cup canola or rice bran oil

2 cups self-raising flour (or self-raising gluten-free flour)

1 tsp sodium bicarbonate (2 tsp if gluten-free)

1 cup sugar

Pre-heat oven to 180°C. Grease a square 20 cm tin. Prepare choko, pears and cashews. Beat eggs until thick and stir in oil. Sift dry ingredients together and combine. Fold in remaining ingredients. Bake 60 minutes, 10 minutes longer for gluten-free. Serve with pear jam or Carrot cake icing (above).

Andra's 'honey' roll

'Better than sticky date pudding' said one failsafe husband. Both wheat and gluten-free options are exceptionally delicious and quick to make.

60 g butter or failsafe margarine (p. 183)

¾ cup golden syrup

¾ cup plain flour

½ cup self-raising flour

2 eggs

1 tsp sodium bicarbonate

¼ cup boiling water

HONEY ROLL FILLING

1 cup pure icing sugar

4 tbsp butter or failsafe margarine (p. 183)

Preheat oven to 180°C. Grease a 26 cm × 32 cm swiss roll pan, or biscuit and slice tray, and line base and sides with baking paper. Beat butter until smooth and creamy, then gradually beat in golden syrup. Stir in sifted flours, then stir in eggs. Quickly stir in combined bicarbonate and water. Spread mixture evenly in pan. Bake about 12–15 minutes. Do not overcook or it will be too hard to roll well. While cake is in the oven, prepare filling: beat icing sugar and margarine in food processor until white and fluffy. (You can make a big batch of filling and leave a tub in the refrigerator; it keeps well.) Peel baking paper off and turn out onto a clean tea towel. Roll up while still warm and let stand for a few minutes to cool. Unroll, then spread filling over cake and carefully re-roll.

VARIATIONS • *Gluten-free*: use 1¼ cups of gluten-free self-raising flour mix (p. 233) • *As a cake*: bake in swiss roll tin, cut in half and sandwich with filling, sprinkle top with icing sugar • *As a dessert*: serve the sandwich variation with Narni's custard (p. 153) or ice-cream (p. 146).

Caramel cake

125 g butter or failsafe margarine (p. 183)
½ cup brown sugar
2 eggs, separated
1 tbsp golden syrup
1½ cups self-raising flour
½ cup milk or soymilk or ricemilk
pinch of salt

Pre-heat oven to 180°C. Grease round ring tin. Cream butter and sugar, separate the eggs and beat in the yolks in the butter mixture. Stir in golden syrup and add the sifted flour alternately with the milk. Whip the egg whites with salt until stiff and fold in. Bake 30–40 minutes until cooked.

Coffee cake

For gluten-free, see Melt and mix coffee cake (p. 241).
75 g butter or failsafe margarine (p. 183)
¾ cup sugar
1 tbsp decaffeinated instant coffee
3 eggs, separated

1 cup flour
4 tbsp cornflour
3 tbsp milk or soymilk
1 tsp baking powder

Cream butter, sugar and coffee powder. Beat in
egg yolks one at a time, then add sifted flour
and cornflour alternately with stiffly beaten egg
whites. Mix well, add milk and last of all baking powder. Bake in two 20 cm
(8 inch) greased sandwich tins for 20–25 minutes at 190°C. Ice and fill with
coffee butter icing (p. 241).

Classic sponge

3 eggs
½ cup caster sugar
½ cup cornflour
2 tbsp self-raising flour

Beat eggs on high speed in the mixer for 5 minutes or until thick and pale.
Gradually beat in caster sugar, beating well after each addition. Continue
beating until sugar has dissolved. Sift flours together three times then quickly
and gently stir into the egg mixture. Do not overmix. Divide batter evenly
between two greased and floured 20 cm sandwich pans and bake for 18–20
minutes at 180°C. Allow to cool in the pans for a few minutes then turn out
onto wire rack to cool. Spread with Birgit's pear jam (p. 186) and whipped
cream, or sandwich together with Honey roll filling (p. 163) and dust with
icing sugar. See also Carob lamingtons (below), Trifle (p. 166) and Trifle cups
(p. 166).

Carob lamingtons

My children love this recipe and make it themselves.

Make Classic sponge (above) in lamington tins. Wait until the next day and
cut into squares. Dip each in carob icing (following) and allow to dry.

Cornflour sponge (gluten-free – p. 242).

Carob icing

2 tbsp butter or failsafe margarine (p. 183)

2 tbsp carob powder

6 tbsp boiling water

1½ cups icing sugar

VARIATIONS • *Gluten-free:* use cornflour sponge (p. 242) • *Chocolate icing:* use flavour-free cocoa powder (amines) instead of carob if tolerated.

Trifle

This dessert is a lot of work, but good for a special occasion.

Classic sponge (p. 165) or gluten-free sponge cake (see p. 242)

tinned pears, sliced

pear jelly (p. 153)

custard (p. 153)

Cut sponge into squares and put into a bowl. Arrange sliced pears on sponge, pour nearly set jelly over sponge, put in fridge to set, pour cooled custard over the top. Serve with whipped cream, yoghurt, soy yoghurt or ice-cream.

Trifle cups

A quick and easy trifle recipe.

1 Classic sponge (p. 165) or gluten-free sponge cake (p. 242)

800 g canned pears in syrup

1 kg yoghurt or soy yoghurt

muesli for topping (p. 33)

Cut sponge cake into cubes and put in 10 clear plastic cups. Drizzle over syrup from pears. Layer pear slices and yoghurt on top. Sprinkle with muesli and refrigerate until ready to serve. Makes 10 cups.

Quick lunchbox biscuit

'My daughter is happy to have one of these at morning recess when all the other kids have cream biscuits. Sometimes I put a face on using carob.' Reader, Perth

2 Arnott's Milk Arrowroot biscuits
1 white marshmallow
carob button (optional)
white icing (p. 196)

Place marshmallow on 1 biscuit and microwave for about 10 seconds – watch carefully. Place carob button and other arrowroot on top, squashing marshmallow and carob button between the two biscuits. Ice top biscuit with white icing.

Commercial biscuits except Arnott's are likely to contain unlisted BHA (320) in vegetable oil. As well, there are added flavours in many biscuits. These are more likely to cause a slow build-up of problems rather than a dramatic reaction. Avoid skim milk powder in biscuits if you are dairy-free. Home cooking is better.

Slice and bake biscuits

250 g butter or failsafe margarine (p. 183)
1¼ cups icing sugar
2 cups plain flour
½ cup rice flour
⅓ cup cornflour
2 tbsp milk or soymilk

Cream butter and icing sugar until light and fluffy. Sift flours together. Mix dry ingredients into creamed mixture. Knead well. Roll into 2 logs. Put into freezer on a cornfloured plate for about 20 minutes (logs can be wrapped in foil and frozen until ready to bake). Slice logs into 1 cm thick slices. Bake at 160°C for about 20 minutes or until pale golden colour.

VARIATIONS • Carob chip: stir through 200 g of crushed carob buttons (no added flavours) with sifted flours • Lemon and poppyseed: beat 1 tsp of citric acid dissolved in 1 tbsp of warm water. Add 1 tbsp of poppyseeds with sifted flours.

Big Anzacs

1 cup plain flour
2 cups rolled oats
¾ cup sugar
125 g butter or failsafe margarine (p. 183)
2 tbsp golden syrup
2 tsp sodium bicarbonate
2 tbsp boiling water

Mix together flour, oats and sugar. Melt butter and golden syrup together. Mix bicarbonate with boiling water and add to butter mixture. Pour into blended dry ingredients and stir to combine. Place large spoonfuls of mixture onto greased oven tray, leaving room to spread. Bake at 160°C for 20 mins.

VARIATIONS • Try piping (put icing in a small freezer bag and snip the corner) zigzag stripes of caramel icing across the Anzacs for a failsafe version of Kensingtons • *Gluten-free*: use gluten-free slice (p. 239).

Butterscotch biscuits

These biscuits are so delicious you will probably want to double the recipe. The gluten-free option is also particularly successful, so I take one or two in a small container when having a decaf in a café.

125 g butter or failsafe margarine (p. 183)
½ cup brown sugar, firmly packed
1 tbsp golden syrup
1¼ cups self-raising flour

Beat butter, sugar and golden syrup in a small bowl. Stir in sifted flour. Roll into balls. Place about 5 cm apart on greased oven trays and flatten with a fork. Bake on greased trays for 15 (soft) to 20 minutes (very crunchy) at 180°C.

VARIATIONS • *Gluten-free:* use gluten-free flour mix (p. 233) instead of self-raising flour • Use as a press-in gluten-free pastry base for cheesecakes and tarts.

Rebecca's gingerless pigs
You won't know the ginger has been left out of these gingerbread animals. Fun to make and good for a plate to take to a party. Icing is essential.

125 g butter or failsafe margarine (p. 183)
⅓ cup brown sugar
⅓ cup golden syrup
3 tsp sodium bicarbonate
1 egg
3 cups plain flour

Preheat oven to 180°C. Dissolve butter, sugar and golden syrup in the microwave or in a saucepan over low heat. When lukewarm, stir in bicarbonate and egg. Place flour in bowl, make a well in the centre and add other ingredients. Knead to form a dough, roll out on a floured surface and cut into shapes. Bake for 15 minutes. Ice with lemon citric icing (p. 197).

Mrs Cattle's biscuits
This hundred-year-old recipe was used by a family who were amazed at the improvement in their children's behaviour during a pioneer-week re-enactment. See story 299 on www.fedup.com.au.

1 cup self-raising flour or plain flour plus
   2 tsp failsafe baking powder (or gluten-free flour)
1 egg
½ cup sugar
3 tbsp butter or failsafe margarine (p. 183)

Mix all ingredients and shape into small balls, put onto tray well-spaced and bake at 180°C for 10–15 minutes, longer for gluten-free.

VARIATION • Press into trays and cover with golden syrup and crumble mix (p. 135) on top. Cut into slices before cooling.

Butter kisses

225 g butter or failsafe margarine (p. 183)

75 g icing sugar

⅓ cup milk

3 cups flour

2 tsp baking powder

Cream butter and sugar. Add milk, beat well, then add sifted dry ingredients.
Put spoonfuls of the mixture on cold greased trays and bake for about
15 minutes at 190°C. When cold, put together with icing (p. 196).

Melting moments

¾ cup butter or failsafe margarine (p. 183)

½ cup icing sugar

½ cup self-raising flour

½ cup plain flour

½ cup cornflour

Cream butter and sugar and mix
in other ingredients. Roll into little
balls and place on greased trays.
Press down each biscuit with a fork.
Bake at 160°C for 10–15 minutes.
Put together with lemon citric icing
(p. 197).

Highlander biscuits

125 g butter or failsafe margarine (p. 183)

¼ cup sugar

1 tbsp sweetened condensed milk

1½ cups self-raising flour

Cream butter, sugar and condensed
milk together. Add flour. Cut off
small pieces and roll into balls. Place
on greased baking tray and flatten
with fork. Bake for 20 minutes at
180°C.

Shortbread

Children enjoy cutting out the shapes in this recipe.

225 g butter or failsafe margarine (p. 183)

½ cup caster sugar

3 cups plain flour or gluten-free flour

¼ cup cornflour

¼ tsp salt

Cream butter and sugar well, add sifted flour, cornflour and salt. Knead well, roll out 12 to 18 mm thick. Cut into shapes. Place on cold greased tray and prick with fork. Bake for about 30 minutes at 180°C.

Marshmallow slice

BASE

125 g butter

1 cup self-raising flour or gluten-free

¾ cup rice crumbs (or crushed Rice
  Bubbles)

½ cup sugar

TOPPING

1 cup sugar

1 tbsp gelatine

1 cup water

BASE: Preheat oven to 180°C. Grease slice tray. Melt butter and add to the dry ingredients. Press into tray and bake 10–15 minutes or until just starting to brown – it should be soft and chewy rather than toasted. Cool in tray.

TOPPING: Place all ingredients in a saucepan, bring to boil and boil for 3 minutes to reduce sulphites. When cool, beat until thick and white. Pour the marshmallow topping over the base and allow to set. Cut into small squares and store in an airtight container.

Carob caramel slice (15 per cent fat, 1700 kJ/100 g)

A bit fiddly but delicious, with or without gluten.

1 cup plain flour or gluten-free plain flour

½ cup brown sugar

½ cup rolled oats or rice flakes if gluten-
  free

125 g butter or failsafe margarine (p. 183)

400 g can sweetened skim condensed
  milk

2 tbsp golden syrup

30 g butter or failsafe margarine

ICING

1 cup icing sugar, sifted

50 g butter

2 tbsp carob powder

Preheat oven to 180°C. Grease a 20 cm square deep baking tray or equivalent. Combine flour, sugar and rolled oats with melted butter, press into base of tray and bake for 12–15 minutes. Set aside for 10 minutes. Combine milk, golden syrup and butter in a large microwavable jug or bowl, then microwave uncovered on high for 3–4 minutes, stirring every minute, until golden and thickened slightly. Pour over the warm base and bake for 10–12 minutes until edges are a deep golden. Cool thoroughly. **ICING**: combine icing ingredients, then add water a little at a time to make a thick icing. Spread smoothly on caramel. Allow to set and cut into tiny squares.

Quick no-bake pear slice

1 packet of Sao biscuits, original or
  wholemeal
1 tbsp cornflour
cold water or pear syrup
750 g stewed pears or diced partially
  drained canned pears

Line a baking tray with greaseproof paper and a layer of half the Sao biscuits. Dissolve cornflour in a small amount of cold water or pear syrup. Add to the pears over low heat, stirring until mixture thickens. Spread evenly over Sao layer, top with the rest of the Saos, ice with white icing. Slice when set. Good as a lunchbox treat.

Sweet treats

No one is pretending these are healthy, but children need treats. For school holidays and parties, these are fun to make and delicious to eat.

We don't recommend artificial sweeteners such as aspartame (951).

Sherbet

1 cup icing sugar

½ tsp citric acid

½ tsp tartaric acid

¼ tsp baking powder (gluten-free if necessary) to make it fizzy

Mix all ingredients together and serve in a small container with a small spoon, or in a large bowl at parties. Keep refrigerated in an airtight container.

Marshmallows

My kids prefer marshmallows frozen.

4 tbsp gelatine

1 cup warm water

4 cups sugar

2 cups boiling water

2 pinches citric acid

icing sugar

cornflour (gluten-free if necessary)

Sprinkle gelatine over warm water and stir to dissolve. Put sugar and boiling water into a large saucepan. Stir in gelatine mixture and boil gently, uncovered, for 20 minutes. Allow to cool until lukewarm. Pour mixture into the large bowl of an electric mixer, add citric acid. Beat fast until very thick and white. Pour mixture into two deep 20 cm square wetted cake tins. Refrigerate until set. When cold, cut into squares with a wet knife and toss in a mixture of icing sugar and cornflour. Store separated with greaseproof paper.

Commercial marshmallows usually contain artificial flavours and, except the white ones, artificial colours. Most people can tolerate Pascall's Vanilla marshmallows (limit 4 per day). It's better to buy the plain vanilla than the pink and white mix.

'We slipped up by keeping the pink marshmallows in the house. My son, aged 8, found them and ate every one. He is now in day 2 of the violent monster stage!' Reader, New Zealand

Rice Bubble treats

4 cups Rice Bubbles
200 g of home-made marshmallows
   (p. 173) or 2 × 100 g packets of
   Pascall's Vanilla white marshmallows
80 g butter or failsafe margarine (p. 183)

Put Rice Bubbles in a large bowl. Line a lamington tin or swiss roll tray with ovenbake paper. Melt marshmallows and butter over low heat, stirring so it doesn't burn. Pour the marshmallow and butter mixture onto the Rice Bubbles. Mix well. Tip into lined tray and press down. This works best with a metal spoon as the mixture cools. Cut into bars before completely set.

Mega-bites

'We cut these into shapes with mini biscuit cutters and rolled them in caster sugar instead of icing sugar. Although some of my family prefer the taste when rolled in icing sugar, this method is for parties and taking to special days at school. They look more like commercially made jellies.' Reader, Victoria

2 cups sugar
1 cup water
3 tbsp gelatine

¼ tsp citric acid
sifted icing sugar for coating

Place the sugar, water and gelatine in a saucepan over low heat and stir until dissolved. Bring to the boil and boil without stirring for 20 minutes. Add the citric acid and pour into a lightly greased tin. Allow to cool and set. Cut into bite-sized squares and roll in icing sugar.

Honeycomb

5 tbsp sugar

2 tbsp golden syrup

1 tsp sodium bicarbonate (make sure this is fresh, especially in the tropics)

Bring sugar and golden syrup to the boil, slowly stirring all the time. Boil 4 minutes, stirring occasionally. Remove from heat and quickly add bicarbonate. Stir in quickly until it froths and pour at once into a greased tray. Break up when cold. Store in airtight jars.

Commercial lollies include • Pascall's white marshmallows • Darryl Lea butterscotch • Smashi lollies (www.smashi.com) • Sweet Treats (www.sweettreats.com.au)

None of these should be eaten in large quantities, except perhaps at parties. Sugar is best eaten as part of a balanced meal than in large amounts on an empty stomach.

Golden nuggets

butter or failsafe margarine (p. 183)

1 cup sugar

3 tbsp golden syrup

3 tsp sodium bicarbonate

Grease a baking tray with butter. Melt sugar and golden syrup together in a saucepan. Stir over medium heat for 10 minutes. Sprinkle over the bicarbonate and mix in with a wooden spoon. Mixture will foam. Carefully drop spoonfuls of the mixture on to the tray. Leave to cool.

Toffee

3 cups sugar

1 cup water

1 tsp citric acid

Put sugar, water and citric acid in a heavy saucepan. Stir over low heat until sugar is dissolved. Increase heat and boil rapidly uncovered for about 15 minutes until a small amount poured into cold water will crack. Remove from heat, then reduce heat by standing saucepan in cold water for one minute. Wait until toffee stops bubbling and pour into paper patty cases.

'I wouldn't dream of giving my daughter coloured sweets, but she's been using coloured toothpaste. I didn't think ...' Reader, NSW

Avoid colours and mint or herbal flavours. Plain Toothpaste (www. plaintoothpaste.com) or Soul Pattinson's Plain Toothpaste is the best. When starting the diet, use a plain wet toothbrush for a few days, then introduce special toothpaste. Encourage teeth cleaning after sweets.

Toffee apples

These are fun if apples are tolerated, but not suitable for your supervised elimination diet.

3 cups sugar

½ tsp citric acid dissolved in 1 tbsp water or 1 tbsp malt vinegar (amines)

1 tbsp butter or failsafe margarine (p. 183)

¼ cup cold water

½ tsp cream of tartar

6 Golden or Red Delicious apples, peeled (salicylates)

Boil all ingredients except for apples together without stirring until a drop snaps in cold water. Remove from heat, stand saucepan in a basin of hot water and dip skewered apples in toffee. Stand apples on greaseproof paper until dry.

Lollipops

'I put these lollipops in a small cellophane bag with a fancy sticker to seal it.'
Reader, New Zealand

1 cup sugar
⅔ cup water
cochineal colour (optional)
wooden sticks

Heat sugar, water and colouring in heavy-based saucepan over low heat and stir with wooden spoon until sugar dissolves. Then bring to the boil and simmer without stirring for 40–45 minutes until a drop snaps in cold water. Arrange rows of small sticks on oiled trays. Drop one teaspoonful of toffee onto pointed end of each stick. Allow to set firmly.

Fairy floss (cotton candy)

Home fairy-floss makers such as Sunbeam are strongly recommended by fail-safers, including my family. Each serve takes one tablespoon of sugar – low compared to a can of soft drink – and ten minutes. Children can operate the appliance themselves for an entertaining holiday treat for family and friends.

Caramels

These sweets are gluten-free but contain dairy. There is no dairy-free option. People who are dairy-free can often tolerate milk like this better when it has been well-cooked.

1 cup caster sugar
90 g butter or failsafe margarine (p. 183)
2 tbsp golden syrup

⅓ cup glucose syrup (e.g. Colonial
  Farms, available in supermarkets)
½ cup condensed milk

Put all ingredients in a heavy saucepan. Stir over a low heat until sugar has dissolved. Increase heat and boil for 10 minutes, stirring constantly. Mixture will be a dark caramel colour. Remove from heat and pour quickly into a well-greased 20 cm square tin before mixture starts to set. Mark squares, allow to cool, then break into squares.

> Glucose syrup may contain sulphur dioxide not listed on the label. Sulphur dioxide is driven off by heat, so make sure glucose syrup is always well-heated before eating.

Butterscotch

2 cups sugar
⅓ cup water
⅔ cup glucose syrup
125 g butter or failsafe margarine (p. 183)
1 tsp citric acid
½ tsp salt

Put sugar, water and glucose syrup in a heavy saucepan. Stir over low heat until sugar is dissolved. Bring to the boil, reduce heat until very low but mixture is still boiling. Boil 8 to 10 minutes or to 150°C on a confectionery thermometer. The mixture should be a light golden brown. Remove from heat, add remaining ingredients and stir until well blended. Pour into a lightly greased 18 cm × 28 cm lamington tin. Mark small squares while still hot, allow to cool, break into squares.

> Commercial caramels, toffees and butterscotch usually contain artificial flavours and can contain artificial colours 102 or 110. Darryl Lea butterscotch is failsafe.

Lachlan's butterscotch

½ cup of water

2 cups white sugar

1–2 tsp butter or failsafe margarine
  (p. 183) (optional)

On low heat, put ingredients into a saucepan in the order listed above, but don't stir. At first, there are bubbles as the mixture boils, but after 5 to 10 minutes the bubbles diminish. Watch carefully for a straw/gold colour and remove from heat. Pour into either paper-lined patty tins, or into a slab tin lined with baking paper (not wax paper or greaseproof). Allow to cool and harden. Store in an airtight container if the kids haven't already finished it off.

Caramel fudge

A favourite holiday recipe from New Zealand. Organise people in shifts with a timer to help with the stirring.

3 cups sugar

½ cup milk

200 g (half a tin) sweetened condensed
  milk

125 g butter or failsafe margarine (p. 183)

¼ tsp salt

1 tbsp golden syrup

Put sugar and milk into a saucepan and bring to the boil. Add condensed milk, butter, salt and golden syrup. Boil for 30 minutes, stirring frequently. Pour into a mixing bowl quickly before it sets and beat for a few minutes. Pour into greased tins. Mark into squares and cut when set. Store in the refrigerator.

As commercial sweets go, Darryl Lea Caramel Fudge is pretty good. It contains cane sugar, glucose syrup, sweetened condensed milk, butter, vegetable oil, emulsifiers (471, lecithin) salt, flavour, water added. Possible unlisted antioxidants (319–321) in the vegetable oil and artificial flavour are the worry with an ingredient list like this.

Snowballs

85 g butter or failsafe margarine (p. 183)
100 g pack of Pascall's Vanilla white
   marshmallows or home-made (p. 173)
¾ cup of milk powder or soymilk powder
2 cups of Rice Bubbles or gluten-free puffed rice
¼ cup icing sugar, sifted
extra icing sugar

Melt butter and marshmallows in a bowl over gently simmering water until both are just melted (this mixture will not blend together). In a large mixing bowl, mix together milk powder, Rice Bubbles, icing sugar and melted butter mixture until well combined. Shape mixture into small balls and place on foil-lined trays. Set and store in the refrigerator. Serve sprinkled with extra sifted icing sugar. Makes approximately 45.

Frozen Rice Bubble bars

These may not be okay for people on a gluten-free diet because Rice Bubbles contain malt.

250 g butter or failsafe margarine (p. 183)
1 cup sugar
2 eggs, beaten
6–7 cups Rice Bubbles

Boil butter and sugar. Allow to cool slightly, add egg and cook together for about 30 seconds. Mix in Rice Bubbles. Place in lined lamington tin and refrigerate. When set, cut into bars and place in container and then freeze. These are best eaten straight out of the freezer.

Dominic's Pop-rocks

'Similar to candied popcorn, these are my kids' favourite sweet treats – they share them with friends at teeball and soccer and their friends love them so my kids feel on top of the world, and not quite so "different" for a while.' Reader, Canberra

1 packet (150 g) of Sunrice Plain Rice Cakes
½ cup water
2 cups white sugar
1 to 2 tsp butter or failsafe margarine (p. 183)

Crumble the rice cakes – not too small as they will break up in stirring. On low heat, put water, sugar and butter into a saucepan in the order listed above, but don't stir. At first, there are bubbles as the mixture boils, but after 5 to 10 minutes the bubbles diminish. Watch carefully for a straw/gold colour. Turn off the heat but do not remove the pan from the hotplate. Using a clean wooden spoon (plastic might melt!) stir the crushed ricecakes into the butterscotch. Mix well until all the rice-cake crumbs are covered. Pour the pop-rock mixture into a baking-paper-lined slab tin and spread out. When cool, break into pieces and store in an airtight container.

Toffee bark

Sprinkle ½ cup sugar evenly over a lightly greased baking tray lined with foil and place under a hot grill. Cook until sugar is dissolved and is a dark caramel colour. Turn the grill tray as it cooks to dissolve sugar evenly. Leave until completely cold and then break into pieces. Make 1–2 days ahead. Store in an airtight container in a cool, dry place.

Sorbitol or other sugar-free sweeteners called polyols can cause bloating, diarrhoea and stomach aches that can be chronic or severe. Sugar-free products such as chewing gum, sweets and vitamin supplements generally have a warning label, *Excessive consumption may have a laxative effect*, but some people can be affected by the smallest amount and daily consumption can lead to a misdiagnosis of irritable bowel syndrome. Intolerance to sorbitol (420) is thought to affect up to 30 per cent of the population. Other polyols include mannitol (421), isomalt (953), maltitol or hydrogenated glucose syrup (965), lactitol (966), xylitol (967), erythritol (968) and polydextrose (1100).

Carob crackles

4 cups Rice Bubbles
1½ cups icing sugar, sifted
5 tbsp carob powder, sifted
250 g butter or failsafe margarine (p. 183)

Combine the Rice Bubbles with the icing sugar and carob powder in a large mixing bowl. Stir in the butter and mix well. Using 2 tsp of the mixture per patty case, divide the mixture between 24 patty case papers placed on a scone tray and refrigerate.

Others

Fats and oils

Failsafe butter

• Pure butter is failsafe. Colour annatto (160b) is permitted in butter and used in the US and South Africa but not in Australia yet – so check labels. • Butter blends are usually not failsafe – if butter contains added vegetable oil, check for antioxidants (310–312, 319–321) in the oil. If the amount of oil is less than 5 per cent, there could be unlisted antioxidants (see 5 per cent labelling loophole, p. 184). There may also be other nasty additives.

Failsafe margarine

• Made with canola, sunflower or safflower. • Avoid preservatives 200–203. • Avoid antioxidants 310–312, 319–321. • Avoid colours 102, 110, 160b, but 160a is failsafe. • Milk-free if necessary. • In Australia, there are several failsafe margarines and at least one failsafe dairy-free margarine (Nuttelex). • Check labels for trans fats, which are considered a health hazard (see below). • See Shopping List.

Trans fats

• Artificial trans fats – or trans fatty acids – are industrially created through partial hydrogenation of plant oils and animal fats in a chemical process developed in the early 1900s. They are known to promote heart disease. • In 2002 the US

National Academy of Sciences concluded that the only safe intake of trans fats is zero. • In 2006 the World Health Organization (WHO) recommended that governments around the world phase out partially hydrogenated oils. • Trans fats are used widely in fast food, snack foods, fried foods, bakery products and some margarines. Many companies are voluntarily removing trans fats from their products. Check the nutrition panel. Trans fats, if listed, will appear underneath saturated fats. Nuttelex is 'virtually free of trans fatty acids'.

Failsafe oils
• Sunflower, safflower and canola oils are failsafe but should not be cold-pressed (olive and other oils are too high in salicylates). • Cold-pressed rice bran oil is suitable for most but not all readers – anyone who is sensitive to the wholegrain of wheat in products such as wholemeal bread and Weet-Bix should avoid daily use of rice bran oil (see Checklist of Common Mistakes). • Avoid synthetic antioxidants (310–312, 319–320) in a few Australian supermarket cooking oils, nearly all New Zealand cooking oils, and virtually all commercially fried products. • When any kind of vegetable oil is used in a product such as biscuits, frozen chips or soymilk, antioxidants in the oil need not appear on the label if the amount of oil is less than 5 per cent (due to the 5 per cent labelling loophole, see below). In that case, to avoid these antioxidants you need to phone the manufacturer or stick to products on the Shopping List (see Checklist of Common Mistakes).

The 5 per cent labelling loophole
• If the amount of canola oil or other vegetable oil in a product such as biscuits, frozen potato chips or soymilk is less than 5 per cent, any nasty antioxidants (usually 319 or 320) in that product don't have to be listed on the label. So to find out what this product contains, you have to phone the consumer hotline to ask. Most consumers don't know it is there, but it is still enough to affect sensitive children, especially if they eat it every day. • The 5 per cent labelling loophole also applies to artificial colours, preservatives and MSG in added 'flavours' in any processed food.

Spreads

Egg spread

1 freshly hard-boiled egg
1 potato, freshly cooked and mashed
salt to taste
1 tsp finely chopped parsley
1 tsp mayonnaise (p. 190)

Mash all together. Good for sandwiches.

Garlic butter

80 g butter or failsafe margarine (p. 183)
1 tsp chopped parsley
4 cloves of garlic, crushed

Whiz in food processor. Refrigerate after use.

Honey substitute: use 5 parts sugar and 1 part water instead of honey in recipes.

Maple syrup jam

3 tsp gelatine
100 ml boiling water
250 ml pure maple syrup
150 ml syrup from tinned pears
small pieces of chopped pear (optional)

Dissolve gelatine in boiling water and boil a few more minutes to drive off preservative. Add maple syrup, pear syrup and chopped pear. Stir well, cover and refrigerate.

Magic spread

This spread tastes like lemon butter and goes well on rice cakes.

90 g butter or failsafe margarine (p. 183)
1½ cups of sugar
3 eggs
2 tsp citric acid in ½ cup warm water

Melt butter in the microwave on HIGH for about 30 seconds. Beat together sugar, eggs and citric acid in water. Stir into melted butter, mixing well. Cook on HIGH, stirring well every 30 seconds until the mixture thickens (about 3 minutes). Makes roughly 2 cups. Keeps about 2 weeks in a glass jar in the refrigerator. Also a delicious topping for yoghurt, ice-cream and cheesecake (p. 157).

VARIATIONS • Make one third quantity for a quicker recipe: 30 g butter, ½ cup sugar, 1 egg, 1 tsp citric acid in 2 tbsp warm water • Thicken with icing sugar for a cream filling for biscuits (p. 170), or for thicker spread • When using margarine, mixture will thicken in refrigerator.

Caramel sauce or spread

'Apart from the obvious use on ice-cream, this is delicious as a cake filling with mock cream, and I have also offered it as a spread on toast for breakfast to our fussiest eater. I sometimes use the egg whites for meringues, and serve them with the caramel sauce and soy/rice milk ice-cream [p. 150].' Member of email discussion group

60g failsafe margarine (p. 183)
1 cup brown sugar
2 egg yolks, beaten
80 ml soy or rice milk

Melt margarine and sugar. Add egg yolks, mixing well. Stir in milk and cook until mixture boils and thickens. Cool and store in refrigerator.

Birgit's pear jam

'Put a tsp of whisky into your jar of pear jam. It will help preserve it and also takes away the very sweet taste.'
Reader, Northern Territory

Pears must be soft and ripe, or your jam will contain some salicylates. Jam-making generally requires roughly equal quantities of sugar and fruit.

1 kg ripe pears, peeled and cut into small pieces (should be about 750 g), or
2 large (825 g) tins soft pears, drained
750 g sugar
1 tsp citric acid
1 × 50 g packet of Jamsetta (pectin and sugar mix, available in supermarkets)

Puree pears. Put in a large saucepan and heat gently. Add sugar and citric, then Jamsetta, stirring with a wooden spoon until sugar is dissolved. Bring to the boil and boil rapidly for five minutes, stirring occasionally. Allow to cool. Pour into sterilised glass jars or plastic storage containers. Store in refrigerator or freezer.

All jams except pear jam are very high in salicylates because even moderate food chemicals become concentrated as the fruit is boiled down. Birgit's pear jam is available by mail order (see website).

Deborah's cashew paste

1 cup (140 g) raw cashews
1–2 tsp salt
failsafe canola or sunflower oil for mixing (about 2–3 tsp)

Put cashews in blender, add salt, blend briefly. Add oil a little at a time and blend until the desired consistency is reached. To compete with commercial peanut pastes, add plenty of salt. You can reduce quantity later when children have been weaned off processed foods. Use as a sandwich spread alone or with golden syrup. Delicious on rice cakes.

VARIATIONS • Add half a tin (200 g) of drained chickpeas for a different texture • Carob cashew spread: omit the salt but use 1 tbsp carob powder, 1 tbsp caster sugar and about 1½ tbsp oil for a Nutella taste-alike. Store in an airtight jar.

Commercial cashew paste made from lightly roasted cashews is not suitable. Cashews must be *raw*. A few sensitive people react even to raw cashews. The limit for cashews is ten per day.

Maple cashew butter

2 cups raw cashews
80 g butter or failsafe margarine (p. 183)
¼ cup pure maple syrup

Process cashews in food processor until finely chopped. Keeping the processor going, add butter then maple syrup until mixture forms a paste. Pour into an airtight jar and store in the refrigerator. Makes 1½ cups.

Freedom Foods soy butter is a useful peanut butter alternative when tolerated but may not be suitable for your supervised elimination diet.

Dips

Basic dip (contains dairy products)

125 g tub light preservative-free cream cheese and equal volume of natural yoghurt or 125 g tub sour cream and preservative-free cottage cheese
salt to taste

Combine all ingredients. Use as a dip, sauce or mayonnaise.

VARIATIONS • Beetroot: 6 slices of drained canned beetroot, pureed (salicylates). Stir in with half yoghurt amount • Asparagus: 6 drained canned asparagus spears (salicylates). Stir in with half yoghurt amount and 3 pinches citric acid • Garlic: one large clove of garlic, crushed. Decorate with parsley • Shallot: 2 shallots, crush white portion, finely slice green portion and stir in with 3 pinches citric acid • Salmon (not for amine responders): 100 g tinned red salmon. Blend in with 3 pinches citric acid and half yoghurt amount.

Failsafe hummus

440 g can chickpeas (garbanzos), drained
and rinsed
2 cloves of garlic, crushed
3 tbsp failsafe canola oil
⅓ tsp citric acid
1 tbsp parsley, chopped
salt to taste

Combine ingredients in a food processor and blend until smooth. Use as a spread on sandwiches and rice cakes or as a dip with preservative-free bread and salad.

Lentil spread or dip

½ cup red lentils
2 garlic cloves roughly chopped or more
to taste
1 tbsp butter or failsafe margarine (p. 183)
1–2 tbsp Birgit's pear ketchup (p. 192) to
taste

Cook lentils in just enough water to minimise excess liquid. When cooked, drain well and blend with butter and pear ketchup. Refrigerate. The spread keeps well in the refrigerator in a screwtop jar and also freezes well. Nice on rice crackers.

Bean dip

1 can (375 g) butter beans
1 clove of garlic
3 shallots
½ pear
4 tbsp plain yoghurt

Blend all together.

Sauces

Quick mayonnaise

400 g tin sweetened condensed milk
equal volume of water
3 tsp citric acid (or more to thicken)
1 tsp salt or to taste

Combine all ingredients in a glass screwtop jar and shake well to mix. Store in refrigerator.

VARIATION • Use malt vinegar instead of water with citric acid if you don't react to amines.

Creamy tofu dressing

300 g light silken tofu
2 tbsp rice syrup
3 cloves of garlic, minced
½ tsp salt
1 pinch citric acid or to taste
1 tbsp finely chopped chives

Blend all ingredients except chives in a food processor or blender until smooth. Stir in chopped chives. Chill. Will keep for about one week in the refrigerator. Use as a creamy dressing for green salads or coleslaw, a dip for raw vegetables or a topping for baked potatoes.

Mighty Mayo (aka Robin's dressing)

An easy-to-make, delicious dressing that really works.

¼ cup maize cornflour
1 tsp citric acid (or more to taste)
1 tsp salt
½ cup sugar
1¼ cups water
2 eggs
175 ml failsafe oil (p. 184)

Cook together cornflour, citric acid, salt, sugar and water. When thickened, pour into blender and while whizzing add eggs and drizzle in failsafe oil. Keeps well in refrigerator for approximately 2 weeks.

Tartare sauce

2 tbsp Mighty Mayo (above)
2 tbsp plain yoghurt
1 shallot, finely chopped
chives, finely chopped

Mix all ingredients together and serve with home-made fish and chips or rosti potato patties (p. 104).

Quick salad dressing

¼ cup failsafe oil (p. 184)
1 tbsp citric lemon juice (p. 194) or
   1 tbsp malt vinegar (if you don't react
   to amines)
1 clove of garlic, crushed
salt to taste

Combine all ingredients in a glass jar with a screwtop lid and shake.

Home-made gravy

This gravy is very high in amines and not suitable for your supervised elimination diet. After roasting meat, pour off most of the fat, add 1 tbsp flour and 1 tsp salt dissolved in 1 cup water to the baking dish, bring to the boil, stirring continuously, and simmer 2 minutes.

Commercial gravy can be very high in salicylates and amines and usually contains added MSG. 'Health food' gravy with ingredients such as onion are not failsafe. Even home-made gravy is unsuitable, because meat juices are very high in amines. As a gravy substitute, you can use leek sauce, failsafe hummus (p. 189), herb sauce, garlic sauce or pear sauce (below), pear ketchup (p. 192), or mushy peas (p. 112) if you can tolerate peas.

Pear sauce

Use pureed canned pears as a sauce, like apple sauce.

Birgit's cheese pasta sauce (p. 129)

Basic white sauce

2 tbsp butter or failsafe margarine (p. 183)
1½ tbsp flour or gluten-free flour
1 cup or more of milk or milk substitute
salt to taste

Put butter in pan and stir until melted. Add the flour to the butter, stir until cooked. The flour and butter have to be well cooked before adding liquid. Add liquid and whisk continually until thickened. Add salt and remove from heat.

VARIATIONS • Herb sauce with finely chopped and stir-fried shallots, leeks and a little parsley • Garlic sauce: Add crushed garlic • Hollandaise sauce: Remove white sauce from heat. Stir in a beaten egg yolk and ¼ tsp citric acid. Reheat but do not boil • Cheese-tasting sauce: 1 tsp of salt in this recipe will fool people into thinking it is a cheese sauce.

Leek sauce

'My son doesn't like the pear puree. But he loves this leek sauce on sausages and anything he used to have tomato sauce on. Sometimes I add 2 tablespoons of Philadelphia cream cheese to make it nice and creamy.' Parent, Darwin

1 large leek, finely sliced
water
1 tsp butter or failsafe margarine (p. 183)
1 quantity of white sauce (above)

Cover microwave dish with leek slices. Add water until leek slices are just covered. Add butter. Microwave on high for 3 minutes. Make a white sauce and add leek mixture. Stir well.

Birgit's pear ketchup
Use instead of tomato sauce.

1 large tin (825 g) of pears and syrup
½ cup brown sugar
2 tsp citric acid
1 tsp salt

Drain and dice pears. Put syrup in a saucepan and simmer until reduced to half. Add pears and remaining ingredients. Simmer about 15 minutes or until mixture thickens. Allow to cool. Puree in blender. Store in an airtight container in fridge.

VARIATIONS • Pear chutney: Skip the puree step. Keeps best in the freezer. It is so soft you can use it while frozen • Add chopped leeks, shallots and garlic to diced pears • For a thicker sauce, thicken with cornflour, gluten-free if necessary.

Whisky cream sauce

1 tbsp whisky
¼ cup sugar
2 egg yolks
300 ml cream

Combine whisky and sugar and allow to stand for 1 hour. Beat egg yolks until thick and creamy and add gradually to whisky mixture, beating well. Cover and stand for 1 hour. Just before serving, whip cream and gently stir into sauce.

Mock maple syrup

1 cup brown sugar
1 cup boiling water
½ cup white sugar
1 tsp butter or failsafe margarine (p. 183)
½ tsp vanilla (see warning about vanilla on p. 136)

Combine brown sugar and water and bring to boil. Caramelise white sugar by heating it in a frying pan until sugar melts and turns brown. Add brown sugar and water mixture and simmer until smooth and thick. Pour into a container containing butter and vanilla and stir until well mixed.

Chocolate-style topping

1½ cups sugar
5 tbsp carob powder
⅔ cup water

Heat sugar, carob powder and water in saucepan or microwave until sugar is dissolved. Use as a drink flavouring, on Rice Bubbles as a treat, or as ice-cream topping.

Hot carob sauce

2 tbsp carob powder
2 tbsp water
2 tbsp sugar
1 tbsp butter or failsafe margarine (p. 183)

Mix all ingredients together. Heat gently over low heat, stirring, until creamy. Pour over ice-cream and serve immediately.

Odds and ends

Citric lemon juice

Real lemon juice contains salicylates and amines. Even a small amount is enough to contribute to a reaction. Use this substitute in any recipe that calls for lemon juice.

4 tbsp warm water
1 tsp sugar
¾ tsp citric acid or to taste
¼ tsp ascorbic acid (Vitamin C) powder, optional

Put sugar in warm water, stir to dissolve. Add remaining ingredients and store in refrigerator.

Alison's failsafe breadcrumbs

'These breadcrumbs are vastly superior in flavour to anything you can buy and once you have eaten food with home-made crumbs you will never want to use any others.' Reader, Queensland

slices of failsafe white bread (see p. 40)

Preheat oven to 180°C. Remove crusts and cut each slice into half. Bake until golden brown. Allow to cool for a few minutes. Whiz in food processor until baked bread is reduced to fine crumbs, or put the bread in a paper bag and crush with a rolling pin.

VARIATIONS • Ask your local preservative-free bread store for fresh breadcrumbs. Some will sell you a bag of crumbs for a small charge • For crunchier crumbs, use crushed Sao biscuits • Use gluten-free rice crumbs (see Shopping List).

> Commercial breadcrumbs usually contain preservative (282) and flavours.

Golden marinade

3 tbsp golden syrup

3 tbsp failsafe oil (p. 184)

2 cloves of garlic, crushed

1 pinch citric acid

1 shallot, chopped

1 tsp finely chopped parsley

salt to taste

Combine all ingredients.

Pear and celery marinade

2 canned soft pear halves

2 sticks celery

1 clove of garlic, crushed

1 tsp salt

1 tbsp brown sugar

½ leek, finely chopped

2 shallots

½ cup pear syrup from canned pears

1 tbsp failsafe oil (p. 184)

Combine all marinade ingredients, whiz in blender. Can be frozen.

Pear and yoghurt marinade

1 cup yoghurt or soy yoghurt

1 peeled pear

1 clove of garlic

1 shallot

Blend all ingredients until smooth. Use this to marinate strips of chicken before grilling.

Rice milk

½ cup hot cooked rice (or frozen cooked rice)

2 cups hot water (if rice is frozen, use boiling water)

½ tbsp failsafe oil (p. 184)

½ tbsp sugar

Put all ingredients in a blender and blend for 5 minutes or until smooth. Strain through cheesecloth or let sit for 30 minutes then pour into a container without disturbing the sediment. Store in refrigerator. Use within 24 hours.

Rice milk is not suitable for infant feeding. Any infant not breastfed to 12 months must be given an appropriate infant formula. Commercial rice milks enriched with chickpeas are not suitable for children or adults with cross-reactivity problems due to nut, legume or soy allergies.

Mock cream

1½ tsp cornflour

½ cup milk

2 tbsp butter or failsafe margarine (p. 183)

2 tbsp sugar

Mix cornflour with milk to make a smooth paste. Put into a saucepan and boil for 3 or 4 minutes. Remove from heat. Mix butter and sugar to a cream. Slowly add the cold cooked cornflour mixture. Beat well.

White icing

1 cup icing sugar (pure icing sugar for gluten-free)

2 tsp butter or failsafe margarine (p. 183), melted

1 tbsp water (approximately)

VARIATIONS • Coloured icing, see natural colours below • Lemon: Dissolve ½ tsp citric acid in the water • Carob: Dissolve 1 tbsp carob powder in the water • Coffee: Dissolve 1 tsp instant decaffeinated coffee powder in the water • Quick caramel: Use golden syrup instead of water • Cream cheese: Substitute ½ cup of preservative-free cream cheese for half of the icing sugar.

Caramel icing

1 cup brown sugar

2 tbsp milk

1 tbsp butter or failsafe margarine (p. 183)

Heat ingredients over medium-low heat in a small saucepan, stirring constantly until smooth and bubbly. Cool. Beat with electric mixer until thickened.

Vienna cream frosting

125 g butter or failsafe margarine (p. 183), chopped

1½ cups icing sugar

2 tbsp milk

3 tbsp carob powder

Beat butter until as white as possible. Sift in half the icing sugar and carob and add all the milk. Beat until smooth, add rest of icing mixture and beat again.

Natural colours (home-made)

Blend some chopped cabbage leaf with water. The cabbage colours can be stabilised by microwaving to hot but still taste of cabbage. Cabbage juice and saffron are permitted. Beetroot juice is easy to use but has an earthy taste. Beetroots contain some salicylates so there could be salicylate problems in extra-sensitive children.

Purple: red cabbage juice
Blue: dilute red cabbage juice with extra water
Deep blue: red cabbage juice with sodium bicarbonate
Pale blue: cabbage juice with sodium bicarbonate
Bright red: red cabbage juice with pinch citric acid
Pink: beetroot juice, or cabbage juice with citric acid
Yellow: saffron

Natural colours (commercial) • Annatto (160b, a yellow colour) is the only natural colour that can cause food intolerance symptoms as bad as artificial colours. • Cochineal (120) is a failsafe pink colour made from beetles, but it can cause true allergies to beetle proteins in allergic families. • Some commercial colours made from plant-derived colours and flavours such as turmeric, anthocyanins and gardenia extract may contain small amounts of salicylates, but are generally fine for special occasions.

Playdough recipe

This failsafe gluten-free playdough has a commercial texture and will last about one week. Refrigerate when not in use.

½ cup rice flour

½ cup cornflour or glutinous rice flour

½ cup salt

2 tsp cream of tartar

1 cup water

1 tbsp sunflower oil

Place all ingredients in a saucepan, mix well and bring to the boil, stirring constantly. Reduce heat and cook, stirring, for three minutes or until the mixture forms a ball.

VARIATIONS • For coloured playdough, add natural colours, above • Add glitter • For other failsafe craft suggestions, see the playgroup factsheet on www.fedup. com.au.

FLAVOURS

When 'flavours' appears on an ingredients label, they are made in a factory, whether described as artificial, natural or nature identical. • **Natural flavours** must be derived from entirely from natural products. • **Nature-identical flavours** are made in a laboratory to be chemically identical to flavouring substances present in natural foods. • **Artificial flavours** are made in a laboratory and not found in natural foods. • Because man-made flavours are cheap, they are often used in far greater concentrations than would ever be found in nature.

Food for Special Occasions

Birthday parties

There are two ways of handling your children's birthday parties. You can provide totally failsafe alternatives such as sausage rolls (p. 46), HFC (p. 90), additive-free crisps (Kettle chips, or see p. 54) and failsafe treats, or a combination of failsafe and other food that isn't too tempting for the birthday child. To make birthdays look colourful, cook a Fete Cake (p. 161) or carob cake (p. 200) with white icing (p. 196), or prepare an ice-cream cake (p. 201) and decorate with coloured plastic decorations, ribbons or paper streamers, or use cochineal pink colouring (salicylates) in the icing.

For birthday parties away, slip in with a bottle of permitted lemonade and a plate of food to share. Cup cakes (p. 161) are good for this. Or join in the theme – for example, a Spot the Dog birthday cake can be accompanied by a small white-iced gluten-free failsafe cake in the shape of Spot's bone (see our DVD cover). It also helps if your child arrives with a full stomach. Parents have reported surviving birthday parties at fast-food burger restaurants by allowing chicken nuggets, chips and water, avoiding the cake and providing their own lolly bag. You can just treat the whole party as a challenge, or you could take your child's failsafe lemonade and failsafe burger and have it presented in store wrapping like all the rest.

Never-fail carob cake

For those who tolerate amines, this cake can be made with unflavoured cocoa and iced with chocolate. We often make it with one half chocolate, the other half carob, to accommodate everyone.

125 g butter or failsafe margarine (p. 183)

1 cup caster sugar

2 eggs

1 cup self-raising wheat flour or self-raising gluten-free flour

2 tbsp carob powder

½ cup milk or soymilk

Preheat oven to 180°C. Grease 20 cm ring pan. Combine all ingredients and beat thoroughly until smooth. Bake for 40 minutes, then allow to stand several minutes before turning out to cool. Ice with Vienna cream frosting (p. 197).

Brenda's microwave carob cake

This is the famous carob cake from the leader of the finB group in Brisbane.

125 g failsafe margarine (p. 183) or butter if tolerated

¾ cup sugar

⅓ cup carob powder (or cocoa, if amines are tolerated)

2 eggs

½ cup ricemilk or soymilk or cow's milk

1 cup of gluten-free self-raising flour

Line a microwave ring pan with a paper towel (cut or tear a cross in the middle of the towel to easily go over the central dome). Melt margarine in a bowl or jug on 100 per cent (800 watts) power for approximately 40 seconds. Add sugar and sifted carob. Stir to dissolve any lumps. Add eggs and milk. Add flour. Stir with a fork until combined. Pour cake mixture into pan. Cook elevated on a rack or an inverted saucer for 5 minutes on high. Cover with paper towel, and stand directly on bench top (i.e. not elevated) for 5 minutes. Turn out onto a wire rack, remove paper towel and allow to cool completely. Ice with carob icing (p. 166).

Vienna fudge cake (eggless)

'A very delicious carob cake for special occasions. A few slices are left in the freezer at kindy if another child has a birthday cake.' Llewellyn, Queensland.

125 g butter or failsafe margarine (p. 183)
1 cup caster sugar
1 cup carob powder
½ cup hot water
¾ tsp sodium bicarbonate
1 cup milk or soymilk
1¾ cups plain flour
1 tsp baking powder
1 tsp sodium bicarbonate, extra
pinch of salt

Preheat oven to 180°C. Grease and line two round sponge tins. Cream butter and sugar. Mix carob in hot water to a smooth paste. Gradually add carob mixture to butter mixture. Add bicarbonate to milk. Sift flour, baking powder, extra bicarbonate and salt and add to creamed mixture alternately with milk. Mix thoroughly. Spoon cake mixture into tins and bake for 30 minutes. Cool and ice with Vienna cream frosting (p. 166) or fill centre with pear jam (p. 186) and whipped cream.

Ice-cream birthday cake

This is an excellent alternative for children who must avoid wheat but can tolerate dairy foods. It can be decorated with plastic candle holders and a toy such as Astro Boy or Spiderman, which then becomes an extra present.

1 litre failsafe vanilla ice-cream
300 ml cream, whipped with 1 tbsp sugar
carob buttons, plastic decorations

Make sure ice-cream is firmly frozen. Remove from container by dipping briefly into hot water and running a knife around the edge. Cover with whipped cream. Decorate and replace in freezer until well frozen. Do this the day before.

Princess bread

For parties, this is an alternative to fairy bread.

Put 2 drops of cochineal with one cup of sugar in jar with lid, toss until all sugar is coloured, then spread on buttered bread.

Christmas cakes and puddings

Traditional Christmas cakes and puddings packed with sultanas and other dried fruit are exceptionally high in salicylates and amines. We use Fete Cake (p. 161) iced with white icing (p. 196), decorated with a sprig of plastic holly and wrapped with red or green paper frills. Alternatives to the traditional pudding and brandy sauce include Bombe Alaska (p. 203), sago pudding (p. 152) with dried pears and bananas, Andra's 'honey' roll pudding variation (p. 163) and our favourite, Dominion pudding, below, with Not brandy sauce.

Dominion pudding

2 tbsp butter or failsafe margarine (p. 183)

½ cup sugar

1 egg

1 cup self-raising flour or gluten-free flour (p. 233)

½ cup milk or soymilk

4 tbsp golden syrup

Cream butter and sugar, add egg and beat well. Add sifted flour alternately with milk. Place golden syrup in the bottom of a greased bowl, pour batter over, tie brown paper or baking paper over the top and steam in a covered saucepan with 2 cm of water for 1¼ hours. Serve with a failsafe version of the traditional brandy sauce (following), cream, ice-cream or Narni's custard (p. 153).

VARIATION • Pour whisky instead of brandy over pudding and set it alight by warming it slightly first in a pan over the stove – but not too hot or the alcohol will evaporate.

Not brandy sauce

4 cups cold water

1 cup brown sugar

4 tbsp cornflour (from corn if gluten-free)

100 g butter or failsafe margarine (p. 183)

½ cup whisky

Mix water, sugar and cornflour in a saucepan. Bring to the boil, stirring constantly until mixture thickens. Reduce heat and cook a little longer, then add butter and brandy. Best made in advance.

Bombe Alaska

An entertaining failsafe substitute for hot puddings, suitable for an Australian Christmas.

1 packet of crushed biscuits (e.g. Milk Arrowroot or Big Anzacs)

4 tbsp of magic cordial drink, diluted to taste

5 egg whites

¾ cup caster sugar

¼ tsp salt

1 litre block of failsafe vanilla ice-cream

pure icing sugar for dusting

Cover the base of an ovenproof serving dish with crushed biscuits or stale cake. Drizzle with magic cordial. Beat egg whites with sugar and salt until stiff. Arrange ice-cream on crushed biscuits to insulate it from the heat. Using a large knife, quickly spread meringue mixture all over the ice-cream. Dust with pure icing sugar (immediately before baking). Bake for 3–4 minutes, no longer, in a very hot oven (250°C) and serve immediately. Can be prepared a few hours in advance and stored in the freezer, but you must warm the dish briefly in water before placing it in the oven.

Easter

Many parents first realise their child's behaviour is affected by foods during the Easter chocolate overload. Amine reactions can be delayed: that is, building up slowly, worst on day three, then slowly improving with occasional flare-ups over a week or even up to a month. Some alternatives:

- Carob Easter eggs, preferably without added flavour.
- White chocolate Easter eggs (white chocolate is much lower in amines than milk or dark chocolate).
- A small plastic rabbit container packed with Pascall's white marshmallows.
- A packet of the very little chocolate Easter eggs for a big Easter egg hunt, so the hunt is more fun than eating the eggs.
- For people who can tolerate amines, beware of regular Easter eggs because they contain too much flavour (salicylates). Nestlé unflavoured dark choc bits or cooking chocolate can be used to make your own eggs by melting (in a double boiler) and using commercial chocolate egg moulds or two spoons.
- For children with nut allergies, there are several brands of nut-free chocolate (see Product Updates on www.fedup.com.au).

Salicylate and amine recipes

Challenges can be harder than they sound, as these examples show. The recipes following can be used during or after challenges.

Example of a challenge diary

This is the salicylate challenge diary for a five-year-old boy who exhibited different kinds of effects – behaviour, rash and bedwetting. Note that effects can be delayed, occur at different times, build up slowly and fluctuate. Behavioural reactions depend on the environment, so if the child is getting his own way he will be fine, but when asked to do something he doesn't like, he will overreact. From story 446 on www.fedup.com.au.

Day 1 – No reaction
Day 2 – Tantrum, kicking, punching (wanted more peppermints)
Day 3 – Punched a peer's arm at kindy
Day 4 – Itchy rash appeared on inside of elbow
Day 5 – Well-behaved
Day 6 – Red blotches and pimples all over lower half of face. Tantrum, screaming and hitting me (didn't want photo taken)
Day 7 – More blotchy and spotty, face sore and raw [End of challenge foods]
Day 8 – Wet bed
Day 9 – Wet bed, sore tummy, sore red anus, constipated
Day 10 – Wet bed, kindy complained of very small attention span, loss of concentration
Day 11 – Face clearing, no wet bed, generally seems to be getting better
Day 12 – Wet bed again

A salicylate challenge story

'Of the foods listed we ate tinned apricots (heaps) in syrup on our Rice Bubbles, preservative-free apple juice, curries or pumpkin soup for dinner and only vegetables recommended for the salicylate challenge. We put away mountains of carrots and similar of grannies in a week as well as large quantities of pumpkin, kumara, corn, capsicum (had forgotten how good that tastes), cucumber, curry, cinnamon, tea and everything else we could find in season that was on the list.

'We went for about the first three days with no reaction at all. Everyone seemed to respond differently. My husband and one son seemed not to react. My 8-year-old son – the reason we started this thing – became fractious and difficult and seemingly continuously involved in conflict with his brothers and sisters, pretty well back to pre-elimination behaviour. Yuk! The youngest two had wet beds and seem a bit anxious and grumpy. I have probably had the most obvious reaction. My flesh felt like it was crawling, my eyes were stingy, I was tired and grumpy. I also had bloating and tummy aches and alternating constipation and loose stools. I got restless legs so badly while I was trying to fall asleep that I would nearly jump off the bed.' Reader, by email

SOME SALICYLATE RECIPES

- Carrot cake (p. 162): You can add 1 tsp cinnamon but not walnuts because nuts contain both salicylates and amines.
- Indian style lamb with the curry option (p. 86): Use powdered spices, not pastes with artificial colours or hidden synthetic antioxidant (320).
- Pear crumble (p. 135): Made with apples, apricots, peaches or cherries.
- Smoothie (p. 61): Made with strawberries and honey.
- Fresh watermelon juice.

Impossible zucchini bake

Called impossible because the flour magically turns into a pie base, this dish can be used during your salicylate challenge. For people who don't have to worry about salicylates, amines and dairy foods, a cup of grated cheese can be sprinkled over the top.

3 cups zucchini, grated (high in salicylates)
1 small onion, chopped (high in salicylates)
1½ cup milk or soymilk
¾ cup flour or gluten-free flour
3 eggs
salt to taste

Preheat oven to 180°C. Grease or spray a 23 cm deep pie dish with canola oil and arrange zucchini and leeks in base. Beat remaining ingredients until smooth and pour over zucchini mixture. Bake about 40 minutes, or until knife inserted near the centre comes out clean. Cool for 5 minutes before cutting into wedges.

SOME AMINE RECIPES

Amine choc-top banana ice-cream

Children who won't eat dark chocolate and ripe bananas will probably eat this delicious recipe.

Very ripe bananas
Dark choc bits, cooking chocolate or dark
  chocolate bars

Peel bananas, wrap in foil and leave in freezer until frozen, then whiz in food processor for a creamy banana ice-cream. Dip in melted chocolate.

VARIATION • Freeze bananas as above but on a wooden stick, then dip banana top in melted chocolate

Amine chocolate mud cake

This very rich and delicious cake has an excellent low amine variation, below.

250 g butter or failsafe margarine (p. 183)
250 g dark chocolate
3 tbsp decaf coffee
300 ml boiling water
4 eggs
2 tablespoons failsafe oil (p. 184)
½ cup cream
1¼ cups self-raising flour
1¼ cups plain flour
½ cup cocoa
½ tsp sodium bicarbonate
2¼ cups caster sugar

Preheat oven to 160°C. Grease a large cake tin. In a large bowl melt butter, chocolate, coffee and water by microwaving for 2 minutes. In a smaller bowl, beat together eggs, oil and cream, add to large bowl and mix. Sieve remaining dry ingredients together and fold in. Bake for 80 minutes. Ice with 250 g dark chocolate melted in ½ cup cream.

VARIATION • For a low-amine version use white Nestlé Melts (no added flavour) and ½ cup carob instead of cocoa.

Amine Banana cake

125 g butter or failsafe margarine (p. 183)

¾ cup sugar

2 eggs

2 mashed ripe bananas (amines)

1 tsp sodium bicarbonate

2 tbsp boiling milk or soymilk

2 cups plain flour or gluten-free flour

1 tsp baking powder

Cream butter and sugar. Add eggs, mashed bananas, then sodium bicarbonate dissolved in boiling milk. Lastly, add mixed flour and baking powder (already mixed). Bake in two greased sandwich tins for 20 minutes at 180°C. Fill with whipped cream and sliced bananas.

VARIATIONS • *Gluten-free*: Use 2 cups gluten-free self-raising flour (p. 233) instead of flour and baking powder • For a higher fibre cake you can use 1 cup of white and 1 cup of wholemeal flour.

Tuna and potatoes

An easy nutritious meal for those who can tolerate amines.

1 large can tuna (in canola oil or brine, no flavours)

1 large potato per person, peeled and boiled

dob of butter

Drain tuna. Semi-mash potatoes with a dob of butter, serve tuna over potatoes and garnish with parsley and chives. Serve with green salad or green beans. Tuna can also be served on cous-cous or pasta.

Canned tuna generally has lower levels of mercury than fresh tuna because they are younger and a smaller species. It is considered safe for all population groups to consume a snack can of tuna (95 grams) every day, assuming no other fish is eaten. More at www.foodstandards.gov.au.

Other amine suggestions

- dried bananas for lunchboxes (but not banana chips that are deep-fried in coconut oil)
- golden bananas (p. 134)
- tuna rolls and sandwiches
- additive-free ham and bacon, usually available only from organic specialists.

Eating out

Find out through your supervised elimination diet which foods affect you the worst, so you can choose what to avoid when you go out. Here is some feedback I've received from readers, with different scenarios:

> 'My sister has been really ill with irritable bowel but she resisted doing the diet for years. Eventually it was either do the diet or give up work. Now she sticks to her diet all the time. She has to go to work dinners two or three times a week so she phones the chef the day before and tells him exactly what she wants. She always has steamed fresh white fish, steamed rice, green beans. She drinks soda water. That's it, nothing else. She's doing really well.' Reader, Sydney

> 'When we go out, we like to sit in cafes, but we just have decaf cappuccinos. We don't eat anything. The food's better at home. And it saves us money.' Reader, Darwin

> 'On Sunday one of the few people we know here said "I'd invite you over for supper but you people are so difficult to feed".' Reader, Victoria

Some answers to the last difficult situation could be: 'Thank you, why don't you come to our place instead? How about next week?' or 'Thank you. We'd love to come. Perhaps we could bring some food to share?'

At home, you have control of the food and can serve anything to suit you, from home-made hamburgers (p. 74) to a simple chicken casserole (p. 94) to a splendid roast lamb dinner with all the trimmings, which you can avoid if you want. If you're going out to someone else's place, a potluck dinner where everyone brings a plate is the easiest way to socialise when you have food intolerance. Otherwise, hosts can talk the menu through with you and let you bring a dish or two, like a chicken and chickpea casserole (p. 99). Barbecues are easy because you can bring your own failsafe sausages. You can bring all kinds of things to share, especially food the kids can snack on like dip and crackers, failsafe sausage rolls, a cake, permitted ice-cream, a cheesecake. As long as there are a few things you can eat, you can then concentrate on enjoying the company.

Takeaways

It's best to avoid takeaways during your supervised elimination diet. After challenges, you can work out what suits you. Some readers take their own toppings and buy baked jacket potatoes from a potato cart. Others buy steamed white rice and an omelette from Chinese restaurants, or fried rice with only shallots and egg strips, no MSG. In a shopping mall, you can buy a failsafe roll from a hot bread shop to go with a plate of sandwich fillings such as egg, shredded lettuce, grated carrot, beetroot and cucumber, when permitted, from a sandwich shop. Or you can sit in a café with a cup of decaf and eat your own brown-bag lunch. If you can find a chicken shop that sells plain rotisseried chickens (no stuffing, no seasoning on the skin) you can combine it with your own fresh rolls and salad. Some people can manage grilled fish and a small serve of chips, but it's easy to overdo BHA (320) in the oil. Again, you can combine the grilled fish with your own rolls and salad to avoid the BHA (320) in the chips.

Fast food chains

For fast food chains, visit their website first to check ingredients. For example, at Subway the ham and bacon contain nitrates, anything with chicken contains flavour enhancers 627 and 631, the Atkins wraps contain bread preservative calcium propionate (282), and there are sorbates or benzoates in pickles and mayonnaise. There are also some artificial colours. Carrot, lettuce, cucumber and Swiss cheese on Italian bread is free of nasty additives, although it does contain some salicylates and amines.

Cafés

It's easiest to find a place that suits you and eat there frequently so they get used to your odd requests. Organic cafés are additive-free but often choose their fruit and vegetables straight from the high end of the salicylate range. My favourite is the café at the Bellingen organic markets with meals such as potato and leek frittata with salad – mostly organic iceberg lettuce with a few other greens – made from fresh local organic food in season. I've seen most of the people there eating a simple lunch of fried eggs on organic rye bread with salad, set in a picturesque green field like something out of the 1950s. I just wish this kind of good food was more readily available.

Failsafe weight loss

Many overweight people lose weight when they do the elimination diet, particularly if they have previously eaten processed foods high in hidden fats and sugars.

Food intolerance can contribute to obesity because food chemicals can be addictive and lead to food cravings. Within the first two weeks of eliminating problem foods, food 'addicts' will experience withdrawal symptoms, and gradually lose their cravings. Any of the usual culprits can be involved, from flavour enhancers (600 numbers) and artificial colours, to salicylates, wheat and milk. Although fruit and vegetables are generally considered the key to losing weight, some people with salicylate sensitivity actually gain weight during their salicylate challenge because their salicylate-induced food cravings make them over-eat.

Food chemicals can cause appetite disturbance. Skipping breakfast, shown to be associated with obesity, is often due to salicylate sensitivity or other food intolerances. When children or adults do the elimination diet, normal eating patterns can appear.

Hints for happy weight loss
• keep a food and exercise diary – research shows this is the single most effective way to lose weight and readers are already doing that • record your weight once

a week • reduce portion sizes to two thirds your normal serve • serve food in smaller plates and bowls • keep it simple – research shows that variety, even different varieties of pasta, will encourage people to eat more • avoid flavour enhancers and added flavours that make food taste irresistible • limit sugar to a one sweet treat per day because sweeteners will make you eat about 10 per cent more than the same meal without sweeteners • eat and drink only while seated at a table • limit TV viewing because your body goes into a state of semi-hibernation and burns fewer calories • avoid TV advertisements about food – watch videos or tape your favourite programs and fast-forward the ads • eat at home and prepare your own meals because processed food is higher in fat • choose whole foods and grains rather than processed foods because wholefoods have a lower glycaemic index so make you feel full for longer • exercise every day because exercise is an appetite suppressant • read slimming magazines instead of indulgence columns • limit alcohol and drink to after rather than before meals to maintain control • limit fats and fatty or fried foods • don't buy unsuitable foods because your home should be a failsafe low-fat haven from the temptations of the world • set a target weight and ask your family and friends for support, not sabotage, so that your success is their success.

A sample failsafe 1200 calorie menu and exercise plan

Howard and I have used this plan successfully. For the first few days, eat your usual quantities of these foods, then reduce the portion sizes.

Breakfast • ½ cup rolled oats or millet (200 calories) • half a drained canned pear (40) • 2 tbsp yoghurt (30) • low fat milk or soymilk (55) • total 325 calories.

During the day • 2 salad sandwiches or equivalent: 4 slices of bread (wholemeal if tolerated, no butter (280)) • 1 egg or 100 g lean chicken (or water-packed tuna if amines are permitted) or kidney and other beans (110) • salad vegetables, e.g. lettuce, finely sliced cabbage, celery, chives, shallots – beetroot, asparagus, carrot, corn (all salicylates) as permitted (50) • for me, a gluten-free lunch, see slimmer's salad following • total 440 calories.

Afternoon tea • 1 cup red lentil and vegetable soup (Red Soup) • total 75 calories.

Dinner • 150 g kidney beans or 150 g grilled fresh white fish, or 100 g lamb steak or 100 g chicken fillet (225) • ½ medium potato, ½ medium choko, 2 medium Brussels sprouts, green beans, steamed cabbage (100) • 2 tbsp Vaalia or soy yoghurt, or 1 tbsp pear ketchup, or Robin's dressing (30) • total 355 calories

GRAND TOTAL • 1200 calories.

Extras • water, decaf coffee or hot carob with low fat milk (22 calories each) • raw vegetables – celery, lettuce, shredded cabbage and carrot without dressing (negligible) • Saltine or Salada crackers (30 each) • peeled pear or dried pear snack (70).

Exercise can give you bonus calories. You can work out how many calories you have to spend and what to spend it on by using a book such as Allan Borushek's *Calorie and Fat Counter* or the automatic calorie counter at http://hp2010.nhl-bihin.net/menuplanner/menu.cgi. We spent our bonus calories from exercise on extras above, weekend meals for socializing such as a roast dinner, whisky and simple desserts such as lemon sago (p. 152), rice pudding (p. 144) or pear crumble (p. 135).

Slimmers' salad

Dried beans, lentils and chickpeas are a slimmer's best friend because they are low in fat, high in fibre and nutrition, and have a very low glycaemic index.

½ cup kidney or other beans
½ cup cooked green beans or other cold cooked permitted vegetables
1 cup of shallots, celery and cabbage
½ cup lettuce, torn up
1 tbsp Howard's bean paste (p. 106) or failsafe hummus (p. 189)
fresh chives, chopped
1 tsp parsley, finely chopped

Toss to mix. For people who don't like to eat raw cabbage due to issues with wind, the shallots, celery and cabbage can be stir-fried together in a little failsafe oil, or with leftovers from last night's dinner.

Travelling, camping and hiking

Airline foods

I once spent two hours on a flight with a toddler kicking the back of the seat next to me after eating the airline's coloured snacks. There are no failsafe meal options. I always request gluten-free and sometimes it's suitable, but mostly it's a plate of high salicylate fruit, so I always carry my own food. Over the years we have carried stacks of home-made chicken salad sandwiches, boiled eggs, cookies, crackers, home-made muffins, rice cakes, PBJs (p. 218), cooked rice, raw cashews, trail mix (p. 217), carob-coated buckwheat, water and soymilk poppers. At airports, decaffeinated coffee, bananas, Delicious apples, yoghurt and mango smoothies are generally available. We always avoid additives, but have had to compromise with salicylates and amines – and paid for it later.

Travelling

Holidays are a time of reduced stress and higher tolerance but are more enjoyable without food reactions. The food in some countries is more naturally failsafe than in others, with the USA the worst and – in our experience – Indonesia and Nepal the best (see the 'Additives around the world' factsheet on www.

fedup.com.au for more details about international failsafe travel). The easiest way to travel in countries with high additive usage is to self-cater. This can be through camping, motor homes, hostels with cooking facilities, cabins, motels with barbeque facilities or microwave ovens, holiday apartments, or by carrying your own backpacker's camping gas stove. Have cereal for breakfast, pack your own lunch with snacks (sandwiches, boiled eggs, cookies), and a quick meal for dinner is manageable. If eating out, steak with jacket potatoes and undressed salad, or fresh fish, are some of the safest meals.

For motel-style travel with minimum cooking facilities, we take or buy rolled oats, millet meal (can be cooked in a microwave), rice cakes (can be crumbled for breakfast cereal), Nuttelex, bread, tinned pears, pear jam, cashew paste (for PBJs, p. 218), trail mix, A2 milk (frozen) or soymilk, a few muffins or biscuits from home, and eggs (you can cook eggs in a microwave in a plastic poached egg cooker, available in any shop that sells microwave cookware). It's worth carrying a microwave container for cooking vegetables such as potatoes, cabbage and Brussels sprouts. You can also cook rice in a microwave, see instructions on back of packet. If there are no cooking facilities we sometimes eat out of tins – kidney beans with peas and corn over cous-cous or polenta (gluten-free but contains salicylates) with boiling water poured over. If driving, you can take your own precooked and frozen meals such as lamb stew (p. 85) or chicken and chickpeas (p. 99) that will last two days in the Esky.

Camping and hiking

The difference between camping and hiking is that campers have access to fresh foods, including bread, fruit and vegetables and meat for barbeques. We have managed many five-day hikes for a family of four by using a home dehydrator to dry our own failsafe mince, Red Soup and pears (see following recipe). Theoretically, home-dried mince should be high in amines but I never have any problems while hiking. Perhaps the lack of stress balances out the amines.

We carry the following foods: rolled oats, leftover cooked rice for gluten-free, preservative-free bread and crackers (e.g. Saladas), rice cakes (gluten-free), mild cheese for those who manage it, sticks of celery, shallots, lettuce or cabbage for the first few days, hikers' tubes of failsafe margarine (p. 183), magic spread (p. 185) or pear jam (p. 186), hard-boiled eggs for the first two days, rice and pasta, home-dried mince made with celery, shallots and red kidney beans, home-dried vegetable soup (made with shallots, cabbage, leeks, celery, red lentils), muesli bars (p. 159), Anzac cookies (p. 168), carob powder or decaffeinated coffee for drinks, carob blocks and carob-coated buckwheat crisps for snacks, toffees or caramel fudge (p. 179), and failsafe trail mix (following). Magic spread (tastes like lemon butter) keeps better than butter and is good on crackers, stale bread and rice cakes. Gluten-free slices (p. 239) can be stacked and wrapped tightly in two layers of foil then plastic-bagged.

Dinky di damper

Traditionally, damper is a round unyeasted bread like a cottage loaf cooked in a Dutch oven or the coals of a fire.

2 cups self-raising flour or gluten-free
  flour
enough water to make a dough

In a billy, mix flour and water together to make a workable dough. We make ours fairly flat and rectangular to fit into a meat grill and toast it over hot coals on both sides until done. Serve with butter or failsafe margarine (p. 183) and golden syrup, or for lunch with savoury fillings.

VARIATION • For doughboys, take a handful of dough and shape it over the end of a blunt stick about the shape of your thumb. Toast over coals until it is golden brown and sounds hollow when tapped, then slide off the stick and you will have a hot, delicious, round container waiting to be filled with butter or failsafe margarine (p. 183) and golden syrup.

Campfire potatoes

1 large potato per person
butter or failsafe margarine (p. 183)
foil for wrapping

Cut a triangular wedge out of the top of the potato and load up the hole with butter. Push the wedge back in and wrap the potato in two layers of foil. Put the potatoes up close to the campfire coals, and move them around the coals so they get roasted evenly. Cook until potatoes are hot and soft. Takes about 40 minutes.

'While on a camping trip I discovered that UHT cream makes great potato casserole, luscious quiche, gluten-free pastry and pancakes with no need for melted butter, and heaps of other uses.' Failsafe camper.

Failsafe S'mores

'This is similar to what Americans call "S'mores", which are a popular campfire treat. We roast the marshmallow over the campfire on a stick, then place it on a piece of chocolate between two graham crackers. The warm marshmallow helps melt the chocolate. My son insists on them when we go camping, so I've had to find an acceptable failsafe substitute.' Reader from USA, visiting Australia

Arnott's Milk Arrowroot biscuits
white marshmallows
carob buttons

Toast marshmallow on a stick over the fire. Add a carob button and squash between two biscuits.

Failsafe trail mix

Equal quantities raw cashews, chopped dried pears and Chickadamias (p. 55). You can add chopped carob pods and, if you can tolerate amines, additive-free dried bananas and pawpaw; see Product Updates on www.fedup.com.au.

Home-dried pears

Make sure pears are very soft and ripe. Pears that are like hard little rocks will cause problems.

2 cans (each 825 g) pears in syrup, or 1 kg peeled, ripe, juicy pears

Cut pears in halves and slice across, making slices 3–4 mm thick. This quantity will fill three trays. Run dehydrator at 55°C until pears are thoroughly dried (12–24 hours).

> Unsulphited peeled dried pears are available from specialty stores. See Shopping List.

PBJs

The extraordinary Larapinta Trail – 230 kms and 19 days through the desert to Alice Springs – has been our toughest challenge yet. We left food drops every four or five days before starting, so there was no possibility of fresh food. An American teenager insisted that PBJs were the ideal trail food. Peanut butter and jelly sandwiches, that is. He was right. This failsafe version is highly portable and tastes good no matter how old or hot they are.

2 rice cakes
cashew paste (p. 187) or Freedom Foods soybutter (may not be suitable for your
   supervised elimination diet)
pear jam (p. 186)

VARIATION • With gluten: make with failsafe fresh bread when available.

Failsafe gardening

A hundred years ago most families grew their own fruit and vegetables, but today only 4 per cent of the food grown in Australia is grown in backyards. Some reasons for growing your own:

- The flavour and nutritional content of organic vegetables freshly picked from your own garden are better than supermarket produce.
- Children are more likely to eat vegetables they have picked themselves.
- Gardening gives you access to old-fashioned varieties no longer sold in super-markets that may be lower in salicylates.

Some scientific studies found that organic produce may be higher in salicylates than supermarket produce, but we have noticed it depends on the variety.

What you grow is determined by your tolerance and climate, in our case now a mixture of tropical and temperate. We plant only produce on the low to moderate end of the salicylate scale to fit in with our tolerances.

Vegetables

We are currently growing or about to grow the vegetables we can eat in unlimited amounts • green beans • shallots • chives • parsley (mostly for garnish) • iceberg lettuce • chokos • potatoes • leeks • green peas (everyone in our family can tolerate them) • cabbages • Brussels sprouts – although we haven't worked out how to grow these organically. We also grow in very small quantities (so we aren't tempted to overeat) • corn – fresh corn on the cob is lower in salicylates than tinned corn • carrots • pumpkins – last summer we grew a Jap by mistake but are about to try a butternut.

Fruit

We are currently growing • rhubarb (a plant with stalks like celery that does well in a temperate climate) • tamarillo (a small tree that prefers a subtropical climate with no frost and is supposed to bear prolific fruit for 3 months of the year, although ours has just started flowering for the first time) • persimmon (an old favourite of mine, if we get too many we can dry them as is done in Japan) • loquat (like a mild apricot – grows easily in Australia) • mangoes (we've planted Kensington Pride, the best of all mangoes in my opinion, but mangoes do much better in a full tropical climate) • pawpaw (papaya) (we are careful to plant the yellow variety as we have found the red variety contains salicylates as well as amines) • bananas (we haven't yet been able to find the small old-fashioned variety with seeds that we've eaten in Bali and Nepal, which seem to be low in both salicylates and amines; sugar bananas – ladyfingers – grow well locally but we've avoided these because they are high in salicylates and have affected us very badly in the past).

Experiments with tomatoes

Like most readers, we miss tomatoes. After 12 years without, we are experimenting with heirloom varieties that we have eaten successfully in developing countries. A prolific cherry tomato that literally grew as a weed was so high in salicylates we had to give all the tomatoes away. So far our greatest success has been with a low-acid yellow egg-shaped heirloom tomato called Ivory. Salicylates are much lower when the tomato is picked very ripe, but then amines can be more of a problem for me, so it's all a balancing act. I peel everything thickly, organic or not, because salicylates are concentrated in the skin zone – in the peel, just under the peel and in the outer leaves of leafy greens like lettuces. For us it's a real treat to have a few slices of fresh homegrown tomato on sandwiches or pizza very occasionally.

Overall, we plant very little other than low salicylate crops, so the temptation to eat too much is limited by the small crop and short growing season – and we are always ready to freeze, dry or give away excess. We don't grow a lot, but what we do eat we really enjoy.

Medications and remedies

Medications are supposed to make us better, but all drugs have side effects, some of them serious. In the US, over a quarter of a million people per year die from the adverse effects of health care, mostly the unintended side effects of prescribed medication. People with food intolerance are particularly vulnerable. As with the side effect of food chemicals, most patients and doctors do not recognise symptoms as drug side effects because they can occur hours, days or longer after starting the drug.

Drugs containing salicylates

If you are sensitive to salicylates, be careful of any drug that lists any kind of salicylate, for example • in many prescription and over-the-counter medications including aspirin, nonsteroidal antiflammatory drugs • many painkillers (not paracetamol) • oil of wintergreen • any medications or skin creams containing salicylates or with a warning for asthmatics in the Consumer Medicine Information sheet • arthritis creams • sports creams like Dencorub • Vicks Vaporub • teething gel and oral gels like Bonjela and Ora-Sed • wart removers • acne cleansers and wipes • some insect repellants. Herbal remedies like echinacea and herbal preparations in multivitamin supplements can cause salicylate reactions, and our family members have had reactions to homeopathic remedies, although it is hard to see how there could be anything at the dilutions used.

Drugs containing Amines

Drugs that can contain amines include • over-the-counter cold tablets, decongestants, nasal drops or sprays • some pain relievers • general and local anaesthetics • some antidepressants.

Additives in drugs

Syrup medications typically contain benzoate preservatives, concentrated flavours such as cherry or menthol that are extremely high in salicylates, and sometimes unlisted artificial colours as well. One mother who had to give antibiotic syrup to her active 4 year-old-complained: 'It is turning him into one very nasty tantrum-throwing s---'.

What you can do

- Don't take medication unless it is really necessary (asthma drugs are necessary).
- Read the consumer medicine information sheet (CMI) from your pharmacist or on the internet, search for 'name of the drug' and 'ingredients' or 'adverse'.
- Assume that any new symptom you develop after starting a new drug – including worsening asthma – might be caused by the drug.
- White tablets (e.g. paracetamol, antihistamines) can be cut into smaller doses. You can discuss the dose for your child with your doctor or pharmacist. The failsafebaby group has a useful recipe for children's paracetamol.
- Mix contents of coloured capsules (e.g. antibiotics) with golden syrup or a tablespoon of ice-cream that numbs the tastebuds. If using adult capsules, your doctor can advise you about the dose for your child.
- Wash hard coloured coatings off pills by rubbing gently under the tap.
- See Vitamin icypoles recipe (p. 68).

People will get well from most illnesses – including colds and flu – without medications. The body itself can usually fight off sickness with rest and good food and perhaps some simple remedies.

Some natural alternatives (always consult your doctor when necessary)

• **Colds, flu, cough:** Drink lots of water, breathe hot water vapours to loosen mucus (head over a basin of very hot water, make a tent with a towel), see hot lemon drink (p. 224). • **Sore throat:** Gargle hot salt water. • **To soothe a ticklish throat:** Suck slowly on a hard sweet like a Werther's Original butter candy.

• **Stuffed-up nose:** Sniff up warm salt water. • **Fever:** Rest, drink plenty of liquids. The latest medical thinking is that fever is the body's way to heal itself. Let the fever run its course. • **High fever:** cool the body with tepid water. Use plain white paracetamol tablets when necessary. • **Sores, pimples:** Scrub with soap and water.

• **Itching, burning, irritations of the skin:** For relief, cold compresses. See soothing failsafe creams for itchy rashes in the 'Eczema' factsheet on www.fedup. com.au. • **Minor burns:** Hold in cold water for ten minutes. • **Cold sores**: Hold ice on blister for one hour at first sign. • **Diarrhoea:** Drink plenty of liquids. When the person is vomiting or feels too sick to eat, give 'sips and chips' – sips of rehydration drink (1 litre water, 2 tbsp sugar, ¼ tsp salt, ¼ tsp sodium bicarbonate; or Gastrolyte) and water, and chips of ice. Progress to clear soups (chicken, meat, bean), icypoles, plain boiled rice. Slowly introduce crackers, bananas, stewed apple, pawpaw, potato; progress to chicken, lean meat, beans, lentils, eggs, no fatty foods. If wheat has ever been a problem, avoid it during diarrhoeal illness. A backpacker's trick I learned in India is 24 hours with nothing but boiled water and boiled rice. • **Constipation:** Drink lots of water and magic cordial, eat more fibre in All Bran (if tolerated), pears, celery, cabbage, other vegetables including dried beans, cashews, rhubarb (salicylates, but the laxative effect is well-known in Chinese medicine), rolled oats, rice bran, gelatine in jellies (p. 153) and marshmallows (p. 173). Distinguish between true constipation (hard, dry stools due to lack of fibre and fluids) and bowels 'set like concrete' due to food intolerance (faeces are sticky and hard to clean up). Use a mixture of rice bran and psyllium husks sprinkled over cereal when needed but also identify and avoid food chemicals that cause the problem (salicylates, additives, amines).

Doctor's Orders
This healing dish appeared on a menu in a trekkers' cafe in Nepal where travellers' diarrhoea is a common complaint.

steamed white rice
steamed vegetables (potatoes, cabbage, green beans)
filtered water

Eat and drink only this for 24 hours.

Hot lemon drink

A soothing drink for colds and flu.

1 mug water
1–2 tbsp magic cordial base (use the
  strong option with 1 tsp citric acid,
  p. 63)
1 pinch plain white ascorbic acid or
  calcium ascorbate (Vitamin C) powder

Heat water in microwave. Add
magic cordial base and Vitamin C.
Stir well.

Antidote for food reactions

Readers have noticed that certain over-the-counter remedies can ease the symptoms of food intolerance for a short time. Calcium supplements (plain Caltrate calcium carbonate) or antacid powder (Eno's: sodium bicarbonate, sodium carbonate, citric acid) can reduce hyperactivity, reflux, stomach aches, irritability, restless legs and difficulty falling asleep. Calming effects begin almost immediately and last for about an hour. As with any medication, there can be side effects so it is essential to stay within recommended doses and best to use only when necessary. Large doses of Eno's will result in diarrhoea so I generally take a half teaspoon or less.

What about nutrition?

Food additives can have anti-nutritional effects. For example, sulphite preservatives (220–228) are known to inactivate folate and Vitamin B1 (thiamine) in the body, with results severe enough to cause death from thiamine deficiency in pet cats and dogs. When families go additive-free, the nutrients in their foods will be more available to them.

If you are prepared to eat permitted vegetables such as Brussels sprouts and hummus, failsafe eating can be very nutritious. An analysis of three-year-old Ethan's menu (p. 39) found that his daily intake of calcium, iron, A, B and C vitamins and other nutrients were all at the recommended levels and folate was higher than the recommended level. One of his favourite meals – Darani's amazing chicken noodle stew (p. 71) – which he ate nearly every day, was found to be highly nutritious.

Vitamin C and Vitamin A can be low for children who can't eat fruit and won't eat vegetables; calcium can be low for children who are dairy-free; and thiamine and iron can be low for children who are gluten-free, especially for vegetarians. If your children are on a restricted diet, you need to have their nutrition checked by a dietitian.

The recent finding that one Red Delicious apple contains as much antioxidant as 1.5 kg of Vitamin C through other antioxidant compounds, and that red kidney beans contain four times more antioxidants than Red Delicious apples, indicates that current Recommended Daily Intakes (RDI) may not be the whole story. It seems logical to eat as many fruit and vegetables from the low end of the range as you can tolerate.

Children's eating habits generally become much healthier after a few weeks and there are numerous hints about how to get vegetables into children throughout this book. Calcium supplements or fortified soy and rice milks are available for those who are dairy-free, and people who are gluten-free are encouraged to eat two serves per day of meat or eggs to keep up iron and thiamine levels.

There are some low-dose multivitamin and mineral supplements that will fit into failsafe eating (see Shopping List). After challenges and establishing a routine, you can encourage more vegetable eating (p. 102) and visit your dietitian for a nutrition check. The recommended daily intake for Vitamin C in Australia for children ranges from 30–50 mg per day. Vitamin C is found in breastmilk, all fresh fruit and vegetables and fortified cereals like Rice Bubbles (10 mg per serve). The amount of Vitamin C in an average failsafe day (potato, green beans, cabbage, lettuce, celery, pears) is more than double the RDI. Two medium potatoes or one serve of Brussels sprouts equals the RDI. Vitamin C is reduced by storage and overcooking. Large doses of Vitamin C supplements may be counterproductive as salicylates and Vitamin C compete for excretion in the kidney. This means that Vitamin C can have the effect of 'damming up' salicylates and causing them to stay in the body much longer, with increased adverse effects.

Calcium

The recommended daily intake for calcium is from 800–1500 mg a day. There is a theory that we need only 200–300 mg daily if we avoid calcium depleters such as • phosphates – in cola drinks and excess animal products

• sodium, especially salt hidden in processed foods (e.g. a bowl of cornflakes contains more salt than a packet of salty crisps) • caffeine • animal protein, including dairy products • tobacco • and a sedentary lifestyle. Some readers have reported constipation or diarrhoea from calcium supplements, so I prefer to buy calcium fortified soymilk or ricemilk than to take calcium as a supplement, but have used it as a chewable antidote (see above). Check with your dietitian or doctor regarding dosages for children.

Low chemical sources of major nutrients	
Nutrient	**Food sources**
Protein	meats, fish, poultry, eggs, dairy foods
Fat	oils, margarine, meat, eggs, dairy foods
Carbohydrates	rice, potato, bread, pasta, cereals, white sugar
Fibre	wholegrain cereals, wholegrain bread, cabbage, Brussels sprouts, lentils, beans, pears
Essential fatty acids (omega-3 fats)	canola, sunflower and safflower oils and margarine, flaxseed oil, egg yolk
Natural antioxidants	foods containing vitamins A and C (below) and Vitamin E (canola, sunflower and safflower oils and margarine)
Vitamin A	dairy foods, eggs, margarine, fish, lettuce, Brussels sprouts, beans, cabbage
Vitamin B1	breads (brown and white), brown rice, wholemeal pasta, fortified breakfast cereals
Vitamin B12	meat, chicken, fish, eggs, milk
Other B vitamins	dairy products, meat, chicken, fish, lentils, wholegrain cereals
Vitamin C	potato, parsley, Brussels sprouts, cabbage, peas, swedes (rutabaga)
Folic acid	Brussels sprouts, lettuce, cabbage, lentils, pulses, wholegrain cereals, fortified breakfast cereals
Iron	meat, chicken, fish, eggs, lentils, wholegrain cereals
Calcium	dairy foods, calcium fortified soy products

Reproduced with permission from *Friendly Food* (by Anne Swain, Velencia Soutter and Robert Loblay, Murdoch Books Australia, 2004)

Changing nutrients

Changes in the way our food is produced and stored have led to decreases in essential nutrients. Comparisons of government food nutrition tables shows that in the last 50–60 years • the iron content of the average rump steak has fallen by 55 per cent • the iron content of milk has fallen by more than 60 per cent • the calcium content of cheddar cheese has fallen by 9 per cent • calcium, magnesium, sodium and copper levels in fruit have declined significantly • potassium, iron, magnesium and copper levels in vegetables have declined significantly • the vitamins in bagged salad are reduced significantly by storage • farmed fish are likely to have a poorer ratio of omega 3 fatty acids to omega 6 fatty acids compared with wild fish, especially if fish feed is based on soy.

It seems likely that our fruit and vegetables are only as good as the soil they are grown in and our animal foods are only as good as the food fed to the animals. Depletion of soil in farms that rely on synthetic fertilisers, and dilution of milk due to the use of high-yield A1 producing cows – compared to the much lower yield A2-producing cows – could be to blame. The message seems to be to choose more natural, old-fashioned, organic farming methods, and less processed foods wherever possible.

Experts recommend that women who are planning a pregnancy or who may become pregnant accidentally should take 400–500 µg daily folic acid supplements before conception and during the first three months of pregnancy to prevent neural tube defects.

Gluten-free Cooking

A tendency to gluten intolerance often runs in families and can develop after a gastro-intestinal infection at any time of life. It is not necessarily associated with diarrhoea and is often overlooked, as in this reader's story:

> 'My son has always been the quiet, dreamy type and was sometimes depressed. He improved a lot when we started the elimination diet, dairy-free and wheat-free, three years ago but he still had learning difficulties. When he was 7, we also eliminated gluten. The improvement was noticeable and within 4 weeks he was reading confidently. He also started gaining weight. We didn't think gluten would be a problem because he had no diarrhoea or stomach aches, although his father has irritable bowel and probably should avoid gluten too.'

It is possible to have gluten intolerance without coeliac disease, but if there is an indication of coeliac disease – such as a coeliac relative – blood tests are recommended before beginning an elimination diet because tests for coeliacs are unreliable in the absence of gluten.

Gluten is a protein that makes cereals like wheat stick together when cooked. It is present in • wheat in bread, flours, biscuits and baked goods • rye • oats unless certified gluten-free • barley • triticale, a wheat-like grain • malt made from the grains above and used in such products as soymilks, rice cereals and whisky • wheaten cornflour found in foods like baking powder, marshmallows, other confectionery and most baking powders • sauces • icing sugar mixture containing cornflour (pure icing sugar is okay) • some thickeners in processed foods, yoghurts, ice-cream and cream • spelt, an early form of wheat with a different kind of gluten, although some people who are gluten intolerant say they can manage it.

Coeliac disease (CD) is a permanent autoimmune disorder in which the lining of the small intestine is damaged by exposure to gluten. Although the majority of coeliacs experience diarrhoea and abdominal complaints, other symptoms of CD include malabsorption especially of iron and folate, low calcium levels, easy bruising of the skin, mouth ulcers, miscarriages and infertility, skin rashes such as dermatitis herpetiformis, defects of dental enamel, altered mental alertness, bone and joint pains, poor weight gain and irritability in children, www.coeliac.org.au.

Failsafe gluten-free alternatives to wheat flours
• Amaranth • arrowroot • besan (chickpea) flour and other flours made from dried beans or lentils • buckwheat • millet • potato flour or starch • quinoa • rice • sago • soy • tapioca • cornflour or maize flour (see below).

Cornflour
Corn and corn products such as yellow cornmeal (polenta) are gluten-free but not permitted due to salicylates. 'Cornflour' can be made from wheat or corn, e.g. White Wings Wheaten cornflour contains gluten. If a product lists cornflour on the label, assume it is wheaten cornflour. Cornflour (maize starch, cornstarch) that is made from corn is permitted because it has been so highly refined that salicylates are no longer a problem.

Sulphites in gluten-free flours
Some crops, including corn, arrowroot, potatoes, sago and tapioca, are soaked during processing in a solution preserved with sulphur dioxide (220), and in rare cases sulphite residues can be enough to affect extra-sensitive consumers.

Gluten-free products

Look for the gluten-free sign, a crossed-out stalk of wheat. The gluten-free market is rapidly expanding with more palatable gluten-free products available on the market now than ever before (see Shopping List).

BREADS • commercial gluten-free breads, frozen breads, premixes and home-made (p. 234).

PASTA AND NOODLES • gluten-free pasta made from rice, buckwheat or soy (see p. 125 for failsafe pasta toppings) • rice noodles, bean vermicelli.

BREAKFASTS • rice cereals without malt, puffed rice, puffed millet or amaranth breakfast cereal (see gluten-free muesli, p. 159) • rolled rice or rolled soy flakes instead of rolled oats for porridge and baking, from health food stores (see gluten-free porridge, p. 32) • cooked brown or white rice with milk and sweetener • gluten-free pancakes (p. 236) • eggs on gluten-free toast • gluten-free toast and pear jam (p. 186) • fruit muffins, p. 161.

Some people are so sensitive to gluten that the smallest quantity will affect them, e.g. breadcrumbs in the family butter or toaster, wheat flour landing on foods while cooking for other members of the family.

RICE • rice: white or brown, short or long grain, glutinous or plain, but not flavoured rice such as basmati, jasmine or wild rice • rice bran • rice malt, which is gluten-free, unlike barley malt • rice crumbs, e.g. Casalare brand, are preservative-free, have an excellent texture and can be used instead of breadcrumbs or biscuit crumbs for dishes like schnitzel and cheesecake bases • rice paper from Chinese shops, e.g. for spring rolls.

GLUTEN-FREE FLOURS • There are some excellent gluten-free flours, pancake and pastry mixes (see Shopping List).

BAKING POWDER • Must be gluten-free, either Ward's brand or home-made. (p. 233).

SOYMILK • Some soymilks are labelled gluten-free, others contain ingredients such as maltodextrin (corn or wheat). While food scientists say that maltodextrin from wheat is so refined it is gluten-free, some coeliacs do not agree. See Shopping List for gluten-free soymilks.

FOOD ADDITIVES • The only food additives that may contain small amounts of gluten are thickeners in the range 1400–1450 (modified starch, dextrins) if made from wheat – this will be listed on the label – and in certain strong added savoury 'flavours' such as chicken. You can't find out what is in flavours because it is a trade secret, but they are not permitted for us anyway. Other additives, such as acidity regulators, anti-caking agents, bulking agents, emulsifiers, firming agents, foaming agents, gelling agents, glazing agents, humectants, propellants, raising agents and stabilisers, are permitted and gluten-free.

BISCUITS • Plain rice cakes (avoid corn or sesame flavours because of salicylates). • Buckwheat crispbreads. • Plain rice crackers should be okay but some 'plain' rice crackers list nucleotide flavour enhancers and many readers have reported problems with various brands (see Checklist of Common Mistakes). • Carob-coated rice or buckwheat cakes are gluten-free but not dairy-free. • Communion wafers: gluten-free wafers are available from coeliac centres.

> Carob-coated ricecakes and buckwheat crisps are handy for travelling but contain 17 per cent fat, most of it saturated. That's higher than in ice-creams.

OTHER • Ask your doctor and pharmacist for gluten-free medications. • Request gluten-free meals in restaurants (most chefs have a good understanding of gluten, unlike salicylates). • Request gluten-free meals on airlines, but you are likely to get a plate of high salicylate fruit – take your own food as a back-up.

Main meals
Meats, fish, chicken, vegetables, fruit and dairy products are gluten-free, so main meals such as stir-fries with rice, grills or roasts with vegetables, are gluten-free or can be made gluten-free with little effort. Problems are most likely to occur in sauces thickened with wheat flour and processed foods containing thickeners, see food additives above. Pasta and pizza require gluten-free alternatives.

Nutrition
Rice is the staple food for more than half the world's population, but a restricted diet of mainly white rice can be low in thiamine (Vitamin B1) and protein while brown rice contains phytic acid that can inhibit the body's ability to absorb calcium and zinc. Some dietitians recommend two serves of meat per day for people on a restricted gluten-free diet. Eating as widely as possible from permitted foods such as meat, seafood, eggs, dairy foods, chickpeas, beans, permitted vegetables, and grains or flours such as buckwheat, besan, millet, amaranth and soy, increases your range of nutrients. Xanthan gum can be a useful source of fibre for people who are gluten-free. Consult your dietitian.

Gluten-free cooking
These products replace the function of gluten in baked goods and are available in health-food stores • Xanthan gum, also called corn sugar gum (code 415) is a thickener made from corn sugar. • Guar gum (412) is an extract from the seeds of a member of the pea family native to India. It is high in fibre and can cause nausea, flatulence and abdominal cramps in large quantities or in extra-sensitive people. Xanthan gum is better tolerated. • Glucono-delta-lactone (GDL, 575) gives gluten-free products a smooth texture. Use about ½ tsp for an average cake, 1 tsp for a double pie crust and 2 tsp per loaf of bread.

Gluten-free baking powder

Ward's baking powder is gluten-free, or make your own:

2 tbsp sodium bicarbonate

4 tbsp cream of tartar

6 tbsp arrowroot

Put all in an airtight container, shake to mix. Note that sodium bicarbonate is also called soda bicarbonate, baking soda, bicarb soda and bi-carb soda.

Deborah's gluten-free flour mix

There are many excellent gluten-free flour mixes available, but people who need to avoid soy will need to make their own. Gluten-free flours generally work better in combination.

1 cup brown rice flour

½ cup potato flour

½ cup tapioca flour

2 tsp xanthan gum or glucono-delta-
  lactone (GDL) from health-food stores

FOR SELF-RAISING

2 tsp gluten-free baking powder

Mix ingredients well. Use in any recipe requiring self-raising flour. For one cup of wheat, substitute 1 cup of gluten-free flour mix plus 1 tbsp rice bran. If you can tolerate soy, it is best to add ½ cup of that also to increase nutrition (see next recipe). You can experiment with mixtures of flours.

Deborah's gluten-free flour mix with soy

1 cup cornflour

½ cup tapioca starch

½ cup brown rice flour

½ cup potato flour

½ cup soy flour

FOR SELF-RAISING

2 tsp xanthan gum or glucono-delta-lactone (GDL) from health-food stores

2 tsp gluten-free baking powder (above)

Gluten-free flour mix

Make up a large batch of this extra-nutritious mix and store in the freezer. Use like white flour.

3 cups white rice flour
1 cup brown rice flour
1 cup potato starch
1 cup tapioca starch
½ cup besan (chickpea) flour
½ cup buckwheat flour
1 cup soy flour (optional)
4 tsp xanthan or guar gum (optional)

Gluten-free bread

It is not possible to make gluten-free breads as good as wheat bread because gluten makes wheat pliable. Since baker's yeast does not always work well with gluten-free flours, some commercial gluten-free breads use baking powder rather than yeast. Gluten-free breads are often too soft, too heavy or too crumbly, and are usually better toasted. There are numerous brands of bread and premixes available in supermarkets and health-food stores. Because they vary so much, it is worth shopping around to find a brand that suits your family.

> Always read the label, as not all gluten-free products are permitted. Avoid gluten-free breads with calcium propionate (282), vinegar, wholemeal maize flour (cornflour or cornstarch is permitted, wholegrain corn or maize flour is not, due to salicylates), and any fruit breads.

Gluten, dairy, soy and yeast-free bread

This easy recipe is heavier than wheat bread but it keeps well, freezes well, can be thinly sliced and doesn't crumble like most gluten-free bread. I like it with failsafe hummus, lentil mash or pear jam.

3 cups riceflour

½ cup cornflour (from corn)

⅔ tbsp xanthan gum

2 tbsp caster sugar

1 tsp salt

1½ tsp sodium bicarbonate

2 tsp cream of tartar

300 ml lukewarm water

2 tbsp failsafe oil

2 eggs

Preheat oven to 200°C. Oil or line a small loaf tin with baking paper. Sift all dry ingredients into a large bowl. Beat the wet ingredients together and pour into a well in the bowl. Mix thoroughly with a wooden spoon. Scrape dough into tin and smooth with the spoon. Bake for about 40 minutes.

VARIATION • *Egg-free gluten-free bread:* Use 2 tsp Orgran egg replacer instead of eggs.

Other gluten-free recipes

Most of the recipes in this book are gluten-free or have gluten-free options. The recipes following are gluten-free but many can be made with wheat or eaten as is by people who don't have to avoid gluten.

Millet has been used in Africa and India as a staple food for thousands of years. It is one of the least allergenic grains and is highly nutritious with nearly 15 per cent protein, high amounts of fibre, B-complex vitamins including niacin, thiamine, and riboflavin, the essential amino acid methionine, lecithin, some vitamin E, and is particularly high in iron, magnesium, phosphorus and potassium. Like many otherwise healthy foods – including Brassica vegetables such as cabbage, soy beans and some fruit including pears – millet contains goitrogens, naturally occurring chemicals that can affect the functioning of the thyroid gland unless there is sufficient iodine in the diet. Dietary sources of iodine include seafood, dairy products, eggs, food grown near the coast, iodised salt and multivitamin supplements. Traditionally, millet is boiled as a grain-like rice, added to soups, cooked as a porridge and used as a flour in flat breads.

Millet porridge

½ cup millet meal per person, preferably
   freshly ground
1 cup water

Bring to boil in a saucepan and simmer for 2–3 minutes, stirring. Serve with pear and milk or yoghurt.

Gluten-free porridge

¼ cup soy or rice flakes per person
½ cup hot water or milk per person
pinch of salt

Place all ingredients in a saucepan, bring to the boil and simmer for 2–3 minutes. Serve with milk and a sweetener.

Gluten-free pancake for one

1 small egg
2 tbsp buckwheat flour or 2 tbsp commercial gluten-free
   mix or 2 tbsp Deborah's gluten-free flour
3 tbsp milk or milk substitute

Break egg into a cup or mug and beat with a fork. Add flour and mix well. Add milk and mix well with a fork or wand blender. Pour into an oiled hot frying pan and cook briefly on each side. Serve with butter or failsafe margarine (p. 183) and pure maple syrup, sugar and citric lemon juice (p. 194), soy yoghurt and pear puree, or savoury toppings.

Rice flour pikelets

1 cup rice flour
1 tsp xanthan gum
1 tsp gluten-free baking powder
2 tsp failsafe oil
1–2 eggs, optional, or replace with 1 tbsp
   failsafe oil per egg
⅔ cup rice milk or soymilk or A2 milk or
   milk

Mix dry ingredients thoroughly. With a fork, whisk in oil, eggs and milk together to form a spongy batter. Place spoonfuls in a hot frying pan, press to a uniform 5 mm thickness, turn over when fully risen. Serve hot or cold with butter. A very easy and reliable recipe.

Besan bombs

Good cold too, if they ever last that long.

⅔ cup besan (chickpea) flour

⅓ cup rice flour

½ tsp gluten-free baking powder

about ¾ cup water or home-made stock, as required

salt to taste

1 cup shallot or leek, very finely chopped

1 clove of garlic, crushed

failsafe oil for deep-frying

Combine flours, add liquid and mix until batter resembles a thick pancake mixture. Add vegetables. Heat enough oil for deep-frying in a deep fryer, wok or saucepan. When the oil is hot, drop in one small spoonful of batter at a time. The batter will cook into puffy balls in 2–3 minutes. Cook both sides until golden and slightly crisp on the outside. Drain well and serve as finger food or an accompaniment to a meal.

Rice hoppers

These southern Indian pancakes, also known as appams (pronounced *up-ums*) have a truly delicious flavour and texture that repays the preparation time. The mix can be frozen in batches or let stand in the fridge for later use.

2 cups plain white rice

1 cup water

1 tsp active dried baker's yeast

1 tbsp sugar

3 tbsp extra water, warm

2 eggs

⅓ tsp salt

1 tbsp extra sugar

⅓ cup extra water

failsafe oil (p. 184) for cooking

Rinse the rice several times then cover with water to a depth of 4 cm and leave to stand overnight or for at least 8 hours. Drain and place rice in blender with 1 cup water and blend to a fine paste, which will still be a bit gritty. Mix yeast, sugar and warm water, allow to stand for 10 minutes until fermenting, then stir into the rice paste. Set aside, covered, for 6 hours. Beat eggs lightly, mix with salt, sugar and extra water, then stir thoroughly into fermented batter, which will have a consistency like a thin pancake. Heat frying pan to medium, lightly oil, pour in ⅓ cup of batter and swirl to a diameter of about 15 cm. Cook for about 3 minutes without turning, when it will be brown and slightly crispy underneath and dry on top. Best fresh: serve immediately with a smear of pear ketchup, or pear jam and yoghurt, or any savoury or sweet topping. Unusual for gluten-free, they are even delicious plain!

Mini chicken pizzas

1 egg for each pizza
1 tsp gluten-free flour per egg
salt to taste
failsafe oil (p. 184)
finely chopped chives
cooked chopped chicken

Put eggs, flour, salt and chives in a bowl. Beat until fluffy. Put egg rings into a lightly oiled frying pan and allow rings to get quite hot. Put some chicken into each ring then pour the egg mixture into rings almost to the top. Allow to fry 3–4 minutes, then place frying pan under a griller until cooked on top.

Pancakes with gluten-free self-raising flour

1 egg
1 cup gluten-free self-raising flour
  (p. 233)
1 cup or more of milk or soymilk or
  ricemilk or water

Mix together in blender, add more liquid if needed to make a batter with the consistency of thick cream. Heat a heavy based frying pan to medium heat and brush with failsafe oil or margarine (p. 184). Pour just enough mixture to cover the base thinly. When top of pancake is just dry, flip over with an egg slice. Brown quickly and serve immediately.

Gluten-free slice

Children will probably prefer this with rice flakes. For a really chewy, wholegrain texture, use soy flakes.

1 cup gluten-free self-raising flour (p. 233)

2 cups rolled rice flakes or rolled soy flakes

½ cup sugar

75 g butter or failsafe margarine (p. 183)

2 tbsp golden syrup

water if needed

Mix together flour, rolled rice and sugar. Melt butter and golden syrup together and add to mixture. Stir to combine. Add water if mixture needs to be wetter. Press into a greased slice tin and bake at 160°C for 20 minutes or until golden brown.

Muesli bars (p. 159)

Yum balls (p. 158)

Pear and apple shortcake squares (p. 136)

Muesli slice

A chewy, high-fibre wheat-free or gluten-free slice.

1 cup rolled oats (for gluten-free use rolled rice or rolled soy flakes)

1 cup rice bran

1 cup oatbran (for gluten-free use extra cup of rice bran)

1½ cups brown rice flour

½ cup cornflour

½ cup tapioca starch

½ cup brown sugar

½ cup white sugar

1 tsp baking powder

1 tsp xanthan gum

300 g butter or failsafe margarine (p. 183)

3 tbsp golden syrup

Combine dry ingredients and sugar. Melt butter and golden syrup. Mix into the dry ingredients. Press into a slice tray and bake for 20 minutes at 180°C. Cut while still warm into bars or rectangles. Leave to cool before removing from tray.

Madeira cake

175 g softened failsafe margarine
  (p. 183).
¾ cup sugar
¼ tsp citric acid
3 eggs
1½ cups gluten-free flour (Deborah's
  gluten-free flour mix, p. 233)
1 tsp xanthan gum
1 tsp gluten-free baking powder

Cream butter and sugar until light and fluffy. Add citric acid. Beat eggs until thick in separate bowl. Sift flours and baking powder together. Add to cream mixture alternately with egg. Spoon mix into greased 20 cm square tin. Or double and do in a sponge roll tin. Bake at 180°C for 40 minutes. Leave in the tin for 10 minutes before turning out on the rack. Ice with 'lemon' icing (p. 197).

Deborah's 'chocolate' cake

175 g softened butter or failsafe
  margarine (p. 183)
1¾ cups sugar
3 eggs
¼ cup carob powder
2 cups of Deborah's gluten-free flour mix
  (p. 233)
2 tsp xanthan gum
2 tsp gluten-free baking powder
1 cup milk or soymilk or ricemilk
carob icing (p. 166)

Cream butter and sugar until light and fluffy. Add eggs, one at a time, beating well after each addition. Sift dry ingredients. Add to creamed mixture alternately with milk. Pour mix into two round greased cake tins. Bake at 180°C for 30 minutes or until cake springs back when touched. Leave in tin for 10 minutes before turning out. When cold, ice with carob icing.

VARIATION • Make as patty cakes, baked for 10–15 minutes, and put an unflavoured carob button on top of each, or chocolate melts (amines) on top for birthday parties.

Sticky gingerbread cake

A moist cake great for school lunches, with no ginger of course.

125 g butter or failsafe margarine (p. 183)

¾ cup golden syrup

¾–1 cup caster sugar

2 cups of Deborah's gluten-free flour mix (p. 233)

2 eggs

1 cup of milk or soymilk or ricemilk

2 tsp gluten-free baking powder

Combine butter and syrup in a large pan and stir over low heat without boiling until butter has melted. Add sugar, flour, eggs and milk and beat until smooth. Pour into a lined 20 × 30 cm pan and bake until done, about 50–60 minutes at 160°C. Test for doneness with a skewer. Allow to cool before icing or dust with icing sugar.

Melt and mix coffee cake

125 g butter or failsafe margarine (p. 183)

⅔ cup brown sugar

⅓ cup caster sugar

½ cup milk or soymilk or ricemilk

2 tsp decaf coffee powder

2 eggs

1½ cups of Deborah's gluten-free flour mix (p. 233)

1 tsp gluten-free baking powder

COFFEE ICING

2 tbsp butter or failsafe margarine (p. 183)

½ tsp decaf coffee powder

¼ cup warm milk or soymilk or ricemilk

1½ cups pure icing sugar

Combine butter, sugars, milk and coffee in a medium saucepan. Stir over a low heat without boiling until butter is melted. Stand 10 minutes. Stir in eggs and flour. Pour into a greased or baking-paper-lined loaf tin. Bake at 180°C for 30 to 40 minutes. Cool on rack and ice.

ICING: heat butter in microwave until just softened, no more. Dissolve coffee powder in milk. Sift icing sugar into butter and add enough of the coffee/milk mixture to make a spreadable icing. Use plain icing if your children don't like the coffee flavour.

Andra's honey roll (p. 163).

Gluten-free plain cakes

½ cup brown rice flour

½ cup soy flour

½ cup arrowroot

3 tsp baking powder

⅔ cup sugar

⅓ cup failsafe oil (p. 184)

⅓ cup soymilk or water

2 eggs

Mix together dry ingredients in bowl. Add rest of ingredients and stir together. Mix with electric beaters for 3 minutes. Bake in a loaf tin for 40–50 minutes at 180°C or in patty cases for 15–20 minutes.

Cornflour sponge

1 cup cornflour

½ tsp sodium bicarbonate

1 tsp cream of tartar

¾ cup caster sugar

4 eggs

Preheat oven to 180°C. Grease and dust two 20 cm round tins with cornflour. Sift together cornflour and rising agents, twice. Separate eggs. Beat egg whites on high speed in clean, dry bowl until quite stiff. Add sugar gradually, keeping mixer speed constant. Add egg yolks one at a time on slower speed, beating well after each addition. Sift cornflour mixture all at once onto top of egg mixture. Stir in gently but thoroughly with spoon. Divide mixture between tins and bake for approximately 20 minutes. Sandwich together with honey roll filling (p. 163) and sprinkle top with icing sugar. Or spread pear jam (p. 186) and top with whipped cream.

Carob lamingtons (p. 165)

Carrot cake (p. 162)

Trifle (p. 166)

Weekly muffins

'I make muffins once a week. Sometimes I replace some of the milk with pear syrup and add diced pears or other fruit. After about 2 months the diet became our normal diet and after nearly 6 months it has been worth it.' Reader, Sydney

2 cups rice flour or other gluten-free flour
½ cup sugar
¾ tsp salt
2 tsp gluten-free baking powder
1 tsp xanthan gum or guar gum
1¼ cups milk or soymilk
1 egg
3 tbsp oil or melted butter or failsafe
  margarine (p. 183)

Combine all ingredients. Place scoops of mixture into well-oiled muffin trays. Bake at 180°C for 10–12 minutes. Ice with white icing (optional).

Gingerbread muffins

1 cup brown rice flour
½ cup potato flour
½ cup cornflour
2 tsp xanthan gum
1 tsp gelatine
1½ tsp gluten-free baking power
1½ tsp sodium bicarbonate
½ tsp salt
2 small eggs, lightly beaten
⅔ cup brown sugar
1 cup pear puree
½ cup golden syrup
3 tablespoons failsafe oil (p. 184)

Preheat oven to 180°C. Oil muffin tins (12 very large muffins) or equivalent. Combine dry ingredients in a small bowl. In another bowl, combine egg, brown sugar, pear puree, golden syrup and oil. Stir in dry ingredients until just moist. Spoon batter into tins. Bake for 15–20 minutes or until cooked. Ice with plain white or citric acid flavoured icing (p. 197) if required.

Self-saucing carob fudge pudding

One of the favourite recipes of the failsafe email discussion group, this very rich, very sweet pudding works well with plain wheat flour too. It can be cooked in individual soufflé dishes.

SPONGE MIXTURE

1 cup gluten-free flour

2 tsp gluten-free baking powder

1 tbsp carob powder

¾ cup white sugar

½ cup milk or soymilk or rice milk

2 tbsp melted butter or failsafe margarine (p. 183)

SAUCE

1 cup sugar

4 tbsp carob powder

2 cups boiling water

Preheat oven to 180°C. For the sponge, sift flour, baking powder and carob powder into bowl. Add sugar, milk and melted butter, mix until smooth. Pour into greased 20 cm pan. For the sauce, mix sugar, carob and boiled water. Gently pour over the top of the sponge, do not stir in. The sponge rises to the top as it cooks, and the fudge is at the bottom. Bake for 20–30 minutes.

Butterscotch pudding

60 g failsafe margarine or ¼ cup failsafe oil (p. 184)

1 cup rice flour

½ tsp xanthan gum

2 tsp gluten-free baking powder

¾ cup sugar

pinch salt

½ cup soymilk or water

1 egg, beaten

butterscotch sauce (p. 155)

Melt margarine, add dry ingredients, milk and egg and mix well. Place in greased dish. Pour sauce on top. Another option is to sprinkle ½ cup brown sugar over cake and 1 cup boiling water over the brown sugar immediately before baking to make self-saucing pudding. Bake at 180°C for 30–40 minutes.

Gluten-free carob and cashew brownies

125 g softened failsafe margarine
  (p. 183)
1 cup sugar
1 egg
¾ cup brown rice flour
½ cup tapioca flour
½ cup cornflour
1½ tsp xanthan gum
1 tsp gluten-free baking powder
pinch salt
1 tbsp carob powder
¾ cup chopped raw cashew

Cream butter and sugar until light and fluffy. Add egg and beat well. Sift dry ingredients, mix into creamed mixture. Add cashews and mix well. Roll teaspoons full of mixture into balls. Place on a greased oven tray. Flatten with a fork. Bake at 180°C for 15 minutes. Makes 30. Note that cooking raw cashews will increase amine content.

Butterscotch biscuits (p. 168)

Lazy biscuits

They are called this because they are easy to make in big batches.

250 g butter or failsafe margarine
  (p. 183)
1 cup sugar
1 tin sweetened condensed milk (400 g)
3 cups rice flour
2 cups soy flour
3 tsp sodium bicarbonate
3 tsp cream of tartar

Preheat oven to 180°C and grease several oven trays. Cream butter and sugar, add milk and beat until creamy. Sift dry ingredients together (or 5 cups self-raising flour if not gluten-free) and beat in. Can be plain, or jam drops with pear jam (p. 186), or press flat with a fork and sprinkle with sugar. Bake about 15 minutes or until golden.

Rice flour biscuits

1½ cups brown rice flour
1 tsp gluten-free baking powder
1½ tbsp arrowroot
125 g failsafe margarine (p. 183)
½ cup sugar
up to ⅓ cup water

Mix rice flour, arrowroot, sugar and baking powder. Mix in butter with fork, or rub in lightly, until a fine texture. Add enough water to make a soft dough. Form into balls and flatten slightly. Place on oven tray and press lightly with fork. Bake for 15 minutes at 200°C. Makes about 30. These can be served plain, iced, or joined in pairs. Make the icing slightly creamier than usual by adding a little extra margarine and beating well.

VARIATION • For a different texture, puffed rice or similar can be added before the water.

Kisses

125 g failsafe margarine (p. 183)
   softened
½ cup sugar
2 eggs
1 cup gluten-free flour
1 tsp xanthan gum
1 cup cornflour
1 tsp gluten-free baking powder

Cream margarine and sugar until light and fluffy. Add eggs one at a time, beating well after each addition. Sift dry ingredients. Mix into creamed mixture, stirring well. Drop small spoonful onto greased oven tray. Bake at 180°C for 8–10 minutes. Sandwich two kisses together with jam (p. 186) or icing (p. 196).

Shopping List

These are the foods you will need to make the recipes in this book, listed by supermarket categories. There will be more products on your dietitian's list including vanilla flavoured custards, biscuits, yoghurts, dairy desserts, cake mixes, creamed rice puddings and sweets that we rarely buy because they can cause problems. Some people may be affected by some items, see Checklist of Common Mistakes (p. 255). The brands mentioned following are what we use. If buying another brand with a vegetable oil component of less than 5 per cent you will need to check with the manufacturer for unlisted antioxidants (p. 183).

Asian foods
Bean vermicelli noodles (e.g. Lion brand, gluten-free)
Japanese buckwheat soba noodles (Spiral Foods are 100% buckwheat, but most contain wheat)
Rice noodles (e.g. Pandaroo, Fantastic, gluten-free)
Rice paper (e.g. Banh Trang, gluten-free)
Wheat noodles (no antioxidants, colours, flavours, e.g. Changs)

Baby needs
Baby pear puree (e.g. Heinz)

Baked beans and spaghetti
None (make your own, see recipes, or use canned butter beans instead)

Baking aids
Baking powder (gluten-free if necessary, e.g. Wards)
Bicarbonate of soda (sodium bicarbonate, e.g. McKenzies)
Citric acid (e.g. McKenzies)
Colours (natural by Queen, for playdough and special occasions)
Cooking chocolates Nestlé White Melts (*Not suitable for your supervised elimination diet: for people who tolerate amines, plain unflavoured chocolate and cocoa e.g. Nestlé dark choc bits, Nestlé baking cocoa*)
Cream of tartar (e.g. McKenzies)
Gelatine (e.g. Davis)
Glucose syrup (contains sulphites driven off when boiled, e.g. Herb Valley)
Pectin (for jam-making, e.g. FowlersVacola Jamsetta)

Vanilla essence (natural or artificial e.g. Queen, we use rarely, see Cleaners)

Yeast (not brewers yeast) e.g. Lowan, Tandaco, Kitchen Collection dried yeast, some brands may contain gluten)

Biscuits, crackers and crispbreads

There are numerous plain and sweet biscuits seemingly made from safe ingredients but you will need to check the following · Arnotts have removed unlisted antioxidant BHA 320 from their vegetable oil, for other brands you will need to ask manufacturers · we prefer to avoid any biscuits listing 'flavour' · if dairy-free, avoid milk powder and preferably butter in biscuits

Biscuits with dairy: Arnott's Sao, Wholemeal Sao, Cruskits, Milk Arrowroots, Scotch Finger, Milk Coffee, Glengarry shortbreads or any other shortbread with flour, sugar, butter, such as Walkers shortbread, Unibic Shortbread Fingers and Petticoat Tails

Biscuits without dairy: Arnotts Original water crackers, Salada, Saltine, Vita-Weat original, Shredded Wheatmeal, Kavli and Ryvita crispbreads

Biscuits without gluten or dairy: Sunrice plain Rice Cakes (not with corn), plain Rice Crackers (no flavour enhancers, no synthetic antioxidants, e.g. Sakata)

Bread

Choose plain white or wholemeal breads without · preservatives or mould inhibitors 280-283 · vinegar · sulphites or dough conditioners 220-228 · seeds except poppy seeds · fruit or flavours, e.g. Brumby's or Bakers Delight plain breads, Mountain bread wraps, Country Life Rye breads, Quality Lebanese wraps, Brumby's white iced finger buns. *See more brands* in Product Updates on the website. For gluten-free breads see Health Foods.

Bread crumbs

None (no preservatives or flavours, see Crumbs in Health Food section)

Bread mix

Numerous brands (without nasty additives especially calcium propionate 282, e.g. Laucke's)

Breakfast cereals

Rolled oats (no additives or flavours, traditional or quick, e.g. Uncle Tobys, Home Brand) · Kellogg's Rice Bubbles, Rice Bran · All Bran, Special K, Uncle Toby's Weeties, Sanitarium Weet-Bix and other plain additive-free wholewheat-based cereals

Cake and pancake mixes

Pastry mix (e.g. White Wings)

Plain pancake premix (many brands, e.g. White Wings Original Shaker pancakes - I prefer to avoid added milk and flavours so mostly use the buckwheat pancake mix, see Health Foods)

Cakes and croissants (bakery)

Woolworths baked in-store croissants

See also Sara Lee Pound Cake and Sara Lee Croissants in Frozen Foods.

Canned fish

None suitable for your supervised elimination diet *(For people who tolerate amines: tuna, salmon or sardines in spring water or failsafe oils, no flavours, e.g. John West sandwich tuna in canola oil)*

Canned fruit

Pears in syrup (not natural juice, e.g. supermarket own brands, eat only the soft pieces of pear)

Coles Diced Pears Fruit Cups in syrup, *see also* pear puree under Baby Needs.

Canned meals and meats

None

Canned and dried vegetables

Canned beans (no spices or flavoured sauces as in baked beans) e.g. red kidney beans, chickpeas, butter beans, borlotti beans, three (or more) bean mixes, green beans, Surprise dried green beans, *see also* dried beans and lentils in Soup Mix section

(Not suitable for your supervised elimination diet: beetroot no spices, asparagus, corn kernels, canned green peas no mint, Surprise dried green peas no mint)

Chips and snacks
Arnott's 'French Fries' potato straws
Colvan plain chips
Kettle Original Salted chips
Pretzels (no flavours, e.g. Parkers)
Red Rock Deli plain chips

Chocolates
Nestlé Milkybar Chocolate (limited)
See also Baking Aids section and carob as a chocolate substitute in Health Foods
(Not suitable for your supervised elimination diet: for people who tolerate amines, plain unflavoured chocolate and cocoa, see Baking Aids section. For nut allergies, Kinnerton and Willow nut free brands)

Cleaners
Dishwashing powder
Microfibre cleaning cloths
Plain low scented dishwashing liquid (e.g. Earth's Choice)
See also sodium bicarbonate and vinegar as natural cleaners
No aerosols, use vanilla-flavoured water in a spray bottle as an airfreshener

Coffee and tea
Decaffeinated coffee (many brands, we use Vittoria natural decaffeinated espresso coffee and Nescafé Instant decaffeinated coffee)
No tea (see carob powder in Health Foods)
(Not for your supervised elimination diet: for people who tolerate amines, unflavoured cocoa powder, e.g. Home Brand)

Confectionery
No colours, preservatives or flavours except limited vanilla. Commercial fudge may contain unlisted synthetic antioxidants in margarine or vegetable fat. Cornflour will contain gluten unless specified from corn. Glucose syrup may contain sulphite residues. The following are for occasional treats not daily use. *See also* www.smashi.com and www.hullabaloofood.com
Home-made fudge (may contain unlisted synthetic antioxidants, check with manufacturer)
Pascall vanilla marshmallows (white)
Werthers Original Butter Candies and Chewy Toffees
White Rabbit sweets (Cane Sugar, Liquid Glucose, Butter, Milk) from Chinese supermarkets

Cook-in sauces
None (see recipes for alternatives)

Cooking oils
Canola cooking spray (e.g. Pro chef)
Canola, sunflower and safflower oil (not cold pressed, no synthetic antioxidants 310-321, e.g. Golden Fields Canola), Soy oil (no synthetic antioxidants, cold pressed OK)
Rice Bran oil (e.g. Alfa one)

Cordial
None (make your own, see Magic Cordial recipe).

Crumpets and muffins
None (make your own muffins, see recipes)

Cosmetics and deodorants
As unperfumed as possible, best minimised (my daughter uses Natio lipstick, mascara and eyeshadow, Revlon eyeliner and eyeshadow, Maybelline Express 3 in 1 foundation and blush, Revlon powder), *see also* Hair Care
Unperfumed deodorant (no aerosols, we use Simple roll-on)

Desserts
Easiyo yoghurt premixes (natural and vanilla flavours)
Sago (e.g. Lion Brand)
Tapioca (e.g. Lion Brand)

Dried fruit and nuts

Cashew nuts (raw, e.g. Naytura Natural Cashew
Kernels)

Dried pears (peeled, no sulphite preservatives
220–228, from health food stores e.g. Totally
Pure Fruits freeze dried pears or home dried, see
recipe)

*(Not suitable for your supervised elimination diet: for
people who can tolerate amines, additive-free dried
bananas e.g. Lion of Sahara Crispy Fruit Banana,
other brands in health food stores)*

Drinks

Gin, unflavoured vodka, whisky

Eggs

Fresh eggs, preferably free range (for egg allergies,
see egg replacers in Health Foods)

Flour

Arrowroot flour (gluten-free, e.g. McKenzies)

Cornflour (gluten-free if made from corn, e.g. White
Wings)

Plain or self raising flour (e.g. Defiance)

Fresh fruit and vegetables

Pears (soft, ripe, peeled, pear-shaped varieties
such as Bartlett and Packham - not apple-shaped
varieties such as Nashi or Ya), potatoes (large,
old, white-skinned), green beans, cabbage, celery,
iceberg lettuce, leeks, shallots, chives, garlic,
Brussels sprouts, swedes, chokos, red cabbage,
mung bean sprouts, bamboo shoots, parsley for
decoration

*(Not suitable for your supervised elimination diet:
for people who can tolerate limited amounts
of salicylates: golden or red delicious apples,
mangoes, rhubarb, tamarilloes, persimmons,
custard apples, carrots, butternut pumpkin,
beetroot, sweet potatoes white or orange,
asparagus, Chinese greens such as bok choy, snow
peas and snow pea sprouts, fancy lettuce such as
butter lettuce, fancy potatoes such as red skinned,
coloured flesh or small new potatoes, corn, marrow,
parsnips, turnips · for people who can tolerate
limited amounts of glutamates: green peas ·*

*for people who can tolerate amines: pawpaws,
bananas except the ladyfinger or sugar banana
variety)*

Frozen foods

Pastry (no preservatives or synthetic antioxidants,
e.g. Pampas Puff Pastry sheets not rolls, Pampas
Butter Puff Pastry sheets not rolls, Borg's Puff
Pastry and Home Brand Puff pastry but not
Pampas shortcrust or fillo)

Sara Lee Croissants, All-purpose Pound Cake

Spring Roll Pastry (e.g. Trangs)

Icecream: (no colours, no annatto 160b e.g. Peter's
Original vanilla, Nestlé Milky Bar, Norco Natural,
Sara Lee French Vanilla, Sara Lee Honeycomb
and Butterscotch, Toppa Hokey Pokey, Pure Chill
organic vanilla from Coles)

*(Not suitable for your supervised elimination diet: for
people who tolerate amines: Sara Lee Chocolate
Bavarian)*

Dairy free icecream: see recipes, or Mototo vanilla
www.mototodairyfree.com at selected IGA stores,
limited to one serve per week due to some
salicylates and amines in the vegetable fat

Fruit and vegetables: green beans, Brussels
sprouts, frozen chips, fries and hash browns (no
annatto 160b, most contain unlisted synthetic
antioxidants, check with manufacturer or see
website)

*(Not suitable for your supervised elimination diet:
green peas not minted, frozen mango pulp, frozen
corn cobs)*

Gardening

Seeds or Grow Your Own kits (e.g. parsley and
chives)

Gravy

None (see recipes for alternatives such as leek
sauce)

Hair care

No perfumed products or aerosols (one teenager
uses beaten eggwhite for shaping his mohawk
instead of hair gel or spray), see also Shampoo
section

Health foods (or health food stores)

All products in this section are gluten-free

Agar Agar (gelatine substitute, e.g. Gold Cup powder from health food stores)

Buckwheat gluten-free pancake mix (Orgran)

Carob buttons (no added flavours, with milk or soy)

Carob coated buckwheat or ricecakes (contain milk, e.g. Naturally Good)

Carob powder for drinking and cooking (e.g. Abundant Earth)

Cashew nuts, raw

Crumbs (e.g. Orgran All Purpose Crumbs, Casalare Rice Crumbs)

Egg replacer (if allergic to eggs, e.g. Orgran No Egg)

GDL glucono-delta-lactone (baked products texturiser)

GF bread (many brands, e.g. Brighter Life HF Bendy Bread, Country Life gluten-free rolls but not gluten-free bread [vinegar] or rice bread [gluten], R&R Bakery Wholegrain Rice Bread, Dinner Rolls, Pizza Bases, www.rrbakery.com.au)

GF bread mixes e.g. Orgran Bread Mix

GF crackers, pretzels and rice cakes (no corn, no rye e.g. Eskal crackers, Eskal Pretzels, Sunrice Original Rice Cakes, Naturally Good Buckwheat Crispbreads)

GF flour mixes (plain or self raising e.g. Orgran, Freedom Foods, FG Roberts)

GF flours, e.g. rice (McKenzies), buckwheat (Kialla), millet (Lotus), besan (Lotus)

GF pasta, many brands e.g. Orgran GF spaghetti, San Remo GF lasagna sheets

GF pastry and pizza mixes e.g. Orgran Pizza and Pastry Multi-mix, FreeFrom Pizza Dough Mix

Lecithin granules (from soy)

Millet (e.g. Lotus French hulled millet, Demeter whole millet for home grinding)

Puffed rice, millet, buckwheat, amaranth (many brands, e.g. Good Morning, Micronized Foods)

Rice flakes (no added fruit or juice, e.g. Rice Flakes Medium from JK International)

Rice malt (e.g. Colonial Farm) and Rice syrup (e.g. Nature First)

Roasted chickpeas (e.g. Chic Nuts garlic flavour)

Soy butter (peanut butter substitute by Freedom Foods, possibly not for supervised elimination diet)

Soy flakes

Xanthan gum (e.g. Nu-Vit) and Guar Gum (e.g. Lotus)

Indian foods

Besan (chickpea) flour, also in health food stores

Dried chickpeas, lentils

Pappadums (may contain unlisted BHA 320, e.g. Sharwood's plain Ready to Cook, not Ready to Eat snacks)

Jellies and puddings

None (make your own, see recipes)

Juices

None (see recipe for magic cordial and other suggestions)

Laundry needs

No perfumed products, aerosols or enzymes (we use Omo Sensitive, Planet Ark and Lux Flakes)

Longlife milk

See Soymilk, ricemilk and longlife milk

Mayonnaise

None (make your own, see recipes e.g. Mighty Mayo)

Meat, poultry and fish (refrigerated section)

Meat: buy fresh or freshly vacuum packed meat (preferably not supermarket meat that may have been vacuum packed for up to three months - ask your specialist butcher if he has fresh meat) and use the day you buy or freeze and eat within one month · beef or lamb e.g. preservative-free mince (you can test for preservatives with sulphite test strips from our website), beef roast, T-bone or sirloin steak for pan frying, lamb leg for roast, diced lamb for stew, lamb steak, lamb loin chops for grilling, chump chops for stewing · rabbit · veal for schnitzel · failsafe sausages (excellent frozen sausages are available on Australia's East

Coast by courier from www.honestbeef.com.au or ask your specialist butcher if he will make up the recipe (p. 75) or see Product Updates on the website for butchers who will make sausages to order)

Chicken: Whole fresh or frozen chicken (no seasoning, stuffing, self-basting or manufactured meat), chicken breast fillets, thighs, pieces (no marinade or flavour enhancers)

Fish: Very fresh (not frozen or canned) white fish or seafood e.g. snapper, barramundi, whiting, crab, lobster, oysters, calamari, scallops (but not salmon, tuna or prawns). Best from specialty fish shops, ask for the freshest and eat that day

(Not suitable for your supervised elimination diet: for people who can tolerate amines: pork chops, roast pork, additive-free ham and bacon from organic butchers or health food stores, chicken skin e.g. wings, offal e.g. steak and kidney, lamb's fry and chicken livers, frozen and canned fish. Not prawns which contain sulphite preservatives, not imitation crab sticks, seafood salad mix or seafood extenders which contain flavour enhancers.)

Mexican foods

None (make your own tortillas and burritos, see recipes)

Milk

See Soymilk, ricemilk and longlife milk, and Refrigerated section

Muesli bars

None (make your own, see recipes)

Noodles

See Asian foods

Nuts and snacks

Cashew nuts (raw, not roasted, not suitable for people with nut allergies)

Pretzels (no flavours, e.g. Parkers Baked Wheat Pretzel Twists)

Pasta

Cous-cous (e.g. San Remo), see Health foods for gluten-free pasta

Plain pasta in any shape (no colours, flavours, fillings, e.g. spaghetti, twists, alphabet)

Refrigerated section

Cheese: cream cheese (no preservatives 200-203, e.g. Philadelphia Cream Cheese in blocks not tubs, own brands), cottage cheese (no preservatives, e.g. Jalna from Health Food stores), ricotta cheese (no preservatives, e.g. Pantalica), mascarpone cheese (no preservatives, e.g. Clover Creek) *(Not suitable for your supervised elimination diet: for people who tolerate amines: additive-free mild cheddar cheese, mozzarella cheese, for people who tolerate amines and some glutamates, tasty cheese, parmesan cheese, blue cheese, soft ripe cheese such as camembert)*

Cream, sour cream

Margarine (no sorbates 200-203, no antioxidants 310-321, no artificial colours, no annatto 160b, e.g. Meadowlea Original with dairy, Nuttelex dairy-free margarine)

Milk (unflavoured, we use A2 milk www.A2australia.com.au)

Pure butter (e.g. Mainland Butter Soft, Home Brand), butter blends only if additive-free

Yoghurt (natural or vanilla, no artificial colours, no annatto 160b, no preservatives, e.g. Vaalia natural)

Dairy free: Soy cream cheese (e.g. Kingland), Tofu (plain and silken e.g. Pureland), Soy yoghurt (natural, e.g. Soygurt)

Rice

Plain rice (e.g. Sunwhite, medium or long grain, Arborio, Doongara, glutinous rice but not flavoured such as basmati, jasmine or wild rice)

Salad dressings

None (make your own from oil and citric acid, see recipes)

Salt and pepper

Sea salt or rock salt preferably iodised (no
vegetable or flavoured salts – we use
MasterFoods sea salt grinder on the table and
Saxa iodised salt for cooking)
No pepper

Sauces

None (make your own, see recipes e.g. Leek sauce,
Birgit's pear ketchup)

Shampoo

Preferably no perfume (we use Dermaveen shampoo
and conditioner from pharmacies and EnviroCare
body and hair cleanser or Melrose Everyday
shampoo and conditioner from health food stores)

Skin care and sun care

Sorbolene (preferably no perfume, we use Redwin
Sorbolene moisturizer with Vitamin E, or see your
dietitian's list)
Sunblock (preferably unperfumed and free of
benzoates or parabens, we use Megan Gale
Invisible Zinc from health food stores and Cancer
Council Everyday sunscreen, or see your dietitian's
list)

Soap

Handwashing Liquid (no perfume, we use Redwin
Sorbolene Handwash or EnviroCare body and hair
cleanser from health food stores, or see your
dietitian's list)
Soap (no perfume, we use Simple Pure Soap)

Soft drinks

Lemonade (no preservative 211, e.g. Schweppes
bottled, only for occasional parties due to
salicylates and amines in natural lemon flavour, or
make your own, see the Magic Cordial recipe)
Soda water (no flavours, no additives)
Sparkling mineral water (no flavours, no additives)
Tonic water (no preservative 211, e.g. Schweppes,
as above)

Soup and soup mixes

Dried beans and lentils (e.g. red, brown and green
lentils, chickpeas, split peas, red kidney and all
other dried beans except broad beans)
Pearl barley (e.g. McKenzies)
Soup mix (e.g. McKenzies)

Soymilk, ricemilk and longlife milk

Longlife milks (e.g. Nestlé sweetened condensed
milk, Nestlé canned reduced cream)
Dairy free: soymilk (be careful with flavoured
soymilks and unlisted antioxidants in oils. I
prefer calcium enriched, these are the brands we
drink: Sanitarium So Good, Sanitarium So Good
Soyaccino, SoyLife Original, PureHarvest Organic
Soymilk gluten-free) · ricemilk (e.g. Vitasoy,
gluten-free)

Spices and cooking needs

Garlic powder or granules (e.g. MasterFoods)
Poppy seeds (e.g. MasterFoods)
Saffron threads (powder can be adulterated with
artificial colours) e.g. MasterFoods

Spreads, honey, jam etc

Golden syrup (CSR)
Malt Extract (e.g. Saunders)
No honey, no jam (make your own pear jam), no
Vegemite, no peanut butter (make your own
cashew butter or see soy butter under Health
Foods)

Sugar

Caster sugar
Icing sugar (pure icing sugar is gluten-free, icing
sugar with cornflour is not)
Light brown sugar (not raw, no molasses for
colouring)
White sugar

Tissues and toilet paper

Preferably no perfumes (e.g. Sorbent hypoallergenic)

Toothpaste and dental care

Plain dental floss (not mint flavoured)

Unflavoured toothpaste (e.g. Soul Pattinson's Plain toothpaste from Soul Pattinson pharmacies, Oral Hygiene Solutions Plain toothpaste www. plaintoothpaste.com or use a wet toothbrush)

Toppings and icecream cones

Betta natural icecream cones

Gluten-free icecream cones, see www. hullabaloofood.com

Nestlé Caramel Top'n'Fill

Pure maple syrup (no added flavour e.g. Camp, sometimes in the Health Food section)

Vinegar

None (except as a household cleaner)

Vitamins

Multivitamin and mineral supplement (additive-free, free of herbal ingredients, bioflavonoids and flavours, we use Amcal One-a-day multivitamin and mineral supplement from pharmacies)

Vitamin C for cooking (we use Melrose ascorbic acid powder from pharmacies)

Water

Spring water (all brands, e.g. Mount Franklin), still mineral water, see also Soft drinks

---

Always read labels: ingredients change!

Check Product Updates on www.fedup.com.au or subscribe to our free newsletters (email failsafe_newsletter-subscribe@yahoogroups.com with 'subscribe' in the subject line). For readers outside Australia: your local failsafe group may have a shopping list of suitable foods in your country.

Checklist of Common Mistakes

All of these mistakes have been made by readers. Each one was enough to stop the diet from working, but difficult to identify because effects build up slowly. The most frequent mistakes are at the top of the list. If the diet isn't working, read the list below. You can also ask your dietitian or email support group to check every item for you. For more details, see the Checklist of Common Mistakes on www.fedup.com.au.

Accidental or deliberate mistakes • one or two serves of hot chips, takeaways, Vegemite or any other mistakes per week can be enough to prevent improvement.

Child sneaking food at school • supportive schools ban lunch swapping • UK juvenile offenders did the diet successfully while on home detention • you can start during school holidays.

Too many salicylates • beware the advice 'an apple a day can't hurt you'. Some extra-sensitive people cannot tolerate any fruit • some people even have problems with low salicylate items such as shallots, leeks, golden syrup or brown sugar.

Pear juice is not permitted because commercial pear juice contains the peel and therefore salicylates • pears canned in juice instead of syrup are *not* permitted • pears (fresh, tinned, pureed, jam and ketchup) are limited to two pears or equivalent per day, less for some people • pears must be ripe, soft and peeled.

Flavours • artificial and natural flavours and even vanilla can cause problems. If your child is not improving, avoid 'flavours', 'vanillin' or 'vanilla' in commercial products such as marshmallows, jelly beans and LCMs, vanilla-flavoured yoghurt, custard, soymilk, caramels, biscuits, carob and lollies. Home cooking is safer, but avoid vanilla in that too.

Annatto 160b natural yellow colour in many dairy foods such as yoghurt and ice-cream (especially if labelled 'lite', 'creamy' or 'wholesome'), as well as cheese slices, frozen or crumbed products, biscuits, breakfast cereals and a wide variety of other processed foods.

Cashew paste must be made from raw cashews. • Commercial cashew paste from lightly roasted cashews is not okay.

Chicken with seasoning or stuffing • it is not okay to eat the meat and avoid the skin of BBQ or roast chicken with seasoning or stuffing • beware of stuffed fresh chickens in supermarkets.

Carob • beware of added flavours in carob products, and milk powder if you are sensitive to dairy foods • readers have reported problems with carob powder that has a bitter taste.

Toothpaste • mint-flavoured or herbal toothpastes such as fennel are not permitted, because herbs contain salicylates • coloured toothpaste is not okay (see p. 176 for alternatives or use a wet toothbrush instead).

Cold-pressed oil is not okay, except soybean oil and possibly rice bran oil (see p. 184).

Wholegrains • many children with behaviour and other problems are affected by wholegrains in Weet-Bix, Vitabrits, Weeties, All Bran, wholemeal bread • set limits (e.g. 2 Weet-Bix every second day) or, if no improvement, avoid • rice bran oil may be another possible problem • Alternative sources of fibre include rolled oats, dried beans such as kidney beans, and permitted vegetables • Xanthan gum is a good source of fibre if you are gluten-free.

Too much fibre in foods such as whole grain products, raw rolled oats, dried beans, uncooked cabbage and other vegetables can cause cause bloating, stomach aches and diarrhoea, especially in people with irritable bowel symptoms or when introduced suddenly in large amounts.

Product changes occur frequently • read labels especially with a packaging change • vegetable oils, soymilk, lemonade, pastry, margarine, butters, cream cheese, cooking oils and rice crackers are some of the most changeable • read about changes in Product Updates on www.fedup.com.au or in the newsletters (email: failsafe_newsletter-subscribe@yahoogroups.com with 'subscribe' in the subject line).

Illegally unlisted additives • unlisted additives can occur in any product. If you think a product is affecting you, avoid it and reintroduce. If convinced, contact us so that we can tell others, e.g. sulphites in mince (see p. 81).

Contamination such as added flavours can occur on production lines of such items as plain chips. Discard any product with a flavour that tastes wrong.

Antioxidants in oils are often not listed on the label, in any product that contains any kind of vegetable oil, including biscuits, margarines, snack foods, breads, pizza bases, and frozen potato products such as ovenfry chips • check the Shopping List for safe products or phone the consumer hotline • if there is no improvement on the diet, avoid any commercial product containing any kind of vegetable oil such as canola, 'vegetable oil', vegetable shortening, vegetable fat, beef fat or tallow unless you are absolutely certain it is okay.

Unlisted sulphites • sulphites are widely used in unlabelled foods such as sausages, prawns, and potato products such as hot chips (but not crisps) because potatoes are often soaked in a sulphite solution after peeling to prevent browning.

Natural fruit flavours in vitamins or children's syrup medications, such as paracetamol, cold medications, antibiotics, chewable vitamin tablets, iron supplements, don't have to be listed on the label (see p. 221).

Medications, herbal remedies and supplements • colours, flavours, preservatives and active ingredients in syrups, capsules or lotions, herbal remedies including echinacea and supplements including fish oils can cause problems (see p. 221). Supplements can be reintroduced as challenges.

Eyedrops • preservatives and colours from diagnostic or therapeutic eyedrops and preserved contact-lens solutions are easily absorbed through the eye and can cause problems.

Dental treatment • take your own toothpaste • plaque-disclosing tablets contain artificial colours.

Worm treatment • there are no permitted worm tablets – if necessary, worm your children before starting the diet.

Raw sugar, dark brown sugar • white, soft brown, icing and caster sugars are permitted • raw sugar, honey and dark brown sugar coloured with molasses contain salicylates • avoid commercial products that contain raw sugar (soymilk, cereals).

Whey powder can be cultured with natural propionate (282) preservatives • avoid whey powder in bread and other bakery products • whey powder is okay in non-bakery products such as ice-cream and yoghurt.

Vinegar is not permitted and must be avoided, even in small amounts in products such as bread.

Amines in meat • eat meat as fresh as possible (see p. 73) • fresh meat that has been hung by your butcher for a week or two is acceptable • supermarket meats are now vacuum-packed for up to three months, avoid if possible.

Amines in fermented products • found in wine, beer, soy sauce, tempeh, miso, chocolate, cheese, sauerkraut and even strong yoghurt and sourdough bread • despite seemingly failsafe ingredients (e.g. flour, water, salt), yeast-free bread can be made by a long rising process, which encourages fermentation and can be a problem for the extra-sensitive • bakers' yeast is permitted and yeasted bread can be safer than yeast-free bread for this reason • **fetta cheese** is not permitted • bland fresh white cheeses, such as preservative-free cottage, ricotta and cream cheeses and mascarpone, are permitted; sharp fermented white cheeses are not.

In the USA • cornflour means corn starch, that is, refined white starch from corn. This is permitted but may contain residual sulphites for those sensitive to them • yellow flour from cornmeal is not permitted • if gluten-free, check that the corn starch is not made from wheat.

You may need to exclude more foods • people with severe symptoms or extra sensitivity may need to avoid some of the following • dairy foods (see p. 266) • wheat or gluten (see p. 268) • soy • eggs • citric acid • cashew nuts • canola oil (sunflower is safer) • potatoes • rice • gelatine (see following) • even Nuttelex can cause problems • some people report that more than one cup of decaf coffee a day is too much • if not improving and you don't know why, consult your dietitian and don't eat these foods every day.

Gluten-free • malt contains gluten, so check labels on puffed rice cereals, soy-milks, etc • assume cornflour in confectionery, baking powder and other products is wheaten cornflour unless otherwise specified • avoid contamination, e.g. from family members' toast crumbs in the Nuttelex • when eating out avoid gravies, sauces and anything with thickener • spelt flour is not gluten-free (see p. 229).

Sulphites in gluten-free flours • most people can tolerate the tiny amounts of sulphites in gluten-free flours, but failure to improve on diet, or worsening of symptoms including asthma and eczema when gluten-free, may be sulphite-related • rice, rice flour, rice noodles, plain rice cakes, buckwheat, millet and organic products do not contain sulphites (see p. 229).

Sulphites in gelatine • high levels of sulphites (220) are permitted in gelatine but dissipate with heat and storage, see p. 68.

Challenges can be inconclusive if the dose isn't big enough • it is better to use high salicylate foods than moderate salicylate foods • don't use very high foods such as oranges and tomatoes because they also contain amines (see p. 12).

Exposure to perfumes, industrial chemicals and heavy metals • avoid perfumed toiletries, cosmetics, aftershave, washing powders, shampoo and conditioner, aerosols, deodorants, sunblock for all family members (see p. 247) • avoid household cleaners (see p. 247), essential oils, 'naturally fragranced' products • avoid food dyes in playdough (see p. 198), bubble baths, finger paints, preschool paints and glues • avoid paints, solvents and other renovating fumes • avoid smells of new or newly cleaned soft furnishings, upholstery, carpets, new mattresses • avoid shopping malls, hairdressing salons – alternatives include fast cuts or home hairdressing services – pet shops, cigarette smoke • avoid workplace chemicals • avoid chemical smells of new cars, appliances including computers and CD players and furniture – display or second-hand models are safer • avoid strong-smelling plants, e.g. herb plants, strongly fragrant flowers, and trees, e.g. eucalypt, camphor laurel, pine, particularly freshly cut as in a Christmas tree • avoid freshly sawn timber and new timber for renovations • avoid the smell of wood and smoke from wood fires • avoid lawn clippings and mower fumes • avoid the smell of strongly spicy food – don't cook it for others • fumes are generally worse in hot conditions.

Too much stress, confrontational parenting or teaching styles. Reduce stress by

• avoiding confrontations (the *1-2-3 Magic* video or book from Amazon or www.parentshop.com.au in Australia can show how to do this) • laughter therapy, such as watching family comedies together • family walks, bike rides or camping holidays – preferably with no shops or advertising, e.g. in a national park • relaxation tapes or music – instead of radio and TV, play any music by Mozart for a calming effect • encourage positivity in the family by treating each other with kindness and respect and remember the good times by going through old photos together • for adults, meditation is considered to be the single most effective stress reduction method – see any book by Boston cardiologist Dr Herbert Benson.

Non-food factors such as an absent parent, a new baby, moving, house renovations, illness, changes in medication, a new school, bullying, criticism, punishment or lack of friends. Children on the diet need a failsafe house, support, love, praise, exercise and time with parents.

See www.fedup.com.au for updates as well as hints for extra-sensitive amine or salicylate responders.

Frequently Asked Questions

Q. My specialist has advised me to do the elimination diet. I am a little confused about why I would be doing it – isn't the diet aimed at behaviour problems?

A. The diet helps with a wide range of symptoms (p. 269) in both adults and children and is relatively easy for determined adults. Families of children with behaviour problems are the focus of this book because it is much harder to do an elimination diet – or anything else – with a difficult child.

Q. Do children 'grow out' of food intolerance?

A. Symptoms of food intolerance can change throughout life, so, for example, a baby who has problems with milk may appear to have grown out of it but has probably grown into something else, such as learning delay. A hyperactive pre-schooler may become a teenager with depression. However, children do develop better tolerance as they grow bigger and some boys seem to develop better tolerance during their late teens.

Q. Is the elimination diet expensive?

A. Most families say they spend less on food because they buy less processed food and takeaways.

Q. Why do we have to do challenges – can't we just add back in one food at a time and see what happens?

A. One food at a time will show if you have an allergy to a food but not necessarily an intolerance. Even if you ate, for example, apricots every day for a week, you couldn't conclude that apricots are okay because it depends what else you are eating. If you then introduce more high salicylate foods, eventually you could react to the salicylates in apricots plus whatever else you are eating. This is why so many food-intolerant babies develop problems around the time of introduction of solids, yet their mothers don't realise what has happened.

Q. How can I find out about foods that aren't listed in the *Friendly Food* lists – such as Asian fruits like rambutans, jackfruit and mangosteens?

A. Unlisted foods are not permitted on your supervised elimination diet. Assume that all fruits contain some salicylates. The more you like them, the more likely they are to contain salicylates. No reaction after one dose doesn't mean you can eat large quantities every day, it means you can probably eat one dose occasionally but you always have to be careful of a build-up of effects.

Q. We are doing the elimination diet for behaviour problems in my 9-year-old son. I only want to eliminate dairy if you agree that it can help with behavioural problems and is worth trying.

A. In my experience, dairy foods can be strongly associated with oppositional defiance and other behavioural symptoms. The trouble with not eliminating dairy foods is that they are generally consumed many times a day every day, so if you don't avoid them you won't know how good your child could be. See p. 266 for signs that dairy foods could be a problem.

Q. My doctor told me to 'do the diet but don't do it too seriously'.

A. That's an excellent way to make sure the diet doesn't work. For best results with any elimination diet, the diet must be followed strictly. You can request our list of supportive doctors and dietitians from confoodnet@ozemail.com.au.

Q. Just wondering if you can tell me how much salicylate is in a sugar banana? My 3-year-old was accidentally given one earlier in the week and had a slight wobble. Nothing earth-shattering but I thought it interesting that one banana could do it.

A. Sugar bananas are quite high in salicylates and problems are often reported because salicylate-sensitive children generally assume all bananas are safe for them.

Q. Should children be punished for bad behaviour after inadvertently eating food that affects them?

A. When this question was a talking point in a failsafe newsletter, one mother wrote: 'My husband and I argue about this – he believes bad behaviour is simply unacceptable and our son needs to get "consequences" but I think it's unfair to give a child drugs and then punish him for the way he behaves. When my 5-year-old threatened to hurt his teacher, I said to my husband "Imagine if someone spiked your drink with a hallucinogen and then sent you off to school? How would you behave, and how would you feel if you were punished for your behaviour?" When the food reaction was over, we discussed my son's behaviour, explaining that it was totally unacceptable in no uncertain terms, and he understood. I think it's best to communicate acceptable and unacceptable behaviour with children very clearly, but not to punish them for being on drugs.' For more contributions, see Failsafe Newsletter #50 on www.fedup.com.au.

Q. I'm in my twenties, failsafe, working and going to uni. I know I'm under a lot of stress but I wish I could eat some more foods.

A. Exam time is not a good time to widen your diet. Stress, illness, lack of sleep, female hormones, medication, and chemical exposure can all contribute to intolerance. The reverse is that you can eat a wider range of foods if you reduce stress, get more sleep, have a holiday or go camping in a national park, which gets you away from chemical exposure – assuming you don't carry nasty sunblock and pesticides with you. You might also like to join one of the failsafe email groups for support, as it really helps to talk to others who are in the same situation – or go to a gluten-free, additive-free café such as Silly Yaks in Melbourne occasionally and break your diet just a little.

Q. I saw Velcorin listed on a fruit-juice label. Is it a safe additive?

A. There are new additives introduced into our food supply constantly. Velcorin is an antimicrobial agent chemically known as dimethyl dicarbonate (DMDC). It is used for the cold sterilisation of non-alcoholic beverages and can reduce the need for nasty preservatives such as sodium benzoate (211) or sodium metabisulphite (223). Once added to the product, Velcorin breaks down quickly into small amounts of carbon dioxide and methanol, which occur naturally in most beverages, including fruit juice. It is too early for us to be sure, but it seems likely that Velcorin will not cause children's behaviour, learning problems and other symptoms of food intolerance. Readers would still have to consider salicylate and amine content of the product.

Q. It has been just over a week since we started our supervised elimination diet and so far there hasn't really been an improvement in my son at school.

A. Children respond differently to foods. Some improve within days, others take weeks. Some improve at home first, others at school. It is common for mothers to go through second-week blues – all that effort and no results yet. But when improvements do start, it is very exciting and the child will then keep on improving for months, as long as you don't make mistakes (see Checklist of Common Mistakes).

Q. I'm confused about sulphites in gluten-free flours.

A. Most people can manage the small amounts of sulphites in commercial gluten-free mixes, but it's best to be aware that extra-sensitive people can get worse when they go gluten-free. It's very rare, but if it happens to you it's important. You can check whether you are sensitive to sulphites by going sulphite-free – rice, rice cakes, buckwheat and millet do not contain sulphites.

Q. How will the preservative in lemonade be likely to affect my overactive 4-year-old?

A. Unlike true allergic reactions that typically start quickly (e.g. 'within minutes she had a rash and swelling across her face'), there are three main kinds of reactions to food chemicals • **same day reaction** can start within half an hour and can be all over in a few hours (typically the overexcited behaviour from food colours) • **next day** (for example, child wakes up grumpy and has a bad day with occasional outbursts and difficulty falling asleep that night) • **long reaction** (can start straight away or build up very slowly, may be most obvious on the third day, and can last for a week or more, slowly improving with occasional outbursts). For most children, I would expect a next day reaction to benzoate preservatives, but there are many exceptions.

Q. How do I know if I have to avoid dairy foods or gluten?

Statistically speaking, additives and salicylates are more likely to cause problems than dairy foods or gluten, but there are still significant numbers of people affected by both, including for behavioural problems. If dairy and wheat or gluten do cause symptoms, they are a major problem because they are consumed so frequently. Discuss this with your dietitian and see the following.

MILK

Some signs that dairy foods may need to be avoided include (although these may be due to other food chemicals or causes as well) • pale face • dark circles under eyes • stuffy or runny nose • frequent nosebleeds • breathes through mouth • constant throat clearing • another family member is sensitive to milk • problems with milk as a baby • frequent ear infections • grommets • would live on milk if you let him or her • drinks litres of milk or other dairy products a day and would hate to give them up, or hates milk • serious symptoms of any kind including behaviour, defiance, autism or any of the physical symptoms • eczema or other food intolerance symptoms in a breast- or cows' milk formula-fed baby.

> Whatever you are most reluctant to give up is most likely to affect you.

Babies need breastmilk or baby formula and there are special formulas such as Neocate for babies with food intolerance available by prescription only. Speak to your dietitian, our lactation consultant (listed under local contacts on www.fedup.com.au) or ask others in the failsafebaby group for more information.

SOYMILK, RICEMILK, ALLERGIES AND INFANT FEEDING
- Rice and soymilks enriched with chickpeas are not suitable for children or adults with cross-reactivity problems due to nut, legume or soy allergies.
- Ricemilk is not suitable for infant feeding. Any infant not breastfed to 12 months must be given an appropriate infant formula.

A2 is a protein in most milks from goat, sheep, buffalo, camel, Asian cows and most Jersey cows, but nearly all supermarket milks contain A1 protein because A1-producing cows yield more milk (see www.a2australia.com.au). A2 milks seem to be better tolerated by some people with allergies and intolerances. Some dietitians say that people who improve on A2 milk will do better on soy or ricemilk, but it has been a godsend in my family where two of us are enjoying A2 milk after 12 years on soymilk. Switching to A2 milk along with additive-free bread is the easiest of all diet changes to make. Although using soy or ricemilk from the start could be the quickest way to do the diet, families who are reluctant to go dairy-free may find it easier to switch to A2 milk first, then switch to soy or ricemilk later on if necessary.

Issues with soy • some people are allergic to soymilk as well as cows' milk • ingredients change constantly in soymilks and are sometimes not failsafe (see Checklist of Common Mistakes) • some people worry about health risks of soy, especially for infants. See www.cspinet.org/nah/soy/soy.html.

Lactose-free milk is not helpful for milk-related problems other than lactose intolerance, which is the inability to digest lactose, a type of sugar found in milk. Lactose intolerance is caused by a deficiency of the enzyme lactase and is characterised by bloating, diarrhoea and abdominal cramps. It is relatively rare in Westernised countries with a long history of dairy farming, although common in Africa, Asia and other non-Westernised countries. Short-term lactose intolerance can be induced by gastrointestinal infections, but 'lactose intolerance' in babies may actually be cows' milk protein intolerance (see www.breastfeeding.asn.au/bfinfo/lactose.html). A long period of complete dairy avoidance may result in losing the enzyme called lactase and hence the ability to break down or tolerate lactose. For people avoiding all dairy foods, it may be helpful to break your diet regularly with small amounts of dairy products to maintain the enzyme.

Cows' milk substitutes: people who are dairy-free will probably have to avoid cow's milk, milk powder, yoghurt, ice-cream, cheese, cream and butter, where milk, milk powder and yoghurt are the most important. Soymilk, ricemilk and oat milk can be substituted (see Shopping List).

WHEAT OR GLUTEN

Many people mistakenly think they are sensitive to wheat when it is really the bread preservative 282 that affects them. Nevertheless, wheat and/or gluten can be associated with the full range of food intolerance symptoms and dietitians generally recommend going gluten-free for anyone with serious symptoms, especially autism.

Going gluten-free is much easier now than it was 10 years ago due to the proliferation of gluten-free flours and products on the market. However, a gluten-free diet is difficult and can be less nutritious than a wheat-based diet (see p. 232).

If coeliac disease is a possibility (see p. 228) experts recommend a blood test before starting a gluten-free diet, because the test only works when there is wheat in the system. It is possible to have reversible gluten intolerance, which can be induced by antibiotics or gastrointestinal infections.

Statistically speaking, gluten is less likely to cause problems than additives, salicylates or amines, so some families find it easiest to leave wheat or gluten avoidance for a few weeks until they are settled into the diet. By then many children will have improved so much it will be obvious they don't need to worry about avoiding wheat or gluten.

Symptoms of Food Intolerance

Listed on the following pages in alphabetical order are many of the most common symptoms of food intolerance.

Abnormal tingling – see Loss of sensation

Adenoids – see Ears, nose and throat

ADHD and ADHD-type behaviours

Symptoms such as irritability, restlessness, inattention and sleep disturbance will improve in children with or without Attention Deficit Hyperactivity Disorder. Diet is not a cure for ADHD, but by reducing problematic symptoms it gives families a chance to enjoy the more positive aspects of ADHD children or adults, such as a quirky sense of humour, ability to think outside the box, intuitive approach and ability to react quickly in emergencies. ADHD children without hyperactivity can improve too, but, contrary to popular opinion, the 'quiet ones' are generally more food sensitive than their hyperactive peers. Most people think artificial colours are the biggest culprits, but salicylates and preservatives are as important as colours for most of these children, with other additives, flavour enhancers, amines, dairy and gluten (in that order) also contributing. See also **Oppositional defiance** and the 'Diet and ADHD' factsheet on www.fedup. com.au.

Allergic shiners

A common name for dark circles under the eyes, allergic shiners can be related to any of the usual culprits. For many people, along with **pallor** (pale face) they are a reaction to dairy products.

Angina-type pain – see Heart palpitations

Angio-oedema

This is the medical name for swelling of the eyes, lips and/or tongue that may occur with or without a rash. The area may swell alarmingly within minutes or hours and can restrict breathing. Causes can be the same as any of the **itchy skin rashes** including **eczema** and **ribo rash**.

Anxiety – see Depression

By his mid-sixties, Bernard from NSW had suffered from painful and crippling arthritis for nearly 30 years, when he was told that if his disease was not controlled by daily use of NSAIDs (nonsteroidal anti-inflammatory drugs), he had 'only four or five years of active life left'. Bernard chose instead to try an elimination diet and achieved remarkable results. He warns that arthritis sufferers may need up to 12 weeks before challenges, and reactions to challenges may be  delayed. It wasn't until the eighth day of his salicylate challenge that Bernard noticed any reaction at all – he found his arthritis had returned with such a vengeance that it took him an hour to get out of bed. Even food colouring, usually a quick reaction, took two days to aggravate his arthritis.

Arthritis

It is not medically recognised that arthritis can be associated with food. However, we have received reports from readers of all ages whose arthritis has improved. The mother of an 8-year-old in the Northern Territory wrote that after three weeks on the diet her daughter was pain-free for the first time in years. A woman in Brisbane whose arthritis was so bad at the age of 19 that she would soak her hands in hot water each morning 'to get them okay to work' found her arthritis disappeared totally when she went on the diet. Challenges showed it was related mainly to salicylates and sulphites, and, to a lesser extent, amines and MSG.

ASD (Autistic Spectrum Disorder) – see Autism

Asperger's syndrome – see Autism

Aspirin-induced asthma – see Samter's triad

Asthma

The incidence of childhood asthma has risen from about 10 per cent in the 1970s to 30 per cent in the 1990s. Any or all of the usual culprits can be involved, but sulphite preservatives (220–228) are the additives most strongly associated with asthma. Sulphites are consumed in large amounts, especially in dried fruit, cordials and fruit drinks, sausages and mince (illegal but it often happens) by young children who have the highest asthma rates. The World Health Organization (WHO) has recommended phasing out the use of sulphite preservatives where possible due to effects on child asthmatics. If that happened overnight the prevalence of childhood asthma would probably halve, but progress is glacially slow. Parents do not realise that many children can be turned into asthmatics just by what they eat. A 7-year-old with no known asthma who reported 'it was a bit hard to breathe' after eating 10 dried apricots would be an asthmatic on daily medication if he ate that level of sulphites every day, as many do.

Benzoate preservatives (210–218) in drinks and syrup medications are another asthma culprit consumed in very high amounts by young children. The 30-minute rule applies to asthmatics: instead of an obvious asthma attack straight after eating, it is more likely that the airways are irritated with no obvious symptoms and asthma doesn't happen until exposure to a trigger, such as cold air, exercise or a virus. The trigger gets the blame, but if they avoid additives these kids can be exposed to triggers without having asthma. When families go on diet because of a child's behaviour problems, any asthmatics in the family generally improve. To join our asthma group, email failsafeasthma-subscribe@ yahoogroups.com with 'subscribe' in the subject line. See 'Food additives and asthma', 'Dangers of dried fruit', and 'Sulphite preservatives' factsheets at www. fedup.com.au. Asthmatics doing challenges must be supervised by a dietitian.

Autism, Asperger's syndrome, ASD

Children with autism can display any of the symptoms of food intolerance, including tantrums and speech delay, but they also have some symptoms of their own, such as lack of eye contact, inflexibility, hand-flapping, rocking and face-blindness. If these children are put on a diet at all, it is common to use a gluten-free casein-free diet, but in our experience it is much more effective to trial a supervised elimination diet free of additives, low in salicylates, amines and glutamates, gluten-free, dairy-free and avoiding perfumed products.

A study in the USA with 49 autistic people used diet plus avoidance of Volatile Organic Compounds – VOCs – chemicals that form a gaseous state at room temperature so they are easy to smell, including perfumes, cleaning products, solvents and pesticides. Children were kept in a special 'clean room' that was free of VOCs, and the researcher reported that a 'broad spectrum of severe and chronic autistic symptoms' are 'fully reversible' – 'the children in the program … returned to normal'. This is an extraordinary claim, but we do see huge improvements in autistic children on the diet. As mothers point out, it is not possible to lock children up in a clean room forever, but it is possible to reduce their exposure to VOCs at home and at school by being very careful. See **Perfume sensitivity** and the 'Autism and Asperger' factsheet at www.fedup.com.au.

Bad breath – see Digestive system

Bedwetting – see Bladder

Behaviour

Behaviour falls into two main categories: the quiet ones (see **Inattention**, **Depression**) or the restless ones (see **Irritability**, **Restlessness**, **ADHD-type behaviours**). It's possible to have symptoms from both categories, and symptoms can change throughout the lifespan. Parents of children with learning delays due to inattentive behaviour often say 'My child isn't hyperactive so we don't have to worry about diet', yet such children are likely to be more food sensitive than their hyperactive siblings. See also **Autism** and **Oppositional defiance**.

Bladder: bedwetting (enuresis), urinary urgency, urinary incontinence

It is common for mothers to report that bedwetting improves within days or weeks of starting the diet. If diet alone is not enough to resolve the problem, parents have reported that the bell and pad system is much more effective combined with diet than when used alone. During my bread preservative study, two young children with bedwetting and daytime urinary incontinence improved on the diet and worsened remarkably during a double blind placebo-controlled challenge of the bread preservative. Senior citizens have also indignantly reported urinary incontinence associated with the bread preservative. 'Everyone should know about this!' one elderly man insisted. Foods and chemicals often associated with bedwetting include additives, salicylates and dairy foods, but any of the usual culprits, including amines, can be involved.

Bloating – see Irritable bowel symptoms

Body odour

Aspirin and some other medications are known to cause excessive sweating, and some readers report that their excessive sweating or body odour improve on the diet. Any of the usual culprits, including salicylates, can be involved.

Catarrh – see Ears, nose and throat

Chinese restaurant syndrome

The classic signs of this condition are headaches, flushing, sweating, sense of facial pressure or swelling, breathing difficulties, tightness in the chest or light-headedness related to ingestion of MSG. Chinese restaurant syndrome is now considered to be disproved by industry-funded medical researchers, the FDA and industry-funded nutrition organisations, but readers don't agree.

Chronic fatigue syndrome (CFS)

Lethargy, foggy brain and a feeling of constant hangover can be associated with food intolerance. Some people with lethargy have reported that their problem was largely due to the bread preservative calcium propionate 282, but people with lethargy as a symptom are often extra sensitive to most of the usual culprits in foods and environmental chemicals including salicylates in both foods and perfumed products. See 'Chronic fatigue' factsheet on www.fedup.com.au

'Clumsy child' – see Fine motor-skills delay

Colds and flu

Colds, flu, tonsillitis, bronchitis, sinusitis, cystitis, croup and similar illnesses may occur frequently in families with food intolerance and decrease when families are well-established on the diet. Presumably the known anti-nutritional and immunosuppressive properties of certain food chemicals such as artificial food colours and propionate bread preservative may contribute. During the first two weeks of your supervised elimination diet, these illnesses sometimes appear as withdrawal symptoms, causing added complications due to additives in medication (see p. 221).

Colic in babies and adults – see Irritable bowel symptoms

Colitis – see Ulcerative colitis

Constipation

Straightforward constipation can be due to lack of dietary fibre and fluids, but food intolerance can also be an important cause of constipation and/or diarrhoea. Salicylates and milk (dairy foods) have been strongly associated with constipation, along with the usual culprits – additives, amines, gluten (see also **Incomplete evacuation**). See the factsheet 'Constipation or incomplete evacuation?' on www.fedup.com.au.

Coordination disorder – see Fine motor-skills delay

Cradle cap – see Itchy skin rashes

Cystitis – see Kidneys and bladder

Depression, anxiety, panic attacks, self harm, suicidal thoughts, obsessive tendencies

Most people are unaware that depression and other symptoms of mental illness can be related to food, yet when families do an elimination diet to support their difficult child, relatives with depression – adults or children – often improve. One father from the NT chose to do the amine challenge first because he felt he wouldn't react. 'How wrong can you get!' he wrote in his account of the challenge:

> 'I had a violent reaction within a few hours and have never felt so awful in all my life. Here are some of the symptoms: depression, suicidal tendencies, not just thoughts, melancholy, looking for an argument, feeling the whole world was against me, lethargy, shakes, pressure on the skull and tingles in the extremities, feeling of hangover, inability to focus on thoughts, ringing in the ears, inability to sleep. The hung-over feeling lasted until the next day. Not the best 24 hours, but at least I know there is a cause for symptoms that I have experienced in the past. On a positive note, it is remarkable that once you know certain food groups cause a problem you don't really miss them!'

The most likely chemical culprits with depression include salicylates, additives, amines, dairy and gluten in roughly that order. See **Self-harm**, and the 'Depression' factsheet on www.fedup.com.au.

Dermatitis – see Itchy skin rashes

Diarrhoea – see Irritable bowel symptoms

Difficulty falling asleep (DFA) – see Sleep

Dysaesthesia – see Loss of sensation

Ears, nose and throat: frequent middle-ear infections, glue ear, need for grommets, runny or stuffed-up nose, frequent throat-clearing, frequent tonsillitis, enlarged adenoids, nasal speech, mouth-breathing, bad breath, snoring

With these symptoms, dairy foods are frequently implicated, but any of the usual culprits can be involved, including benzoate preservatives, salicylates, colours and perfumes. 'The diet saved us thousands of dollars', wrote one mother who opted for a three-month dietary trial before surgical removal of adenoids. See also **Sleep apnoea** and **Tonsillitis**.

Easily distracted – see Inattention

Eczema

A mother from Melbourne described how her 6-year-old son had suffered from eczema all his life, so severe that he was once hospitalised for three days with wet dressings like a burns victim. Two months after he started an elimination diet, his skin was soft and rash-free. For some children, simply avoiding preservatives can make a huge difference, while for others a supervised elimination diet is better. Your dietitian may recommend skin-prick testing for allergy as well. The most common provoking food chemicals for eczema are preservatives and salicylates, with gluten far less so. Also see **Ribo rash** and the 'Eczema' factsheet on the website www.fedup.com.au.

Encopresis – see 'Sneaky poos'

Enuresis – see Bladder

Epilepsy

Epilepsy in children and adults is frequently associated with ADHD-type behavioural symptoms. Trials of both the Few Foods and the ketogenic low carbohydrate diet have found that symptoms of both behaviour and epilepsy can improve on restricted diets, although epilepsy without behaviour problems is unlikely to improve. A medically supervised ketogenic diet for children with difficult-to-control epilepsy is available through the Children's Epilepsy Program at Royal Children's Hospital in Melbourne. Many children on the ketogenic diet eventually switch to failsafe eating for behaviour control after they are able to come off their epilepsy medication. Any of the usual food-chemical culprits can be associated with seizures. Epilepsy medications can contain artificial colours and preservatives known to be associated with seizures. See the 'Epilepsy' factsheet on www.fedup.com.au.

Excessive sweating (hyperhidrosis) – see Sweating excessively

Fatigue – see Chronic fatigue syndrome

Fine motor-skills delay, poor handwriting, letter and number reversals, gross motor-skills delay, 'clumsy child', coordination disorder, round-shouldered posture, low muscle tone

Low muscle tone is probably responsible for many of the manifestations of food intolerance, depending on which muscles are affected (hands, mouth, bladder, bowel, etc.). Dramatic changes can occur within hours. Drawing and handwriting are some of the easiest ways to notice changes – see 4-year-old Laura's drawings made on diet (left) and a few hours after a ham sandwich (right). A ham sandwich can contain up to eight nasty additives. Any or all of the usual culprits can be involved in the usual order: salicylates and additives, amines, dairy, gluten.

'Foggy brain' (disorganised and forgetful, inattentive, unable to concentrate, memory impairment, unmotivated)

All of these symptoms apply equally to children and adults so mothers who developed amnesia during pregnancy that didn't go away after the birth probably have food intolerance themselves. Any of the usual culprits can be involved, most likely preservatives, salicylates and other additives, amines, dairy and gluten in that order.

Geographic tongue (benign migratory glossitis)

In this condition, bald spots surrounded by white edges make the tongue look like a map of the world. It's in the same category as irritable bowel symptoms, since the mouth is the beginning of the digestive system. Any of the usual culprits can be involved, including salicylates and dairy products.

Giftedness

It can be a mistake to blame giftedness and boredom for bad behaviour. One mother wrote that her gifted son was doing well at school but 'has a severe temper, is disruptive, tearful, moody and makes silly noises'. After her son started on the diet he became easier to live with, did better socially, and for the first time in his life became good at and enjoyed participating in sport. Any of the usual culprits can be to blame but the most likely are preservatives, salicylates, other additives, amines and dairy foods in that order, the least likely but still to be considered is gluten. See 'Diet and ADHD' factsheet on www.fedup.com.au.

Glue ear – see Ears, nose and throat

Grommets – see Ears, nose and throat

Gross motor-skills delay – see Fine motor-skills delay

Growing pains

Primary-school-aged children may complain of 'aching legs', especially at night, in the front of the thigh muscles, in the calves and behind the knees. The pain can be severe enough to wake a child from sleep. Parents generally report that the growing pains disappear with diet and reoccur when the diet is broken. Nitrate preservatives (249–252) in processed meat and the bread preservative (282) in particular have been reported, but any of the usual culprits can be involved.

Head-banging

This symptom is one of the childhood problems, such as restless legs and hyper-activity, that has increased dramatically since the spread of processed foods in the 1970s. Although never mentioned in parenting books 30 years ago, head-banging is now considered to be a normal behaviour of toddlers, estimated to affect up to 20 per cent of healthy children in the USA, and 5–15 per cent of children in Australia. Children who frequently engage in head banging can develop a bald spot or long lasting bruising as a result.

In my experience, head banging can be related to any of the usual food chemicals, especially annatto natural colour 160b. Children aged three and under are unable to explain how they feel, although when they avoid certain food chemicals, their head banging stops. One mother who was already avoiding artificial colours reported that her two-year-old's head banging dropped from 10 episodes per day to only one within days of avoiding annatto. Although head banging is thought to be an RMD (rhythmic movement disorder), some older children who have reverted to head banging during food challenges explain that it is due to overwhelming headaches. See the 'Head banging' factsheet on the website www.fedup.com.au.

Headaches – see Migraines and headaches

Hearing loss – see Ménière's Disease

Heart palpitations, tachycardia, angina-type pain, pseudo heart attack

Heart palpitations are an awareness of the beating of your own heart. It can be too fast (tachycardia), too slow, irregular (skipping a beat or with extra beats) or normal (due to exercise or fear). Palpitations can range from mild to what feels like a heart attack, with sweating, dizziness and chest pain. 'A feeling of doom' is a common experience, and even pain down one arm. The food chemicals most often reported to us in relation to heart palpitations are MSG and nucleotide flavour enhancers (627, 631, 635), with a smaller number reporting propionate preservatives (280–283) and salicylates, but any of the usual culprits can be involved. Palpitations can be a side effect of some medications and high-dose Vitamin B supplements. See p. 221, and the 'Heart palpitations' factsheet on www.fedup.com.au.

Hives – see Itchy skin rashes

Hyperactivity
Hyperactivity – meaning overactivity – occurs mostly in younger children. As they grow, hyperactivity is more likely to become restlessness, inability to sit still and fidgeting. Hyperactive adults may change jobs, homes and partners more often than usual, or just feel restless. Most likely culprits are artificial colours, some preservatives, salicylates, other additives, amines, dairy foods and gluten in roughly that order. See also **ADHD**.

Hyperacusis – see Ménière's disease

Hypoglycaemia
Hypoglycaemia is a deficiency of glucose in the bloodstream causing muscular weakness and loss of coordination, mental confusion and sweating. It occurs most commonly in diabetics as a result of insulin overdose and can be life-threatening. Salicylate-induced hypoglycaemia has occasionally been reported in the medical literature associated with relatively small amounts of salicylates in drugs. Some readers report that early hypoglycaemic symptoms such as sugar craving, shakiness, weakness, hunger, dizziness, nausea and confusion due to lack of food or exercise can occur due to salicylates in foods. See 'Candida, yeast, sugars, hypoglycaemia' factsheet at www.fedup.com.au.

Inattention, easily distracted, unmotivated, easily bored
Inattention is one of the main effects of food chemicals. These are the children who are told they 'could do better if they tried'. But it's not lack of trying, it's

the food chemicals these children are eating that prevent them from paying attention. Any of the usual culprits can be involved, with the main suspects being salicylates, additives, amines, dairy and gluten, roughly in that order. Improvements in attention can be difficult to recognise on a daily basis unless you are looking at a particular type of homework every day. It is easier to see long-term results on report cards.

Incomplete evacuation ('sticky poos', 'sluggish bowel')

These symptoms can be difficult for mothers to understand. A mother who took her 7-year-old to the doctor because of 'diarrhoea, accidentally soiling in her pants, tummy ache and bloated tummy' reported that all the tests came back negative but 'a tummy X-ray showed her bowel and colon were jam-packed with waste food enough for three full meals for a grown man. I couldn't understand how something could be so compacted and yet she could have diarrhoea as well.'

Suspect salicylates and additives first, although amines or any other of the usual culprits can be the problem. I hear frequently about children with chronic constipation on a high fruit diet that clearly isn't working, and the same for incomplete evacuation. High fruit means high salicylate, and prunes used for constipation are one of the highest salicylate items of all. When children like this go on an elimination diet, their symptoms often resolve within days. 'Now I feel as if all the poo comes out', said one little boy. See factsheet 'Constipation or incomplete evacuation?' at www.fedup.com.au.

Indigestion – see Irritable bowel symptoms

Insomnia – see Sleep

Irritability

This is the main behavioural effect of food chemicals. A child who is feeling irritable will appear normal when doing something that he or she likes, such as playing with Lego or computer games, but will overreact when asked to do something unappealing such as 'share it with your brother', 'get ready for school' or 'do your homework'. See **Oppositional defiance** for the food chemicals most likely to cause these symptoms.

Irritable bowel syndrome, irritable bowel symptoms

It is estimated that irritable bowel syndrome affects up to 20 per cent of people on a Western diet, yet IBS is hardly seen in traditional cultures. Symptoms include reflux or colic in babies and adults, stomach discomfort, bloating, nausea changes in bowel habits, constipation and/or diarrhoea, 'sneaky poos' (encopresis) and incomplete bowel movement or feeling of incomplete evacuation ('sticky poos'). For years, doctors regarded IBS as psychosomatic and referred sufferers for counselling, or suggested a high-fibre diet. It is now known that a high-fibre diet makes 50 per cent of IBS patients worse. Triggers of these symptoms can include antibiotics, surgery and illness, especially gastrointestinal infections such as rotavirus and giardia. Culprits are the usual salicylates, additives, amines, dairy foods and gluten, in roughly that order, but there is an extra group of additives as well: sorbitol or other sugar-free sweeteners called polyols can cause bloating, diarrhoea and stomach aches that have been misdiagnosed as IBS due to daily consumption. See p. 182 and factsheet 'Sugar-free sweeteners' at www.fedup.com.au. See also **Sneaky poos** and **Incomplete evacuation**.

Itchy skin rashes, hives (urticaria), eczema, dermatitis, cradle cap, angio-oedema (swollen lips, eyes, tongue), itching (pruritis)

Rashes such as hives, eczema and dermatitis may be an intolerance to chemicals such as preservatives or salicylates in foods or medications, a true allergy to foods such as milk or peanuts, an environmental allergy, for example to dustmites, or a chemical sensitivity, for example to washing powder. Any of the usual culprits can be involved. See **Eczema** and **Ribo rash**.

Kidneys and bladder: recurrent inflammation (cystitis, interstitial cystitis, idiopathic nephrotic syndrome)

Symptoms of cystitis (urinary urgency and pain) and inflammation of the kidneys due to unknown causes in children and adults may be related to food intolerance. The most likely culprits are the same as for other digestive-tract symptoms. Salicylates play a major role, which probably explains why cystitis self-help groups notice that tea, coffee, alcohol, fruit juice and highly spiced dishes can aggravate their condition.

Learning disabilities, reading delay

In 1986, following the introduction of a low-additive policy for school meals in more than 800 New York schools over four years, the number of students classified as learning disabled dropped from more than 12.5 per cent to less than 5 per cent. Ten years later when I carried out my bread preservative study I was sorry I hadn't measured reading ability before and after diet, because nearly all the mothers reported dramatic improvements, such as 'reading a novel for the first time ever'. The only child who didn't improve was already a gifted reader. Removal of artificial colours and antioxidants such as BHA (320) were the reason for improvement in the NY schools above, but any of the usual culprits can be involved and, as usual, salicylates are one of the prime suspects.

Letter and number reversals – see Fine motor-skills delay

Loss of sensation, abnormal tingling (pins and needles), numbness (paraesthesia), abnormal and sometimes unpleasant sensations (dysaesthesia)

These symptoms can be associated with the side effects of medication and food chemicals. One woman with frequent, unpleasant 'pins and needles' sensations related to salicylates in foods noticed that her condition started while she was taking long-term high doses of salicylate-containing medications. Most likely culprits include salicylates and additives, amines, dairy foods and gluten, in roughly that order.

Low muscle tone

Low muscle tone is probably responsible for many of the manifestations of food intolerance, depending on which muscles are affected (mouth, hands, bladder, bowel, etc.). Dramatic changes can occur within hours. Most likely culprits include additives and salicylates, amines, dairy foods and gluten, in roughly that order. See also **Fine motor-skills delay.**

Lupus

Lupus is a chronic auto-immune disease with a wide variety of symptoms including skin rashes, arthritis, aching joints, extreme fatigue and mouth ulcers.

Diet is not a cure but readers with lupus report improvement in their symptoms. Most likely culprits include salicylates and additives, amines, dairy foods and gluten, in roughly that order.

Ménière's disease

This involves repeated attacks of **vertigo**, **tinnitus** and **hyperacusis** with fluctuating but progressive hearing loss. Ménière's sufferers often come from a food-intolerant family and have other symptoms of food intolerance, as I have seen myself since my father lost the hearing in one ear due to Ménière's. It is now understood that Ménière's sufferers need to avoid all salicylate-containing drugs and lotions and to reduce intake of salicylates and other food chemicals, but some specialists recommend that challenges are avoided or minimised due to the possibility of severe reactions. As well as salicylates, any of the other usual culprits can be involved.

Middle-ear infections – see Ears, nose and throat

Migraines and headaches

A relative with migraines is a sign of a food-intolerant family, so, for example, a grandmother with migraines suggests that a child's behaviour is probably food related.

People with headaches or migraines can be affected by any or all food chemicals, but the most likely culprits are salicylates, preservatives, MSG and amines. Dairy foods, wheat or gluten are less likely to cause problems. Some people find they only have to avoid one additive, such as nitrates in ham, propionate preservative in bread, sulphites in beer or MSG in Chinese or tasty packet foods. Others are sensitive to multiple food chemicals.

'In the last five years I have suffered constantly from mild headaches to severe migraines,' one woman wrote. 'After avoiding additives and salicylates, I became headache-free in three weeks.' Another reported an improvement in the frequency her migraines after going on a low-amine diet, but it took a 'really, really bad' migraine associated with dried fruit to show her that sulphite preservatives were a problem too.

Young children are not able to describe head pain, but from characteristic migraine-related childhood behaviour, such as hiding under a bed, it is now realised that migraines can affect children of any age, even babies.

Mood swings

These can be strongly related to food. The most likely culprits are some preservatives, salicylates, other additives, amines, dairy and gluten, in roughly that order. For some families, just avoiding the bread preservative 282 can make a noticeable difference. See also **Depression** and **Hyperactivity**.

Mouth-breathing – see Ears, nose and throat

Multiple sclerosis (sensory symptoms)

The sensory symptoms of multiple sclerosis can be affected by foods. A reader with daily fatigue and sensory symptoms due to MS reported feelings of cold, particularly in her legs. 'They are not cold to touch, but I perceive them to feel like ice blocks,' she wrote. She experienced the sensation on a range from minimal (limited to the smallest spot on one leg and hardly noticeable – rated 2 on a scale of 1–10) to very noticeable (both legs feeling cold, rated 8 on a scale of 1–10). 'When I went 100 per cent failsafe after a period of not being so strict,' she wrote, 'after 4 weeks my cold sensations had reduced dramatically to about 1–2 out of 10.' People with MS are likely to be sensitive to most of the usual culprits, including salicylates, additives, amines, dairy, gluten, as well as a range of perfumes and other VOCs. See the 'Multiple Sclerosis' factsheet on www.fedup.com.au.

Myalgia (muscle pains) associated with lethargy and chronic fatigue syndrome (CFS)

These symptoms can be associated with food intolerance, although the lethargy improves better on diet than myalgia. See **Chronic fatigue syndrome**.

Nasal polyps – see Samter's triad

Nasal speech – see Ears, nose and throat

Nausea – see Irritable bowel symptoms

Night terrors – see Sleep

Nosebleeds
Frequent nosebleeds have been reported due to dairy foods, salicylates and amines, but any of the usual culprits can be involved. For more about nosebleeds and salicylates see also the 'HHT (Hereditary haemorrhagic telangiectasia) and salicylates' factsheet on www.fedup.com.au.

Numbness (paraesthesia) – see Loss of sensation

Nystagmus (eye movements)
Improvements in nystagmus (rapid uncontrolled involuntary movement of the eye, often from side to side) related to the additive-free low salicylate diet were described by Dr Feingold nearly 30 years ago. Nystagmus may be so subtle it is unnoticeable but will contribute to reading delay. Any of the usual culprits can be involved, with salicylates and additives the prime suspects. See also **Strabismus** and **Visual acuity**.

Obsessive tendencies – see Depression

Oppositional defiance
Oppositional defiance disorder (ODD) can exist with or without ADHD. Children with oppositional defiance feel irritable and frequently say 'no'. Other symptoms include losing temper, arguing with adults, refusing adult requests or defying rules, deliberately annoying other people, blaming others for their own mistakes, touchy or easily annoyed, and angry or resentful. Medications for ADHD can make these children worse because they are better able to focus on being defiant. Children with oppositional defiance need careful handling because authoritarian management can exacerbate the problem. A quiet, calm approach works best. Avoid confrontations and hitting because when they are big enough they will hit you back or lash out at others. All of the symptoms of oppositional defiance can improve on the diet. The most likely culprits are salicylates and

additives, amines, dairy foods and gluten, in roughly that order. See the 'Oppositional Defiance Disorder (ODD)' factsheet on www.fedup.com.au.

LIFE WITH AN OPPOSITIONAL CHILD

'Before my son started the diet, if he was doing something he wanted to do, everything was hunky dory, but every school day was a struggle from the minute he woke up, just to get him out of bed, eating breakfast, dressed, ready and into the car. At the school, some mornings were fine, others I would have to physically drag him into the classroom.

'The diet has changed all of that. He is up and dressed often before us, breakfast, chores done and into school happy. Occasionally he tries it on but it is always short-lived. I wouldn't say he has turned into a saint, but he is now "normal" and does his chores with only the occasional whingeing.' Reader NT

Pallor (pale skin)

Dairy products are often reported as a cause of pale skin, but pallor can be associated with any of the usual culprits – additives and salicylates, amines, dairy and wheat. See also **Allergic shiners**.

Panic attacks – see Depression

Perfume sensitivity

Some people are more sensitive than others to volatile organic compounds – perfumes, pesticides and other smelly industrial chemicals. Trust your nose. A person who is sensitive can be affected by a smell that others can't detect. See a list of possible problem fumes and perfumes on p. 260. One mother delivers her child to his classroom each morning. If there is a child, teacher or parent with perfume she takes her son home again because he will not learn anything that day. Her son is doing well in mainstream schooling, but she says: 'He would be classified as autistic if he was on the average Australian diet.'

Persistent night waking – see Sleep

Pins and needles – see Loss of sensation

Poor handwriting – see Fine motor-skills delay

Postnatal depression – see Premenstrual tension

Premenstrual tension (PMT), premenstrual syndrome (PMS), postnatal depression

Symptoms of PMS can disappear on diet. Readers have also reported complete disappearance of postnatal depression – see the 'Depression' factsheet on www. fedup.com.au. Some readers report a reduction of period pain and the clotting that is thought to contribute to period pain; others have reported that PMS is related to food chemicals, but pain is related to the level of fat in their diet. Most likely culprits include salicylates and additives, amines, dairy foods and gluten, in roughly that order.

Pruritis – see Itchy skin rashes

Pseudo heart attack – see Heart palpitations

Psoriasis

Psoriasis is an autoimmune disease that causes chronic or recurring red scaly patches on the skin. It can also cause inflammation of the joints, abnormalities of the fingernails and toenails, and increase the risk of heart attack. There are numerous reports of improvements from readers and a well-recognised gluten connection so it is worth trying the elimination diet including avoidance of gluten and dairy. See a remarkable story of failsafe recovery from psoriatic arthritis including psoriatic nail disease at http://members.ozemail.com. au/~btrudget/Bernards_Story/my_arthritis_story1.htm and under **Arthritis** in this section.

Reading delay – see Learning disabilities

Recurrent mouth ulcers

Mouth ulcers (aphthous ulcers) are usually small, painful ulcers that heal in about 7–10 days. They can occur singly or in groups. Aphthous ulcers are a medically recognised symptom of gluten intolerance in coeliacs, but it is less well understood that any of the usual food-intolerance culprits can be involved, especially salicylates and additives.

Reflux or heartburn or Gastroesophageal Reflux Disease (GERD)

In recent years there has been a dramatic increase in the number of babies and adults diagnosed with Gastroesophageal Reflux Disease in Western countries, compared to Asian countries where the Western lifestyle has not yet displaced traditional foods and regurgitation is regarded as a common symptom in healthy infants that decreases spontaneously with age. Readers find that reflux is strongly related to diet with additives and salicylates being the main offenders but the other usual culprits can be involved too. Colours, flavours and preservatives in reflux medication for babies can be part of the problem so some mothers have had to use plain adult medication in appropriately reduced doses. Breastfeeding mothers may need to undergo a supervised elimination diet and formula-fed babies may need special prescription-only formulas (p. 266).

Restless legs syndrome (RLS)

RLS is a relatively new disorder characterised by crawling, burning or uncomfortable feelings in the legs and an uncontrollable urge to move the legs in an attempt to relieve these feelings. Symptoms are worse during periods of immobility: for example, sitting in a classroom, meeting or cinema, travelling on trains or planes or while lying down and trying to go to sleep. People with RLS often move constantly in an effort to feel more comfortable: pacing, fidgeting, moving their legs while sitting, or tossing and turning in bed. Symptoms can range from mild to severe, and can interfere with sleep, work and relationships. RLS symptoms can be associated with the side effects of medications, food chemicals and exposure to environmental chemicals and are exacerbated by overtiredness. See the compelling story on our DVD (p. 298) about a woman whose RLS symptoms are strongly related to food chemicals as well as perfumes and perfumed products. Any of the usual culprits are likely to be involved:

salicylates including perfumes, additives, amines, dairy foods and gluten, in roughly that order.

Restlessness

Restlessness, including hyperactivity, inability to settle, constantly leaving seat in the classroom, fidgeting and 'can't sit still' is one of the main behavioural effects of food chemicals. The most likely culprits are artificial food colours, other additives and salicylates, amines, dairy foods and gluten, in roughly that order. See also **Hyperactivity**.

Ribo rash

As well as the traditional causes of itchy skin rashes, a new group of additives have been strongly associated with itchy skin rashes as well as the full range of food intolerance symptoms, including children's behaviour problems.

Introduced about ten years ago, flavour enhancers of the nucleotide group (disodium inosinate 627, disodium guanylate 631, disodium ribonucleotides 635) are used to make MSG taste up to 15 times stronger. They can appear in products labelled 'No MSG' although usually there is a natural form of MSG such as yeast extract, hydrolysed vegetable protein or similar. In our experience, readers have different reactions to MSG and ribonucleotides. Both can cause any of the usual food intolerance symptoms, but the most commonly reported reaction to ribonucleotides is itchy rash and/or swelling of the lips, tongue or eyes known as angio-oedema. Reactions can start anywhere from immediately to several days later and can last for a week or more, sometimes coming and going and moving around during that time.

Because of the delayed onset, some consumers have suffered from a distressing ribo rash for up to ten years before discovering the cause of their problems. For example, a cup of 635-containing soup for Friday lunch can result in an itchy rash at 8 pm on Saturday evening. These flavour enhancers are used extensively in tasty packet foods, instant noodle-flavour sachets, soups, stocks, stock cubes and sauces, sausages, rotisseried or fresh stuffed chickens, ready meals, seasoned fresh meat from butchers, restaurant meals, flavoured salt and takeaways. See the 'Ribo Rash' factsheet on the website www.fedup.com.au.

Round-shouldered posture – see Low muscle tone

Runny or stuffed-up nose – see Ears, nose and throat

Samter's triad (asthma, nasal polyps, aspirin sensitivity)
About 20 per cent of asthmatics are affected by salicylates, including asthmatics with Samter's triad, also called aspirin-induced asthma (AIA). Samter's patients improve on a low salicylate diet which uses the latest results. Any of the usual culprits can also be involved.

Selective mutism – see Speech delay

Self-harm
Self harm or Deliberate Self-Harm (DSE) is defined as intentionally injuring your own body without suicidal intent, most commonly by cutting, hitting or burning. Although previously considered to be associated with severe mental illnesses, the rate of self-harm behaviour is now known to be more common among the general population and seems to be increasing in younger generations. Readers report that self-harm is related to food intolerance. One 6-year-old whose self-harm stopped as soon as he began his supervised elimination diet responded on day 8 of the salicylate challenge by going to bed as normal then 'began to write swear words all over his bed, his sheets and his body' ('I was angry with you because I couldn't fall asleep'). The most likely culprits include some preservatives, salicylates, other additives, amines, dairy foods, gluten and perfumes, in roughly that order. See the 'Self-harm' factsheet on www.fedup.com.au.

Silly noises, talks too much (empty chatter), loud voice
Loud voice (no volume control) and silly noises – chicken, duck, animal, truck, tuneless humming, anything else that drives parents mad – are some of the symptoms most commonly reported to clear up on the diet. Most likely culprits include additives and salicylates, amines, dairy foods and gluten, in roughly that order.

Skin rashes – see Itchy skin rashes

Sleep: difficulty falling asleep (DFA), persistent night waking, insomnia, night terrors, sleepwalking

Food chemicals can affect sleeping patterns in various ways. Although parents may not realise it, children who go to bed at 7 pm but don't fall asleep until 9 pm are not being naughty, they may genuinely have difficulty falling asleep. This can affect any age group, from breastfed babies – since food chemicals are passed on through breastmilk – to adults. Some people can fall asleep quickly but wake frequently during the night, or wake and then are unable to get back to sleep. Chronic insomnia, unsettled babies, **restless legs syndrome**, night terrors and sleepwalking can all be related to food chemicals, especially salicylates, preservatives and artificial colours but any of the usual culprits can be involved. If suffered frequently, sleep deprivation can contribute to depression. See also **sleep apnoea**, below, and the 'Diet, sleep disturbance and insomnia' factsheet at www.fedup.com.au.

Sleep apnoea

It is not medically recognised that sleep apnoea can be associated with food intolerance, yet improvements due to diet have been reported in all ages from babies to seniors. Any of the usual culprits can be involved. For an account of sleep apnoea and narcolepsy related to amines, see http://home.comcast.net/~exmlclass/pdf/tofamily.pdf. See also **Ears, nose and throat**.

'Sneaky poos' (encopresis)

Previously known as soiling or kids who poo in their pants, this condition is strongly related to food intolerance and children often become symptom-free within days of starting an elimination diet. Prime suspects are the usual culprits: salicylates and additives, amines, dairy and wheat or gluten, in roughly that order.

Snoring – see Ears, nose and throat

Speech delay, stutter, selective mutism, vocal tics, word and phrase repetition, talks too much (empty chatter)

Speech delay in young children can improve within days of starting diet. With one 12-year-old whose mouth muscles were affected by amines it was obvious if he had been breaking his diet because his speech became more difficult to understand. His mother presumably had the same problem because she reported that her mouth felt numb when she ate amines, but any food chemical can be responsible: additives, salicylates, amines and glutamates as well as dairy foods, wheat or gluten. Many readers report that stuttering clears up when they start the diet, see also **Silly noises**, **Tic disorder** and the 'Stuttering' factsheet on the website www.fedup.com.au.

'Sticky poos' – see Incomplete evacuation

Stomach ache – see Irritable bowel syndrome

Strabismus (squint)

Diet-related improvements in strabismus (eyes not pointing in the same direction) were described by Dr Feingold nearly 30 years ago. Any of the usual culprits can be involved, with salicylates and additives being prime suspects. See also **Nystagmus** and **Visual acuity**.

Stutter – see Speech delay

Suicidal thoughts – see Depression

Sweating excessively (hyperhidrosis)

Aspirin and some other medications are known to cause excessive sweating, and some readers report that their excessive sweating or **body odour** improve on diet. Any of the usual culprits, including salicylates, can be involved.

Tachycardia – see Heart palpitations

Talks too much (empty chatter) – see Silly noises

Tantrums

Temper tantrums, including whining, crying, screaming, hitting, kicking, breath holding and even vomiting, are part of normal development in young children. On average, children aged 1–4 throw about 5–8 tantrums per week with most tantrums lasting for less than 5 minutes, but 25 per cent of tantrums last longer and some children are more prone to tantrums than others. Food additives have been found to cause tantrums in toddlers, even in those with no history of hyperactivity. While artificial colours and preservatives have been the focus of most research, all of the usual culprits – especially salicylates – need to be considered.

Throat-clearing – see Ears, nose and throat

Thrush

Many people think that the way to treat thrush is with the candida (yeast-free and sugar-free) diet, but the candida diet is not scientifically proven. Readers report that a low-salicylate low-amine diet is more effective and easier to follow than the candida diet. See the 'Candida, yeast, sugars and hypoglycaemia' fact-sheet on www.fedup.com.au.

Tic disorder

Improvements in motor and vocal tics related to the additive-free low-salicylate diet were described by Dr Feingold nearly 30 years ago. Any of the usual food chemical culprits can be involved. Readers have reported tics from flavour enhancers, salicylates and 'junk food'. The mother of an 8-year-old diagnosed with Chronic Tic Disorder – due to tics in his face, neck, shoulders and arms so severe that he couldn't sit still – realised that the tics were due to synthetic antioxidant 320 (BHA) in hot chips he had been eating as a treat. When he stopped eating hot chips, the tics went away. When he ate hot chips again, the tics recurred. MSG, preservatives and artificial colours have also been reported, but any of the usual culprits can be involved – salicylates and other additives, amines, dairy and gluten.

Tinnitus

Tinnitus is a ringing or roaring sound in the ears. Tinnitus, **vertigo** and reversible hearing loss are regarded as the first signs of salicylate toxicity in adults. Any of the other usual culprits can be involved. See also **Ménière's disease**.

Tonsillitis

More than 50 years ago, Dr Feingold argued that when tonsillitis is a manifestation of food sensitivity, surgical removal of enlarged tonsils or adenoids in the absence of infection will not fix the problem because it is not addressing the cause. His opinions are still relevant and we often hear from surprised parents who have discovered that surgery is no longer needed as a result of the elimination diet. Dairy foods, salicylates and/or additives are likely to be a major problem, but everyone is different and all of the usual culprits need to be considered.

Tourette symptoms – see Tic disorder

Ulcerative colitis

It is not medically recognised that ulcerative colitis can be food-related yet many readers say that their symptoms improve on the diet. A woman who discovered she was sensitive to salicylates and amines went from 'ulcerative colitis with associated liver problems and spontaneous bruising … the doctors were talking about a possible liver transplant in ten years' to recovery with 'quite good liver function' on the diet. Another found that wheat and gluten were a problem. Any of the usual culprits can be involved.

Unable to concentrate – see 'Foggy brain'

Unexplained fatigue – see Chronic fatigue syndrome

Unmotivated – see 'Foggy brain'

Urinary incontinence, urinary urgency – see Bladder

Urticaria – see Itchy skin rashes

Vertigo
Vertigo is a loss of balance that can range from unsteadiness while walking to a sudden severe spinning sensation that can cause nausea or vomiting. With **tinnitus** and reversible hearing loss it is regarded as one of the first signs of salicylate toxicity in adults. Any of the other usual culprits can be involved. See also **Ménière's disease**.

Visual acuity
Diet-related improvements in visual acuity were described by Dr Feingold nearly 30 years ago. Readers have reported 'thinking I needed a new prescription for my contact lenses' while inadvertently off-diet and an optometrist has reported diet-related changes in visual acuity in people with CFS. Any of the usual culprits can be implicated, with salicylates and additives as the prime suspects. See also **Nystagmus** and **Strabismus**.

Vocal tics – see Speech delay

Vomiting – see Irritable bowel symptoms

Word and phrase repetition – see Speech delay

Support and Further Information

The Food Intolerance Network at www.fedup.com.au provides:

- independent information about the effects of food on behaviour, health and learning ability in both children and adults, and
- support for families using a low-chemical approach, free of additives, low in salicylates, amines and flavour enhancers (FAILSAFE) for health, behaviour and learning problems.

Quarterly **Failsafe Newsletters** are available free (Email with 'subscribe' in the subject line to failsafe_newsletter-subscribe@yahoogroups.com) or can be seen on the website.

You can join one of several free failsafe support groups, where experienced people can provide information and assistance. Special groups include failsafebaby, failsafeadult and failsafeasthma. See **email support groups** on www.fedup.com.au for up-to-date information.

There are many local contacts and regional email groups that can provide information about local foods and dietitians. See **local contacts** and **email support groups** on www.fedup.com.au.

Email confoodnet@ozemail.com.au for our list of **supportive dietitians**.

BOOKS

General information about food intolerances, along with comprehensive charts showing the content of natural salicylates, amines and glutamate in most common foods is available in *Friendly Food* (by Anne Swain, Velencia Soutter and Robert Loblay, Murdoch Books, Australia, 2004). *Friendly Food* and additional information about the RPAH Elimination Diet and challenge protocols can be obtained online via the RPAH Allergy Unit website (www.cs.nsw.gov.au/rpa/allergy).

Additive Alert: Your guide to safer shopping, Julie Eady, Additive Alot Pty Ltd, 2004, **ISBN** 9780977517619 (available at www.additivealert.com.au and through bookstores).

Sue Dengate's earlier books are all out of print but may be found in many public libraries:

Different Kids: Growing Up with Attention Deficit Disorder, Sue Dengate, Random House, Australia, 1994, **ISBN** 9780091830519

Fed Up: Understanding how food affects your child and what you can do about it, Sue Dengate, Random House, Australia, 1998, **ISBN** 9780091836986

Fed Up with Asthma: How food affects asthma and what you can do about it, Sue Dengate, Random House, Australia, 2003, **ISBN** 9781740510561

Fed Up with ADHD: How food affects children and what you can do about it, Sue Dengate, Random House, Australia, 2004, **ISBN** 9781740512305

DVDS

Fed Up with Children's Behaviour: How food and additives affect behaviour, Sue Dengate, 2006 **ISBN** 9780646459257 (available through www.fedup.com.au, Australia Online Bookstore www.bookworm.com.au, Capers Bookstore www.capersbookstore.com.au, or by ordering at any Angus & Robertson bookstore).

1-2-3 Magic: managing difficult behaviour in children 2–12, Dr Thomas Phelan, 2004, **ISBN** 9781889140162 (available from www.parentmagic.com or in Australia from www.parentshop.com.au).

SCIENTIFIC REFERENCES

There is a detailed list of current scientific references on www.fedup.com.au.

Notes and References

Most of the abstracts and some of the full texts of cited articles are available from www.pubmed.com.

Are You Affected by Food Chemicals?

p. 1   What we eat has changed – see 'The Idler' conversation with Joanna Blythman at http://www.idler.co.uk/archives/?page_id=88 and Blythman J, *Shopped: the shocking powers of British supermarkets*, London, Fourth Estate, 2004.

p. 1   Children have changed – 'for almost every single indicator, except death', our children are doing worse, see Professor Fiona Stanley on 'the epidemic of the 21st century which is mental health problems, behaviour problems, kids who are falling out of the school system, kids who are going into drug addiction, suicide ...' http://www.abc.net.au/stateline/sa/content/2003/s900445. htm; Stanley F and others, *Children of the Lucky Country? How Australian society has turned its back on children and why children matter*, Sydney, Pan Macmillan Australia, 2005.

p. 3   Research 'favourable to the source of funding' – Lexchin J and others, 'Pharmaceutical industry sponsorship and research outcome and quality: systematic review', *British Medical Journal*, 2003;326(7400):1167–70; Daniells S, *Transparency is the key to the science kingdom*, http://www.foodproductiondaily.com/news/printNewsBis.asp?id=71815.

p. 3   'Independent scientists', see Jacobson MF and Schardt MS, *Diet, ADHD and behaviour: a quarter-century review*, Washington DC, Centre for Science in the Public Interest, 1999 (free full text of 37 page report or Executive Summary on pages 5–6), http.cspinet.org/diet.html.

p. 3   Jamie Oliver at Wingfield Primary School, *Jamie's School Dinners* DVD (Episode 4), Fresh One Productions, 2005, www.jamieoliver.com.

p. 3   Appleton Central Alternative High School, Wisconsin USA, healthy eating program, see http://www.feingold.org/PF/wisconsin1.html.

p. 5   Updated recommendations for possible prevention of allergy due to precautions during pregnancy and breastfeeding, see http://www.allergy.org.au/aer/infobulletins/food_allergy.htm.

p. 5   Food intolerance and food allergy – see the Australasian Society of Clinical Immunology and Allergy info bulletin at http://www.medeserv.com.au/ascia/aer/infobulletins/food_intolerence.htm; Clarke L and others, 'The dietary management of food allergy and food intolerance in children and adults', *Australian Journal of Nutrition and Dietetics*,1996;53(3):89–94. In Europe, food intolerance is often called pseudoallergy.

p. 6   Consumers will make the connection between what they eat and how they feel 'only if the reaction occurs within 30 minutes' – McDonald JR and others, 'Aspirin intolerance in asthma: detection by oral challenge', *J Allergy Clin Immunol*, 1972;50(4):198–207.

p. 7   'People from low income areas ... eat more junk food' – people living in areas from the poorest socioeconomic category have been found to have 2.5 times the exposure to fast food outlets than people in the wealthiest category, see Reidpath DD and others, 'An ecological study of the relationship between social and environmental determinants of obesity', *Health Place*, 2002;8(2):141–5.

p. 8   Babies and perfumed products – infant diarrhoea and earache were associated with air freshener use, and diarrhoea and vomiting were associated with aerosol use in Farrow A and others, 'Symptoms of mothers and infants related to total volatile organic compounds in household products', *Arch Environ Health* 2003;58(10):633–41.

p. 9   'Introduced by Dr Ben Feingold in the 1970s' – in a book (Feingold BF, *Why your child is hyperactive*, New York, Random House, 1974) and 27 medical journal articles indexed by pubmed, unavailable in electronic form except for Feingold BF, 'Tonsillectomy in the allergic child', Calif Med ,1949;71(5):341–4 (free full text available, as relevant today as when it was written more than 50 years ago) and Feingold BF, 'Dietary management of nystagmus', *J Neural Transm*, 1979;45:107–115 (abstract only, ditto), www.feingold.org/bio.html.

p. 9   'Australian researchers' – see *Friendly Food* (by Anne Swain, Velencia Soutter and Robert Loblay, Murdoch Books Australia, 2004). *Friendly Food* and additional information about the RPAH Elimination Diet and challenge protocols can be obtained online via the RPAH Allergy Unit website (www.cs.nsw.gov.au/rpa/allergy).

p. 9   The Few Foods diet has achieved some excellent results in Europe but is extremely difficult to do, see Pelsser LM and Buitelaar JK, 'Favourable effect of a standard elimination diet on the behavior of young children with attention deficit hyperactivity disorder (ADHD): a pilot study', *Ned Tijdschr Geneeskd*

2002;146(52):2543-7. The diet I recommend is much easier but can achieve similar results when done properly.

p. 9   Additive creep – from 1955, production of artificial food colours in the USA increased fourfold over four decades (in Jacobson MF and Schardt MS, *Diet, ADHD and behaviour: a quarter-century review*. Washington DC: Centre for Science in the Public Interest, 1999); between 1960–1970 there was a 30–70 per cent increase in the amounts of several sulphite preservatives used in the USA (Taylor SL and others, 'Sulfites in foods', *Adv Food Res*, 1986;30:1–76); MSG was introduced into western food in 1948 and its use has continued to increase since then (Samuels A, 'The toxicity/safety of processed free glutamic acid (MSG): a study in suppression of information', *Accountability in Research*, 1999;6(4):259–310); the nucleotide flavour enhancers including 635 were introduced to the world in the late 1990s (Sommer R, *Yeast extracts: production, properties and components*, 9th International Symposium on Yeasts, Sydney, 1996); in 2001 Australian food regulators approved an increase in the maximum permitted level of the bread preservative calcium propionate 282 to the highest in the world despite knowing of consumer concerns (FSANZ, *Food Standards Code*, Food Standards Australia New Zealand, 2001, www.foodstandards.gov.au).

p. 11   'Lunch is a bundle of chemicals' – quote from Tom Jaine in the introduction to Drummond JC and Wilbraham Anne, *The Englishman's Food*, Pimlico, London, 1994.

p. 11   'Side effects of aspirin' – Azer M, Salicylate toxicity, www. emedecine.com/med/topic2057.htm.

p. 11   'Protean manifestations' of chronic salicylate toxicity – Bailey RB and Jones SR, 'Chronic salicylate intoxication', *J Am Geriatr Soc*, 1989;37(6):556-61.

p. 11   Knife attack while 'under the influence of salicylates' – Bywaters E, Comment on salicylate toxicity in Lamont-Havers RW, Wagner BM (eds), 'Proceedings of the Conference on Effects of Chronic Salicylate Administration', New York City 1966, US Dept of Health, Education and Welfare, National Institute of Arthritis and Metabolic Disease, 1968, p. 176.

p. 11   'Australian researchers published a new analysis of salicylate contents in foods' – Swain AR, Dutton SP, Truswell AS, 'Salicylates in foods', *J Am Diet Assoc*, 1985;85(8):950–60. You can see the list at http://www.purr.demon.co.uk/Food/Salicylate. html, but note that some foods such as cauliflowers are given very different ratings in the RPAH elimination diet.

p. 12   Amines – see Amine factsheet on www.fedup.com.au. People who are taking certain drugs including recreational hallucinogens such as Ayahuasca have to avoid some amine-containing foods. Hence the list at http://www.biopark.org/peru/maoi-1.html of 'foods to avoid when taking monoamine oxidase inhibitors'. It's similar to but not the same as the RPAH elimination diet list.

p. 13   World Health Organisation estimates that 20–30% of asthmatic children are affected by sulphites – Fifty-first meeting of the Joint FAO/WHO Expert Committee on Food Additives. Safety Evaluation of Certain Food Additives: evaluation of national assessments of sulfur dioxide and sulfites and addendum. Geneva: World Health Organisation, 1999. This is a low estimate considering that Towns and Mellis found nearly 70% of asthmatic children reacted to an oral sulphites challenge in 'Role of acetyl salicylic acid and sodium metabisulfite in chronic childhood asthma', *Pediatrics*, 1984;73(5):631–7.

p. 13   Dingle school, UK – the trial included testing by Professor Jim Stevenson from Southampton University Psychology Department: www.spcottawa.on.ca/ofsc/food_additives.html.

p. 15   For more information about food additives, see Hanssen M, *Additive Code Breaker*, Melbourne, Lothian, 2002.

p. 15   Cochineal allergy – Chung and others, 'Identification of carmine allergens among three carmine allergy patients', *Allergy*, 2001 56(1):73-7.

p. 21   The behaviour management program *1–2–3 Magic* by Dr Thomas Phelan really does work like magic once the diet kicks in, and can double the effect of the diet (www.parentmagic.com or www.parentshop.com.au).

Breakfasts

p. 31   Gluten in oats due to contamination -- Hogberg L and others, 'Oats to children with newly diagnosed coeliac disease', *Gut*, 2004;53(5):649-54.

p. 35   Inulin can cause allergic reactions such as throat swelling, nasal itching, coughing and breathing difficulty. Inulin occurs naturally in leeks and garlic, some other vegetables and in processed foods including yoghurt, see Franck P and others, 'Anaphylactic reaction to inulin: first identification of specific IgEs to an inulin protein compound', *Int Arch Allergy Immunol*, 2005;136(2):155-8.

Lunches and Snacks

p. 60   Overconsumption of fruit juice has been associated with toddler diarrhoea, short stature and obesity – Dennison BA and others, 'Excess fruit juice consumption by preschool-aged children is associated with short stature and obesity', *Pediatrics*, 1997;99(1):15-22.

p. 65   Benefits of kefir: Rodrigues KL and others, 'Antimicrobial and healing activity of kefir and kefiran extract', *Int J Antimicrob Agents*, 2005;25(5):404–8. As living organisms, kefir grains need care similar to goldfish, see *Kefir Grains: the essential manual* by Dominic N Anfiteatro on http://users.sa.chariot.net.au/~dna/Makekefir.html.

Lunches

p. 68   Sulphur dioxide in gelatine – from Sulphur dioxide in sausages and other products, ACT Health Services Food Survey Reports 1996–97, http://www.health.act.gov.au/c/health?a=da&did=10017393&pid=1053855655.

Main Meals

p. 70   Iodised salt is recommended – *FSANZ seeks public comment on mandatory iodine fortification of food*, press release, 18 August 2006, www.foodstandards.gov.au.

p. 75   Vacuum packing can inhibit the growth of bacteria but does not necessarily retard the development of amines – Nadon CA and others, 'Biogenic amines in vacuum-packaged and carbon dioxide-controlled atmosphere-packaged fresh pork stored at -1.50 degrees C', *J Food Prot*, 2001;64(2):220–7.

p. 81   Sulphites in pet meat can cause life-threatening thiamine deficiency – Australian Veterinary Association press release, *AVA warns of deadly preservatives in pet food*, 5/5/06, http://www.ava.com.au/news.php?c=0&action=show&news_id=165; Steel RJ, 'Thiamine deficiency in a cat associated with the preservation of 'pet meat' with sulphur dioxide', *Aust Vet J*, 1997;75(10):719–21.

p. 81   The illegal use of sulphur dioxide was found in 58% of samples tested in October 2004 by the NSW Food Authority, www.foodauthority.nsw.gov.au, showing that sulphite preservatives will be used unless monitoring is constant and strict.

p. 90   Psychologist Steve Biddulph recommends that a boy of 10 should be able to prepare an entire evening meal for the family in *Raising Boys*, Finch Publishing Sydney, 1997, see pages 95-96.

p. 102   'parents give up ... after two or three attempts' from a Newspoll survey commissioned by Kelloggs, Fussy eaters: research, www.kelloggs.com.au. Another study found that daily tasting for 14 days is an effective way of increasing children's acceptance of a new vegetable: Wardle J and others, 'Increasing children's acceptance of vegetables', *Appetite*, 2003;40(2):155–62.

p. 102   Vegetables and nutrition – for excellent nutrition information, see   http://www.healthyeatingclub.com/info/books-phds/books/foodfacts/html/data/data-fs.html or talk to your dietitian.

p. 105   Antioxidant power of dried beans, fruit etc – Melton L, 'The Antioxidant Myth', *New Scientist*, 2563, 05 August 2006; 40–43.

p. 109   Brussels sprouts contain a chemical called sinigrin (sinagrin) which suppresses the development for pre-cancerous cells with an effect so powerful that researchers from Norwich Park Institute of Food Research think the occasional meal of sprouts could destroy these cells in the colon. Unfortunately, plant breeding to make sprouts taste milder reduces the cancer fighting effect. Smith TK and others, 'Effects of Brussels sprout juice on the cell cycle and adhesion of human colorectal carcinoma cells (HT29) in vitro', *J Agric Food Chem*, 2005;53(10):3895–901; http://www.ifr.ac.uk/public/foodinfosheets/brassicas.html.

p. 119   Bagging salads destroys nutrients – Serafini M and others, 'Effect of acute ingestion of fresh and stored lettuce (Lactuca sativa) on plasma total antioxidant capacity and antioxidant levels in human subjects', *Br J Nutr.*, 2002;88(6):615–23.

p. 121   Nutritional value of eggs – Song WO and Kerver JM, 'Nutritional contribution of eggs to American diets', *J Am Coll Nutr*, 2000;19(5 Suppl):556S-562S.

p. 127   'Vine ripened' tomatoes picked at the breaker stage as described by Howard Wener, a Vegetable Consultant with AgriSupportOnline – 'Battle of the tomato brands' by Steven Carruthers, *Practical Hydroponics and Greenhouses*, issue 72, Sept/Oct 2003, http://www.hydroponics.com.au/back_issues/issue72.html.

Something Sweet

p. 134   Antioxidants in Red Delicious apples – *New Scientist*, issue 2251, 12/8/2000, p. 50.

p. 137   Rhubarb as a bestseller – http://www.foodnavigator.com/news/ng.asp?id=66460-rhubarb; rhubarb's laxative effects are due to its natural sennosides content – Peigen X and others, 'Ethnopharmacologic study of Chinese rhubarb', *J Ethnopharmacol*, 1984;10(3):275–93; rhubarb has been found to reduce inflammation and promote gastrointestinal motility in gastric surgery patients – Cai J and others, 'Effects of perioperative administration of rhubarb on acute inflammatory response in patients with gastric cancer', *Zhong Xi Yi Jie He Xue Bao*, 2005;3(3):195–8.

p. 139   'Sugar doesn't cause hyperactivity' – the following researchers found no behavioural effects due to sugar and I agree with them. The behavioural effects that sugar is blamed for are generally due to salicylates (see next item) and additives. Wolraich ML and others, 'Effects of diets high in sucrose or aspartame on the behavior and cognitive performance of children', *N Engl J Med*, 1994;330(5):301-7.

p. 139   'a link between salicylates and sugar' – the 'hypoglycemic effect' of salicylates is discussed in Arena FP and others, 'Salicylate-induced hypoglycemia and ketoacidosis in a nondiabetic adult', *Arch Intern Med*, 1978;138(7):1153-4.

p. 159   Commercial muesli bars can contain more kilojoules than Mars Bars, and fruit 'more likely to have come from a laboratory than an orchard', see 'Healthy lunch snacks? Mars offers better diet' by Kelly Burke, 26/9/06 http://www.smh.com.au/news/national/healthy-lunch-snacks-mars-offers-better-diet/2006/09/25/1159036472167.html and the Choice test on muesli bars, www.choice.com.au.

p. 173   We don't recommend artificial sweeteners such as aspartame (951) because many scientists consider their safety is unproven, see Olney JW and others, 'Increasing brain tumor rates: is there a link to aspartame?', *J Neuropathol Exp Neurol*, 1996;55(11):1115-23.

p. 182   Sorbitol intolerance thought to affect up to 30% – Jain NK and others, 'Sorbitol intolerance in adults: prevalence and pathogenesis on two continents', *J Clin Gastroenterol*, 1987;9(3):317-9. Some pediatric iron supplements contain sorbitol. See Sugar-free sweeteners factsheet on www.fedup.com.au.

Others

p. 183   Annatto 160b in butter – Mikkelsen H and others, 'Hypersensitivity reactions to food colours with special reference to the natural colour annatto extract (butter colour)', *Arch Toxicol Suppl*, 1978(1):141-3.

p. 183   For more about trans fats, see the Trans Fat report on the Australian Consumer Association website, www.choice.com.au.

p. 198   Nature identical flavours – see definitions of added flavours on the Food Standards Australia New Zealand website, www.foodstandards.gov.au.

Food for Special Occasions

p. 208   Mercury in fish – if you eat more than 2–3 serves of fish per week it is important to limit intake of fish high in mercury such as flake/shark, particularly for pregnant women and young children, see the Mercury in Fish brochure on www.foodstandards.gov.au or available from FSANZ phone 02 6271 2241.

p. 218   Organic gardening more nutritious, higher in salicylates – see Nutritional Considerations by the Organic Trade Association, 2006, http://www.ota.com/organic/benefits/nutrition.html.

p. 221 Deaths from adverse effects of health care – Starfield B, 'Is US health really the best in the world?' *JAMA*, 2000;284(4):483-5; http://www.health-care-reform.net/causedeath.htm.

p. 222   'People will get well from most illnesses', see *Where There is No Doctor* by David Werner ('perhaps the most widely used health care manual in the developing world'), Chapter 5: Healing without Medicines, http://hesperian.info/assets/WTND/WTND_Chapter_5.pdf.

p. 224, 274   Antinutritional effects of food additives – Stammati A and others, 'In vitro model for the evaluation of toxicity and antinutritional effects of sulphites', *Food Addit Contam*, 1992;9(5):551-60; Steel RJS, 'Thiamine deficiency in a cat associated with the preservation of 'pet meat' with sulphur dioxide', *Aust Vet J* 1997;75:719-721; Koutsogeorgopoulou and others, 'Immunological aspects of the common food colorants, amaranth and tartrazine', *Vet Hum Toxicol*, 1998;40(1):1-4. Propionic acid causes in vitro immunosuppression, Wajner M et al, 'Inhibition of mitogen-activated proliferation of human peripheral lymphocytes in vitro by propionic acid', *Clin Sci* (Lond), 1999, 96(1),99-103.

p. 224   Folate (also called folic acid) is probably the most common vitamin deficiency according to nutritionist Dr Rosemary Stanton in *Eating for Peak Performance*. For more about folate and pregnancy, ask your doctor, dietitian or see the Folate report at www.choice.com.au.

p. 225   Salicylates and Vitamin C compete for excretion in the kidney – Basu TK, 'Vitamin C-aspirin interactions', *Int J Vitam Nutr Res Suppl*, 1982;23:83-90.

p. 227   Decreases in essential nutrients – Lobstein T, 'Plants lose their value', *Food Magazine*, 64; Jan/Mar 2004: 12-13, www.foodcomm.org.uk/PDF%20files/plants_lose_value.pdf; 'Meat and dairy: where have the minerals gone?', *Food Magazine*, 72; Jan/Mar 2006, www.foodcomm.org.uk/PDF%20files/meat_dairy2.pdf; 'Vegetables without Vitamins', *Life Extension Magazine*, March 2001, www.lef.org/LEFCMS/aspx/PrintVersionMagic.aspx?CmsID=34628; bagged salads, see Serafini and others, above (p. 301).

Gluten-free Cooking

p. 228   Coeliac disease – Duggan JM, 'Coeliac disease: the great imitator', *Med J Aust*, 2004;180(10):524–6 (http://www.mja.com.au/public/issues/180_10_170504/dug10818_fm.html). Selby W, *Gluten enteropathy*, http://www.australianprescriber.com/magazine/24/2/38/40/.

p. 231   Gluten in food additives – Sue Shepherd, 'Food Additives', *The Australian Coeliac Magazine* (quarterly publication of the Australian Coeliac Society), Dec 2003, http://www.coeliac.com.au/FoodAdditives.aspx.

Symptoms of Food Intolerance

p. 269   ADHD-type behaviours – children do not have to be diagnosed with a 'condition' to improve behaviourally on diet. In my bread preservative study, 100% of children who completed two to three weeks of their elimination diet improved significantly. They had all been referred to paediatricians for behaviour problems and some were diagnosed with ADHD. All scored in the top 15% on rating scales for irritability, restlessness, inattention or sleep disturbance. Dengate S and Ruben A, 'Controlled trial of cumulative behavioural effects of a common bread preservative', *J Paediatr Child Health*, 2002;38(4):373–6. 'Salicylates and preservatives are as important as colours... in that order' – Swain A, Soutter V, Loblay R, Truswell AS. 'Salicylates, oligoantigenic diets, and behaviour', *Lancet*, 1985;2(8445):41–2; Loblay RH, Swain AR. 'Food intolerance', in Wahlqvist ML, Truswell AS, *Recent Advances in Clinical Nutrition*. London: John Libbey, 1986, pp. 169–177.

p. 270   Allergic shiners and pallor related to dairy products – this is in my experience.

p. 270   Angio-oedema and Ribo Rash – as far as we know, the Food Intolerance Network was the first in the world to report dramatic itchy rashes and angio-oedema related to flavour enhancer 635 (ribonucleotides) soon after its introduction and we coined the name Ribo Rash. We regularly receive emails from the UK and USA from ribonucleotide victims whose health professionals have been unable to help them.

p. 270   Arthritis – the diet connection is rarely recognised in the medical literature. See Bernard's account of psoriatic arthritis overcome by diet at http://members.ozemail.com.au/~btrudget/Bernards_Story/my_arthritis_story1.htm

p. 271   Sulphites most associated with asthma – Fifty-first meeting of the Joint FAO/WHO Expert Committee on Food Additives, *Safety Evaluation of Certain Food Additives: sulfur dioxide and sulfites,* Geneva: World Health Organisation, 1999; effects of benzoates – Balatsinou L and others, 'Asthma worsened by benzoate contained in some antiasthmatic drugs', *Int J Immunopathol Pharmacol*, 2004;17(2):225–6.

p. 272   Autistics and VOCs – Slimak K, 'Reduction of autistic traits following dietary intervention and elimination of exposure to environmental substances', Proceedings of 2003 International Symposium on Indoor Air Quality and Health Hazards, National Institute of Environmental Health Sciences, USA, and Architectural Institute of Japan, Tokyo, Japan 2003;2:206–216.

p. 273   Bedwetting and urinary urgency – Egger J and others, 'Effect of diet treatment on enuresis in children with migraine or hyperkinetic behaviour', *Clin Pediatr* (Phila), 1992;31(5):302–7 and my own experience in the bread preservative study (Dengate and Ruben, 2002, see above).

p. 273   Chinese Restaurant Syndrome symptoms are described in http://www.nlm.nih.gov/medlineplus/ency/article/001126.htm#Symptoms. Research results are likely to be favourable to the source of funding, see Samuels A, 'The toxicity/safety of processed free glutamic acid (MSG): a study in suppression of information', *Accountability in Research*, 1999;6(4):259–310, www.truthinlabeling.org.

p. 274   Constipation associated with dairy foods – Iacono G and others, 'Food intolerance and chronic constipation: manometry and histology study', *Eur J Gastroenterol Hepatol*, 2006;18(2):143–50; associated with salicylates, see Loblay and Swain, above, p. 303.

p. 275   Depression and food intolerance – Parker G and Watkins T, 'Treatment-resistant depression: when antidepressant drug intolerance may indicate food intolerance', *Aust NZ J Psychiatry*, 2002;36(2):263–5; and see depression factsheet on www.fedup.com.au.

p. 276   Ears, nose and throat – Feingold BF, 'Recognition of food additives as a cause of symptoms of allergy', *Ann Allerg*, 1968;26:309–313; Pacor ML and others, 'Monosodium benzoate hypersensitivity in subjects with persistent rhinitis', *Allergy*, 2004;59(2):192–7.

p. 278   The following study found that people with asthma or rhinitis (not necessarily due to allergy) are more likely to have geographic tongue than the general population – Marks R and others, 'Geographic tongue: sensitivity to the environment', *Oral Surg Oral Med Oral Pathol*, 1984;58(2):156–9.

p. 279   Heart palpitations related to MSG and salicylates – Gann D, 'Ventricular tachycardia in a patient with the "Chinese restaurant syndrome"; *South Med J,* 1977;70(7):879–81; Mukerji V and others, 'Cardiac conduction abnormalities and atrial arrhythmias associated with salicylate toxicity', *Pharmacotherapy,* 1986;6(1):41–3; Bhan AK and Brody C, 'Propionic acidemia: a rare cause of cardiomyopathy', *Congest Heart Fail,* 2001;7(4):218–219.

p. 280   'Salicylate's hypoglycaemic activity' – Arena FP and others, 'Salicylate-induced hypoglycemia and ketoacidosis in a nondiabetic adult', *Arch Intern Med,* 1978;138(7):1153–4.

p. 282   Irritable bowel symptoms – Gunn MC and others, 'Management of irritable bowel syndrome', *Postgrad Med J,* 2003;79(929):154–8, http://pmj.bmj.com/cgi/content/full/79/929/154; salicylates and irritable bowel symptoms, see Loblay and Swain above, p. 303.

p. 282   Kidneys and bladder – Laurent J and others, 'Is adult idiopathic nephrotic syndrome food allergy? Value of oligoantigenic diets', *Nephron,* 1987;47(1):7–11; Pelikan Z and others, 'The role of allergy in interstitial cystitis', *Ned Tijdschr Geneeskd,* 1999;143(25):1289–92; cystitis groups recognise food effects – www.hebs.scot.nhs.uk/services/pubs/pdf/Cystitis.pdf.

p. 283   Learning disabilities – the number of children classified as learning disabled dropped from over 12 per cent to less than 5 per cent with the removal of 16 food additives from school food in Schoenthaler S and others, 'The impact of a low food additive and sucrose diet on academic performance in 803 New York City public schools', *Int J Biosoc Res,* 1986;8(2):185–195.

p. 284   Migraine – Egger J and others, 'Is migraine food allergy? A double-blind controlled trial of oligoantigenic diet treatment', *Lancet,*1983;2(8355):865–9; Millichap JG, Yee MM, 'The diet factor in pediatric and adolescent migraine', *Pediatr Neurol,* 2003;28(1):9–15; see Loblay and Swain, above, p. 303.

p. 286   Nystagmus – Feingold BF, 'Dietary management of nystagmus', *J Neural Transm,* 1979;45:107–115.

p. 287   Exposure to perfumed products and other volatile organic compounds has been linked to asthma, autism, depression, eczema, infant diarrhoea and ear ache, migraines and many other food intolerance symptoms, see Sherriff A and others, 'Frequent use of chemical household products is associated with persistent wheezing in pre-school age children', *Thorax,* 2005;60(1):45–9 (free full text http://thorax.bmj.com/cgi/content/full/60/1/45); Farrow A and others, 'Symptoms of mothers and infants related to total volatile organic compounds in household products', *Arch Environ Health,* 2003;58(10):633–41 and fumes and perfumes factsheet on www.fedup.com.au.

p. 288   A 30-year-old with severe psoriasis has about three times the heart attack risk of a similarly aged person without psoriasis, see http://news.bbc.co.uk/1/hi/health/6033673.stm; gluten and psoriasis – Wolters M, 'Diet and psoriasis: experimental data and clinical evidence', *Br J Dermatol,* 2005;153(4):706–14.

p. 289   Recurrent mouth ulcers and gluten – Bucci P and others, 'Oral aphthous ulcers and dental enamel defects in children with coeliac disease', *Acta Paediatr,* 2006;95(2):203–7.

p. 289   Reflux is increasing in babies and adults – Western doctors say this is due to better diagnostic methods but in Asia, where the Western lifestyle has not yet displaced traditional foods, doctors say that the nature of Western infant reflux differs from that in Asia. Regurgitation is a common symptom in healthy Asian infants that decreases spontaneously with age. For adults, the highest prevalence is in the country with the highest intake of processed food (USA, 42 per cent) and of the countries surveyed, lowest in the country with the lowest intake of processed food (Italy, 9 per cent). Osatakul S and others, 'Prevalence and natural course of gastroesophageal reflux symptoms: a 1-year cohort study in Thai infants', *J Pediatr Gastroenterol Nutr,* 2002;34(1):63–7; Miyazawa R and others, 'Prevalence of gastro-esophageal reflux-related symptoms in Japanese infants', *Pediatr Int,* 2002;44(5):513–6; Delaney BC, 'Review article: prevalence and epidemiology of gastro-oesophageal reflux disease', *Aliment Pharmacol Ther,* 2004;20 Suppl 8:2–4.

p. 291   Self harm – Klonsky ED and others, 'Deliberate self-harm in a nonclinical population: prevalence and psychological correlates', *Am J Psychiatry,* 2003;160(8):1501–8, free full text at www.pubmed.com for an overview of self-harm.

p. 294   Tantrums 'with no history of hyperactivity' – in 'Additives do cause temper tantrums', from *The Food Magazine,* 25/10/02 http://www.foodcomm.org.uk/additive_2002_full.htm; Potegal M and others, 'Temper tantrums in young children', *J Dev Behav Pediatr,* 2003;24(3):140–54 described in http://raisingchildren.net.au/articles/temper_tantrums.html; video of a typical tantrum at http://www.visit4info.com/details.cfm?adid=9115.

p. 295   Tonsillitis can be food-related – Feingold BF, 'Tonsillectomy in the allergic child', *Calif Med,* 1949;71(5):341–4 (free full text available at www.pubmed.com).

p. 296   Visual acuity related to diet is mentioned in Feingold's paper about nystagmus and strabismus, see above, p. 304.

For more details, see Scientific References on www.fedup.com.au.

Index

1-2-3 Magic (DVD), 298
abnormal tingling, 269
additives to avoid, 15
adenoids, 269
ADHD and ADHD-type behaviours, 269
airline foods, 214
alcohol, 65
Alison's
    crumbed cutlets, 82
    failsafe breadcrumbs, 194
    lunchbox pear or apple pies, 135
allergic shiners, 270
allergy, 5
amaranth, 34
American terms, 29
amine
    choc top banana ice–cream, 207
    chocolate mud cake, 207
    banana cake, 208
amines, 12
    in fermented products, 259
    in meat, 73, 83, 259
    in seafood, 99
Andra's 'honey' roll, 163
Andra's chicken noodle soup, 43
angina-type pain, 270
angio-oedema, 270
annatto 160b natural yellow colour, 153, 256
Anne's easy ice-cream (13% fat), 147
Annette's Spanish omelette, 122
antidote for food reactions, 224
antioxidants in oils, 183, 257
anxiety, 270
Anzac biscuits, 168
Arran's fried rice, 57
arthritis, 270
artificial sweeteners, 173
ASD (Autistic Spectrum Disorder), 270

asparagus, 113
Asperger's Syndrome, 272
aspirin-induced asthma, 271
asthma, 271
Aussie toad in the hole, 37
Australian-American terms, 29
Autism, Asperger's Syndrome, ASD, 270
avoiding dairy foods or gluten, 263, 266, 268
babies, finger food for, 59
babies, Neocate, 266
bad breath, 272
baked
    custard, 155
    pears, 133
    potatoes, 105
baking powder, gluten-free, 233
banana cake, amine, 208
banana ice-cream, amine choc top, 207
banana, golden, 134
barley vegetable casserole, 116
basic dip, 188
basic plain cake, *see* Fete Cake, 161
bean
    and pasta salad, 43
    butter, on toast, 57
    dip, 189
    green and corn bake, 123
    Howard's paste, 106
    mixed salad, 120
    quick vegetable stir-fry, 115
    whole green salad, 120
beans, 105
bedwetting, 272
beef
    and leek pie filling, 45
    Failsafe mince, 76
    Failsafe rissoles, 73
    Failsafe, 73
    kebabs, 84

mince and potato casserole, 82
mince topping, 76
quick stroganoff, 87
roast, 88
see also steak and mince
beer, 65
beetroot, 112
behaviour management, 20, 23, 298
behaviour, 1, 272
behaviour, ADHD and ADHD-type behaviours, 269
benzoate preservatives, 221, 271
besan bombs, 237
big Anzacs, 168
Birgit's
    baked muesli bars, 160
    cabbage rolls, 109
    cheese pasta sauce, 129
    glazed meatballs, 74
    Indonesian style fried rice, 96
    pear glazed steak, 84
    pear jam, 186
    pear ketchup, 192
birthday parties, 199
biscuit, 158
    Anzac, 168
    butter kisses, 170
    butterscotch, 168
    gluten-free carob and cashew brownies, 245
    Highlander, 170
    lazy biscuits, 245
    macaroons, 140
    melting moments, 170
    Mrs Cattle's, 169
    quick lunchbox, 167
    Rebecca's gingerless pigs, 169
    rice flour (gluten-free), 246
    shortbread, 170
    slice and bake, 167
    water crackers, 55
    yum balls, 158

black rice pudding with
    butterscotch sauce, 155
bladder: bedwetting (enuresis), urinary
    urgency, urinary incontinence, 273
bloating, 182, 267, 273
body odour, 273
Bombe Alaska, 203
bombs, besan, 237
bread and butter pudding, 154
bread preservative, 268, 273, 274,
    279, 283, 285, see also whey
    powder
bread, 40, 42, 85
    dinky di damper, 216
    Emma's (in the breadmaker), 41
    garlic, 127
    gluten, dairy, soy and yeast-free,
        234
    princess, 202
    tortilla, 78
breadcrumbs, Alison's failsafe, 194
breakfast, 31
breastfed babies and food intolerance,
    8, 292
breastfeeding, 8
breastmilk, 8, 266
Brenda's microwave carob cake, 200
Brussels sprout puree, 110
Brussels sprouts with sauce, 110
Brussels sprouts, 109
bubble and squeak, 109
burgers, 74
burritos, 77
butter beans on toast, 57
butter kisses, 170
butter, 183
    garlic, 185
    maple cashew, 188
butterscotch, 178, 179
    biscuits, 168
    Lachlan's, 179
    meringue pudding, 143
    pudding, 244
cabbage on the side, 109
cabbage, 108
cafés, 211

cake, 158
    amine banana, 208
    amine chocolate mud, 207
    Brenda's microwave carob, 200
    caramel, 164
    Caroline's classic baked
        cheesecake with dairy-free
        option, 157
    carrot, 162
    classic sponge, 165
    coffee, 164
    cool cup, 162
    cornflour sponge, 242
    Deborah's 'chocolate' (gluten-
        free), 240
    fete, 161
    gluten-free plain, 242
    ice-cream birthday, 201
    Jane's pear dessert, 162
    Madeira (gluten-free), 240
    melt and mix coffee (gluten-
        free), 241
    never-fail carob, 200
    no-bake cheese, 156
    pear shortcake squares, 136
    poko (pear and choko), 163
    sticky gingerbread (gluten-free),
        241
    Vienna fudge (eggless), 201
calcium propionate see bread
    preservative
calcium, 226
campfire potatoes, 216
camping and hiking, 215
canola oil, 184
canteens, school, 50
caramel
    cake, 164
    carob slice, 171
    fudge, 179
    icing, 197
    milkshake, 62
    pears, 134
    sauce or spread, 186
caramels, 177
carob,
    Brenda's microwave cake, 200

caramel slice, 171
cashew spread, 187
chocolate-style topping, 194
crackles, 182
dixie cups (4% fat), 150
gluten-free cashew brownies, 245
hot sauce, 194
icing, 166
icypole, 67
lamingtons, 165
milkshake, 62
never-fail cake, 200
self-saucing fudge pudding
    (gluten-free), 244
Caroline's classic baked cheesecake
    with dairy-free option, 157
carrot cake, 162
carrots, 112
cashew carob spread, 187
cashew paste warning, 188
cashew paste, Deborah's, 187
cashew, maple butter, 188
catarrh, 273
cereal toppings, 32
cereals, processed, 32
challenge, 9, 21, 204, 260, 263
challenge diary, 204
Checklist of common mistakes, 255
cheese topping, 126
cheesecake, Caroline's classic baked
    with dairy-free option, 157
cheesecake, no-bake, 156
chemicals, exposure to, 260, 272, 289
Chickadamias, 55
chicken, 90
    balls, 93
    casserole, 94
    chickpeas, 99
    creamy pasta, 48
    Darani's amazing chicken
        noodle stew, 71
    golden, 92
    HFC (Halliwell Fried Chicken),
        90
    hot roll, 42
    lasagne, 130
    leek stir-fry, 97

mini pizzas, 238
Nana's soup, 72
noodle frittata, 98
noodle snack, 43
noodle soup, Andra's, 43
nuggets, 90, 91, 93
parcels, 98
Rebecca's panfried, 92
risotto, 95
roast, 94
satay, 97
schnitzel, 93
seasoning or stuffing, warning, 256
shaker nuggets, 91
shallot pie filling, 45
stock, 96
topping, 126
yoghurt sauce, 98
chickpeas, 105
Chinese restaurant syndrome, 273
chips, additives in commercial, 104
chips, French fried potato, 104
chocolate-style topping, 194
chokoes, 111
chronic fatigue syndrome (CFS), 274
citric lemon juice, 194
classic
    cheesecake, 157
    pavlova, 140
    sponge, 165
clumsy child, 274
coeliac syndrome, 228, 268
coffee cake, 164
cold-pressed oil warning, 184
colds, flu, cough, 274
coleslaw, 118
colic in babies and adults, 274
colitis, 274
colours, natural home-made, 197
constipation, 274, 281, 282
cool cup cakes, 162
coordination disorder, 274
cordials, additives in, 63
corn and green bean bake, 123
cornflour sponge, 242
cornflour, 229

Cornish pasties, Australian-style, 47
cottage pie, 79
country vegetable bake muffins, 114
cows' milk substitutes, 267
cracked egg pies, 121
cradle cap, 275
creamy
    chicken pasta, 48
    tofu dressing, 190
    vegetable casserole, 116
crisps, commercial, 104
crisps, Failsafe, 54
crunchy potatoes, 53
cups, jelly, 153
cups, magic jelly, 68
custard, baked, 155
custard, Narni's, 153
cystitis, 275
dairy, avoiding, 263, 266
damper, dinky di, 216
Darani's amazing chicken noodle
    stew, 71
dark brown sugar warning, 258
Deborah's
    cashew paste, 187
    'chocolate' cake, 240
    gluten-free flour mix with soy,
        233
    gluten-free flour mix, 233
defiant ones, 7, 286
dental treatment, 258
depression, anxiety, panic attacks, self
    harm, suicidal thoughts, obsessive
    tendencies, 275
dermatitis, 275
diarrhoea, 182, 274, 275, 281
dietitians, 17, 297
Different Kids (book), 298
difficulty falling asleep (DFA), 275
dinky di damper, 216
dip
    basic, 188
    bean, 189
    beetroot, asparagus, garlic,
        shallot, salmon, 188
    Failsafe hummus, 189
    lentil or spread, 189

Doctor's Orders, 223
Dominic's pop-rocks, 181
Dominion pudding, 202
dressing, creamy tofu, 190
dressing, quick salad, 191
drinks, alcoholic, 65
drugs,
    additives in, 221
    containing amines, 221
    containing salicylates, 221
dumplings, golden, 154
DVDs, 298
dysaesthesia, 283
ears, nose and throat: frequent middle
    ear infections, glue ear, need for
    grommets, runny or stuffed up
    nose, frequent throat clearing,
    frequent tonsillitis, enlarged
    adenoids, nasal speech, mouth-
    breathing, bad breath, snoring, 276
easily distracted, 276
Easter eggs, 204
easy rice pudding, 155
eczema, 276
egg, 121
    and vegetable stir-fry, 122
    Annette's Spanish omelette, 122
    Aussie toad in the hole, 37
    cracked egg pies, 121
    Foo Yung, 122
    French toast, 37
    frittata for vegetable haters, 115
    plain omelette, 38
    quick quiche, 123
    rolls, 57
    scrambled, on toast, 37
    spread, 185
elimination diet, 2, 9, 17, 262
email support groups, 297
Emma's bread (in the breadmaker),
    41
encopresis, 276
English toffee pie, 141
enuresis, 276
environmental chemicals, 260, 272,
    289
epilepsy, 276

Ethan's menu, 39
excessive sweating, 293
eyedrops, 258
Failsafe, 9
    bread, 40
    burgers, 74
    Irish Cream (alcoholic drink for the over-18s), 65
    hummus, 189
    margarine, 183
    mince topping, 76
    Newsletters, 297
    rissoles, 73
    sausages, 75
    substitutes, 27
    support groups, 297
    trail mix, 217
fairy floss (cotton candy), 177
fast food chains, 210
fatigue, 277
fats and oils, 183
Fed Up (book), 298
Fed Up with ADHD (book), 298
Fed Up with Asthma (book), 298
Fed Up with Children's Behaviour (DVD), 298
Fete Cake, 161
fibre, 102, 257
filling, beef and leek pie filling, 45
filling, Grandma's caramel tart, 141
fine motor-skills delay, poor handwriting, letter and number reversals, gross motor-skills delay, 'clumsy child', coordination disorder, round shouldered posture, low muscle tone, 277
finger food for babies, 59
fish and chips, 99
fish, amines, 99
five-minute oats, 31
flavour enhancers, 16, 44, 46, 54, 72, 290, 294, see also MSG, Ribo Rash
flavours, 16, 198, 256
flour, gluten-free mixes, 233
'foggy brain' (disorganised and forgetful), 278
food additives to avoid, 15

Food Intolerance Network, 297
food intolerance
    symptoms, 269
    adults, 7
    numbers affected, 13
food reactions, antidote for, 224
French fried potato chips, 104
French toast, 37
frequent colds and flu, 274
Frequently Asked Questions, 262
Fridge list, 26
fried rice, Arran's, 57
fried rice, Birgit's Indonesian style, 96
Friendly Food (book), 298
frittata for vegetable haters, 115
frittata, chicken noodle, 98
frozen Rice Bubble bars, 180
frozen yoghurt iceblocks, 67
fruit flavours, 198
fruit for desserts, 132
fruit ice-cream, 152
fruit juice, 60, 63, 265
fruit, salicylates in, 11, 132, 219
fudge, caramel, 179
garbanzo see Chickadamias, 55
gardening, 218
garlic
    bread, 127
    butter, 185
    meat topping, 125
    pasta, 129
Gastroesophageal Reflux Disease (GERD), 289
gelatine, sulphites in, 68, 132, 146
geographic tongue (benign migratory glossitis), 278
giftedness, 278
gin, 65
gingerbread muffins, 243
glucono-delta-lactone, 232
glucose syrup, sulphites in, 132, 178
glue ear, 278
glutamates, naturally occurring, 2, 9, 111
glutamates, see MSG, Ribo Rash, flavour enhancers

gluten intolerance, 228, 268
gluten, avoiding, 268
gluten, dairy, soy and yeast-free bread, 234
gluten-free cooking, 228, see also variations on most other recipes
gluten-free
    alternatives to wheat flours, 233
    baking powder, 233
    flour, Deborah's mix with soy, 233
    flour, Deborah's mix, 233
    products, 230
golden
    banana, 134
    chicken, 92
    dumplings, 154
    marinade, 195
    nuggets, 175
    pears or apples, 134
Grandma's caramel tart filling, 141
gravy home-made, 191
green peas, 111
grilled meat and three veg, 83
grommets, 278
gross motor-skills delay, 278
growing pains, 278
Halliwell Fried Chicken (HFC), 90
hamburgers, 74
head banging, 279
headaches, 279
hearing loss, 279
heart palpitations, tachycardia, angina-type pain, pseudo heart attack, 279
heartburn, 289
heavy metals, 260
herbed rack of lamb, 89
herbs and herbal remedies warning, 11, 176, 221, 258
HFC (Halliwell Fried Chicken), 90
Highlander biscuits, 170
hiking and camping, 215
hives, 280
home-dried pears, 217
home-made dairy ice-cream (15% fat), 148

honey, substitute for, 185
honeycomb, 175
hot
    carob sauce, 194
    chicken roll, 42
    lemon drink, 224
Howard's bean paste, 106
Howard's pear crumble, 135
hummus, Failsafe, 189
hyperactivity, 280
hyperacusis, 280
hypoglycaemia, 280
IBS, 282
iceblocks, frozen yoghurt, 67
ice-cream, 146
    amine choc top banana, 207
    Anna's easy (13% fat), 147
    birthday cake, 201
    carob dixie cups (4% fat), 150
    home-made dairy (15% fat), 148
    ice-cream maker (10% fat), 148
    icey ricey (non-dairy) (2% fat),
        151
    pear with dairy-free option (7%
        fat), 146
    pure fruit, 152
    soy (non-dairy) (6% fat), 150
    syrup (non-dairy) (3% fat), 149
icecups, 66
icey ricey ice-cream (2% fat), 151
icing
    'lemon', 197
    caramel, 197
    carob, 166
    coffee, 197
    cream cheese, 197
    Vienna cream frosting, 197
    white, 196
icypoles, 66
    carob, 67
    commercial warning, 66
    vitamin, 68
illegally unlisted additives warning, 257
immunosuppressive effects, 274
impossible zucchini bake, 206
inattention, easily distracted,
    unmotivated, easily bored, 280

incomplete evacuation ('sticky poos',
    'sluggish bowel'), 281
Indian style lamb with leeks and
    potatoes, 86
Indian yoghurt drink (lassi), 63
indigestion, 281
Indonesian style fried rice, Birgit's,
    96
industrial chemicals, 260, 287
insomnia, 281
intolerance symptoms, 269
Irish stew, 85
irritability, 281
irritable bowel symptoms, 282
itching, burning, irritations of the
    skin, 223
itchy skin rashes, hives (urticaria),
    eczema, dermatitis, cradle cap,
    angio-oedema (swollen lips, eyes,
    tongue), itching (pruritis), 282
jam
    Birgit's pear, 186
    maple syrup, 185
    salicylates in, 187
Jane's pear dessert cake, 162
Japanese style tofu in sauce, 113
jelly cups, 153
jelly cups, magic, 68
kebabs, 84
kefir drink, 65
Kerry's vegetable-hater soup, 72
ketchup, Birgit's pear, 192
kidneys and bladder: recurrent
    inflammation (cystitis, interstitial
    cystitis, idiopathic nephritic
    syndrome), 282
kisses (gluten-free), 246
Lachlan's butterscotch, 179
lactose-free milk, 267
lamb
Alison's crumbed cutlets, 82
    herbed rack, 89
    Indian style with leeks and
        potatoes, 86
    Irish stew, 85
    kebabs, 84
    roast, 88

lamingtons, carob, 165
lasagne, special occasion, 130
lazy biscuits, 245
learning disabilities, reading delay,
    283
leek sauce, 192
leeks, 108
legumes – chickpeas, lentils and dried
    beans, 105
lemon
    drink, hot, 224
    icing, 197
    juice, citric, 194
    meringue pie, 143
    mousse, 145
    sago cups, 152
lentil, 105
    mash, 107
    pie, 117
    Red Soup, 70
    spread or dip, 189
lethargy, 274, 277
letter and number reversals, 283
lobsters, 99
local contacts, 297
lollipops, 177
loss of sensation, abnormal tingling
    (pins and needles), numbness
    (paraesthesia), abnormal and
    sometimes unpleasant sensations
    (dysaesthesia), 283
loud voice, 291
low muscle tone, 283
lunch, school suggestions, 49
lunchbox
    Alison's pear or apple pies, 135
    Margie's muffins, 161
    quick biscuit, 167
lupus, 283
macaroons, 140
Madeira cake, 240
magic
    cordial, 63
    jelly cups, 68, 153
    spread, 185
mango sorbet, 152
mango, 138

maple
   cashew butter, 188
   syrup jam, 185
   syrup, mock, 193
margarine, Failsafe, 183
Margarita topping, 127
Margie's lunchbox muffins, 161
marinade, 83
   golden, 195
   pear and celery, 195
   pear and yoghurt, 195
marshmallow slice, 171
marshmallows, 173
Mary's potato bake, 104
mayonnaise
   Mighty Mayo (aka Robin's
      dressing), 190
   quick, 190
measures, 28
meat loaf, 82
meat, 73
meatballs, Birgit's glazed, 74
medications, 221
medications, herbal remedies and
   supplements warning, 221
mega-bites, 174
melt and mix coffee cake, 241
melting moments, 170
memory impairment, 278
Ménière's disease, 284
menu, weekly, see Fridge List
meringue, butterscotch pudding,
   143
meringue, lemon pie, 143
middle ear infections, 284
Mighty Mayo (aka Robin's
   dressing), 190
migraines and headaches, 284
milk and alternatives, 266
milk, rice, 268
milkshake, carob, caramel,
   'strawberry', 62
millet, 235
millet porridge, 236
mince
   and potato casserole, 82
   Birgit's glazed meatballs, 74

cottage pie, 79
Failsafe topping, 76
meat loaf, 82
rissoles, 73
mini
   chicken pizzas, 238
   pavs, 139
   pies, Sammy's steak and pea,
      80
mistakes, Checklist, 255
mixed bean salad, 120
mock cream, 196
mock maple syrup, 193
mood swings, 285
mountain burritos, 77
mousse, lemon, 145
mousse, pear, 133
mouth-breathing, 285
Mrs Cattle's biscuits, 169
MSG (monosodium glutamate), 16,
   273, 284, 290
muesli bar
   Birgit's baked, 160
   pear, 159
   rolled oat, 160
   warning, 159
muesli slice, 239
muesli, gluten-free, 34
muesli, toasted, 33
muffins
   country vegetable bake, 114
   gingerbread (gluten-free), 243
   Margie's lunchbox, 161
   weekly (gluten-free), 243
multiple sclerosis (sensory symptoms),
   285
Mum's mash, 110
muscle symptoms, 285
mushy peas, 112
mussels with sauce, 102
myalgia (muscle pains) associated
   with lethargy and chronic fatigue
   (CFS), 285
Nana's chicken soup, 72
Narni's custard, 153
nasal polyps, 285
nasal speech, 285

natural
   colours (home-made), 197
   food chemicals, 10
   fruit flavours warning, 198
nausea, 286
Neocate babies, 266
never-fail carob cake, 200
Newsletters, Failsafe, 297
night terrors, night waking, 286
nitrate and nitrite preservatives, 16,
   50, 279, 284
no-bake cheesecake, 156
no-bake, quick pear slice, 172
non-dairy ice-creams, 149
non-food factors, 261
noodle
   soup, 69
   Andra's chicken soup, 43
   chicken frittata, 98
   chicken snack, 43
   Darani's amazing chicken stew,
      71
noodles warning see Ribo Rash
nose, runny or stuffed up, 276
nosebleeds, 286
not brandy sauce, 203
nuggets, golden, 175
numbness (paraesthesia), 286
Nutella, see carob cashew spread, 187
nutrition, 224
nystagmus (eye movements), 286
oats, 31
obsessive tendencies, 286
oil, salicylates in, 184
oils and fats, 183
omelette, Annette's Spanish, 122
omelette, plain, 38
oppositional defiance, 286
oven fries, 103
oysters natural, 101
paella, Spanish with mussels and
   scallops, 101
pallor (pale skin), 287
pancake, 35
   for one, 36
   gluten-free for one, 236
   rice hoppers, 237

secret, 145
  with gluten-free self-raising
    flour, 238
panfried fish, 100
panic attacks, 287
pasta, 128
  and bean salad, 43
  Birgit's cheese sauce, 129
  creamy chicken, 48
  garlic, 129
  spaghetti Caesar, 129
  special occasion lasagne, 130
  three-minute spaghetti, 128
pastry,
  commercial warning, 46, 116
  short crust, 48
  sweet and/or gluten-free, 48
pavlova, classic, 140
pavlova, mini pavs, 139
PBJs, 218
pear, 61, 133, 256
  Alison's lunchbox pie, 135
  and celery marinade, 195
  and yoghurt marinade, 196
  baked, 133
  Birgit's jam, 186
  Birgit's ketchup, 192
  caramel, 134
  clafoutis, 142
  crumble, 135
  fool, 134
  golden or apples, 134
  home-dried, 217
  Howard's crumble, 135
  ice-cream with dairy-free option
    (7% fat), 146
  Jane's pear dessert cake, 162
  juice warning, 61
  mousse, 133
  muesli bars, 159
  poko cake, 163
  quick no-bake slice, 172
  ricotta pie, 156
  sauce, 191
  shortcake squares, 136
  smoothies, 61
  sorbet, 152

peas, 111
perfume sensitivity, 287
perfumes, industrial chemicals and
  heavy metals, 260, 287
persimmon wine, 65
persimmons, 138
persistent night waking, 288
pie, 44
  Alison's lunchbox pear or apple,
    135
  beef and leek filling, 45
  chicken and shallot filling, 45
  Cornish pasties Australian-style,
    47
  commercial warning, 46
  cottage, 79
  cracked egg, 121
  English toffee, 141
  impossible zucchini bake, 206
  lemon meringue, 143
  lentil, 117
  pear ricotta, 156
  Sammy's steak and pea mini, 80
  vegetable, 117
pikelets, 53
pikelets, rice flour, 236
pins and needles, 288
pizza, 124
  commercial warning, 124, 125
  Margarita, 127
  mini chicken, 238
  yeasted, 124
  yeastless, 125
plain cake, see Fete Cake, 161
playdough recipe, 198
poko cake (pear and choko), 163
poor handwriting, 288
popcorn warning, 55
popples, 58
porridge
  five-minute oats, 31
  gluten-free, 236
  millet, 236
  rice, 33
postnatal depression, 288
potato, 103
  and garlic topping, 126

and mince casserole, 82
and tuna, 208
baked, 105
campfire, 216
commercial warning, 54, 104
crisps, 54
crunchy, 53
French fried chips, 104
Mary's bake, 104
oven fries, 103
rosti cakes, 104
salad, 119
Tex Mex, 105
traditional Scottish salad, 119
wedges, 54
premenstrual tension (PMT),
  premenstrual syndrome (PMS),
  postnatal depression, 288
preschool alternatives to a plate of
  fruit, 49
preservatives to avoid, 15
princess bread, 202
processed cereals, 32
product changes, 257
propionate preservatives, 16, 258
pruritis, 288
pseudo heart attack, 288
psoriasis, 288
pudding,
  black rice with butterscotch
    sauce, 155
  bread and butter, 154
  butterscotch (gluten-free), 244
  butterscotch meringue, 143
  Dominion, 202
  easy rice, 155
  rice, 144
  sago milk cups, 152
  self-saucing carob fudge (gluten-
    free), 244
  self-saucing microwave golden
    syrup, 144
  Yorkshire, 89
pumpkin scones, 52
pumpkin, 112
punishment for bad behaviour, 20,
  264

pure fruit ice-cream, 152
quiche, quick and mini, 123
quick
    beef stroganoff, 87
    lunchbox biscuit, 167
    mayonnaise, 190
    no-bake pear slice, 172
    processor scones, 52
    quiche, 123
    salad dressing, 191
    vegetable and bean stir-fry, 115
quiet ones, 7, 269
rabbit provençal, 89
rashes, *see* itchy skin rashes, Ribo Rash
rating scale, 23
raw sugar, 258
reading delay, 288
Rebecca's panfried chicken, 92
Rebecca's gingerless pigs, 169
recurrent mouth ulcers, 289
Red Soup, 70
reflux, 289
remedies, 221
restless legs syndrome (RLS), 289
restless ones, 7, 272
restlessness, 290
rhubarb, 137
    stirabout, **138**
    stewed, **137**
Ribo Rash, 290
rice, 230
    Arran's fried, 57
    balls, 56
    Birgit's Indonesian style fried, 96
    black rice pudding, 155
    Bubble bar, frozen, 180
    Bubble treats, 174
    chicken risotto, 95
    easy pudding, 155
    flour biscuits, 246
    flour pikelets, 236
    hoppers, 237
    milk, 196
    porridge, 33
    pudding, 144
    puffs, 160
    salad, 120

ricotta, pear pie, 156
ringing in the ears, *see* tinnitus
rissoles, Failsafe, 73
roast chicken, 94
roast lamb or beef, 88
**Robin's dressing (aka Mighty
    Mayo)**, 190
rolled oat bars, 160
rosti potato cakes, 104
roundshouldered posture, 291
Royal Prince Alfred Hospital (RPAH)
    Allergy Unit, 2, 17, 298
RPAH Elimination Diet, 2
runny or stuffed up nose, 291
rusks, 59
sago, lemon cups, 152
sago, milk pudding cups, 152
salad dressing, quick, 191
salad
    bean and pasta, 43
    mixed bean, 120
    potato, 119
    rice, 120
    slimmers', 213
    super rolls or wraps, 42
    tossed, 118
    traditional Scottish potato, 119
    whole green bean, 120
salicylates, 11, 255, 256
Sammy's steak and pea mini-pies, 80
Samter's triad (asthma, nasal polyps,
    aspirin sensitivity), 291
sandwich, steak with the lot, 44
sandwiches, **40**
sauce,
    caramel, 186
    **herb, garlic, Hollandaise, cheese-
        tasting, white**, 192
    hot carob, 194
    not brandy, 203
    tartare, 191
    whisky cream, 193
    white, 192
sauces, *see also* toppings
sausages
    Failsafe, 75
    in foil, 76

    recipe for butcher, 75
    Wade's sausage rolls, 46
school lunchbox suggestions, 49
school lunches for teenagers, 49
schools, how they can help, 50
scientific references, 299
scones, pumpkin, 52
scones, quick processor, 52
Scottish, traditional potato salad,
    119
scrambled eggs on toast, 37
seafood, amines, 99
secret pancakes, 145
selective mutism, 291
self harm, 291
self-saucing carob fudge pudding,
    244
**self-saucing microwave golden
    syrup pudding**, 144
shaker nuggets, 91
shallots, 108
shampoo warning, 260
sherbet, 173
Shopping list, 247
short crust pastry, 48
shortbread, 170
silly noises, talks too much (empty
    chatter), loud voice, 291
skin rashes, 292
sleep apnoea, 292
sleep: difficulty falling asleep (DFA),
    persistent night waking, insomnia,
    night terrors, sleepwalking, 292
slice
    and bake biscuits, 167
    Birgit's baked muesli bars, 160
    carob caramel, 171
    gluten-free, 239
    marshmallow, 171
    muesli, 239
    quick no-bake pear, 172
    rice puffs, 160
    rolled oat bars, 160
slimmers' salad, 213
smoothies, pear, 61
S'mores, 217
snack rings, 56

snacks, 52, 58
sneaky poos (encopresis), 292
snoring, 292
snow peas and snow pea sprouts, 112
snowballs, 180
soap, see Shopping list
sodium metabisulphite, see sulphite
soft drinks commercial, warning, 63
sorbate preservatives, 15
sorbets, mango or pear, 152
sorbitol warning, 182
soup, 69, 72
    Andra's chicken noodle, 43
    Kerry's vegetable-hater, 72
    Nana's chicken, 72
    noodle, 69
    red, 70
soy ice-cream (6% fat), 150
soymilk, 231, 261
    antioxidants warning, 184
    ricemilk, allergies and infant
        feeding, 268
spaghetti, Caesar, 129
spaghetti, three-minute, 128
Spanish paella with mussels and
    scallops, 101
Spanish, Annette's omelette, 122
special occasion lasagne, 130
speech delay, stutter, selective mutism,
    vocal tics, word and phrase
    repetition, talks too much (empty
    chatter), 293
spices, 11, 162
spirits, 65
sponge, classic, 165
sponge, cornflour, 242
sports drinks, warning, 63
spread
    carob cashew, 187
    Howard's bean paste, 106
    lentil, or dip, 189
    magic, 185
spreads, 40, see also toppings, jam
spring rolls, 78
steak
    and pea mini-pies, Sammy's, 80
    Birgit's pear glazed, 84

sandwich with the lot, 44
sticky gingerbread cake, 241
sticky poos, 293
stir-fries, 80
    basic beef, 81
    chicken and leek, 97
    egg and vegetable, 122
    quick vegetable and bean, 115
    tofu, 114
stock, chicken, 96
stomach ache, 293
strabismus (squint), 293
stress, 260, 264
stuffed up nose, 276
stutter, 293
substitute foods, Failsafe, 27
sugar, 60, 139, 182, 258, 280
sugar-free sweeteners, 182, 282
suicidal thoughts, 293
suicidal thoughts, depression, anxiety,
    panic attacks, self harm, obsessive
    tendencies, 293
sulphite preservatives, 81, 258
    and asthma, 13, 271
    anti-nutritional effect, 224
    in cordial, 63
    in desserts, 132
    in dried fruit, 132, 271
    in gelatine, 68, 146
    in gluten-free flours, 229, 260,
        265
    in mince, 81
Sunday roast topping, 126
super salad rolls or wraps, 42
support groups, 297
sweating excessively (hyperhidrosis),
    293
swedes, 110
sweet pastry, 48
sweeteners, 173, 182, 282
symptoms of food intolerance, 269
syrup ice-cream (3% fat), 149
tachycardia, 293
takeaways, 210
talks too much (empty chatter), 293
tamarilloes, 139
tantrums, 294

tart, Grandma's caramel filling, 141
tartare sauce, 191
temper, see irritability, tantrums
testing for food intolerance, 8
Tex Mex potatoes, 105
thiamine, 224
three-minute spaghetti, 128
throat clearing, 294
thrush, 294
tic disorder, Tourette symptoms, 294
tinnitus, 295
tiredness, 274, 277, 285
toasted muesli, 33
toddlers, finger food for, 59
toffee, 176
    apples, 176
    bark, 181
    English pie, 141
tofu, 113
    stir-fry, 114
    creamy dressing, 190
    Japanese style in sauce, 113
tolerance, 21, 262
tonsillitis, 295
toothpaste, 176, 256
topping
    caramel, 186
    cereal, 32
    cheese, 126
    chicken, 126
    chocolate-style (carob), 194
    Failsafe mince, 76
    garlic meat, 125
    Margarita, 127
    mock cream, 196
    potato and garlic, 126
    Sunday roast, 126
    vegetarian, 126
    see also sauces
tortillas, 78
tossed salad, 118
Tourette symptoms, 295
traditional Scottish potato salad,
    119
trail mix, Failsafe, 217
travelling, 214
trifle, 166

trifle cups, 166
tuna and potatoes, 208
two-minute noodles, warning, 44
ulcerative colitis, 295
unable to concentrate, 295
unexplained fatigue, 295
unmotivated, 295
urinary incontinence, urinary urgency, 295
urticaria, 295
USA, 29
vanilla, warning, 136
veal, 73
vegetable oils, *see* oils
vegetable
    and vegetarian meals, 102
    country bake muffins, 114
    creamy casserole, 116
    frittata for vegetable haters, 115
    -hater soup, Kerry's, 72
    parcels, 116
    pie, 117

quick bean stir-fry, 115
    salicylates in, 11, 102, 219
vegetarian topping, 126
vertigo, 296
Vienna cream frosting, 197
Vienna fudge cake (eggless), 201
vinegar, 259
visual acuity, 296
Vitamin icypoles, 68
vitamins and minerals, 226
vocal tics, 296
vodka, 65
vomiting, 296
Wade's sausage rolls, 46
washing powder, see Shopping List
water crackers, 55
wedding whip, 145
weekly menu, see Fridge List
weekly muffins, 243
weight loss, 211
wheat or gluten avoidance, 268
whey powder, 40, 258

whisky cream sauce, 193
whisky, 65
white icing, 196
white sauce, 192
whole green bean salad, 120
wholegrains, 13, 257
wine, 65
    amines in, 12
    persimmon, 65
withdrawal symptoms, 20
word and phrase repetition, 296
worm treatment, 258
www.fedup.com.au, 297
xanthan gum, 232
yoghurt
    frozen iceblocks, 67
    homemade, 35
    Indian drink (lassi), 63
yoghurt, warning, 35
Yorkshire pudding, 89
yum balls, 158

Nasty Additives Wallet List

Cut out along lines as shown, laminate the card, and keep in your wallet or purse. Alternatively, photocopy pages, cut out cards and stick together. For more copies of this card, please see www.fedup.com.au.

Nasty additives
www.fedup.com.au

COLOURS
Artificial
102 tartrazine
104 quinoline yellow
107 yellow 2G
110 sunset yellow
122 azorubine, carmoisine
123 amaranth
124 ponceau, brilliant scarlet
127 erythrosine
128 red 2G

129 allura red
132 indigotine, indigo carmine
133 brilliant blue
142 green S, food green, acid brilliant green
151 brilliant black
155 brown, chocolate brown

Natural
160b annatto, bixin, norbixin

PRESERVATIVES
200–203 sorbic acid, all sorbates
210–219 benzoic acid, all benzoates
220–228 sulphur dioxide,
    all sulphites, bisulphites,
    metabisulphites
249–252 all nitrates and nitrites
280–283 propionic acid,
    all propionates

SYNTHETIC ANTIOXIDANTS
310–312 all gallates
319–321 TBHQ, BHA (butylated
    hydroxyanisole), BHT (butylated
    hydroxytoluene)

FLAVOUR ENHANCERS
620–625 glutamic acid and all
    glutamates, MSG (monosodium
    glutamate)
627 disodium guanylate
631 disodium inosinate
635 ribonucleotides
Yeast extract, HVP HPP (hydrolysed
    vegetable or plant protein)

FLAVOURS
No numbers since they are trade
secrets